Kurdish-English/Enry

Aziz Amindarov

HIPPOCRENE BOOKS, INC.
New York

FOREWORD

This completely modern, up-to-date Kurdish-English\English-Kurdish dictionary provides a quick reference to the Northern dialect of Kurdish and English. Useful for travelers, business people, and students, the dictionary includes over 8,000 entries for both languages in a concise, easy-to-use format. Every entry provides a clear pronunciation guide. Parts of speech are indicated in italics.

Each entry is accompanied by a transcription in the alphabet of the other language: the English words are spelled with Kurdish characters and the Kurdish words with English characters. The author has designed an easy-to-follow system of transliteration customized for the Kurdish and English phonetic systems.

LIST OF ABBREVIATIONS

adj	adjective
adv	adverb
conj	conjunction
f	feminine
interj	interjection
m	masculine
n	noun
num	numeral
part	particle
pl	plural
prep	preposition
pron	pronoun
v	verb

GUIDE TO PRONUNCIATION

Kurdish	English	Example
a	a	hard
b	b	bat
c	dg	edge
ç	ch	reach
d	d	dog
e	ä	apple
ê	e	met
f	f	fat
g	g	gas
h	h	hair
x	kh	khan
ẍ	gh	ghoul
i	y	hit
î	i	meet
j	zh	pleasure
k	k	kitten
q	q	queen
l	l	life
m	m	man
n	n	nap
o	o	fortune
p	p	pan
r	r	rose
s	s	sand
ş	sh	shoe
t	t	time
u	ö	turn
v	v	van
w	w	wing
y	y	young
z	z	zebra

KURDISH-ENGLISH
DICTIONARY

A

aba [aba] *m* father, parent
abad [abad] *m* being, essence; eternity; *adj* eternal, constant
abdar [abdar] *m* horse
abid [abyd] *adj* righteous
abrûdar [abrudar] *adj* famous, celebrated
aciz [adjyz] *adj* weak, helpless, pitiful
açar [achar] *m* rye; key
ad [ad] *m* oath
ada [ada] *f* island
adab [adab] *m* honor, shame, conscience; politeness, good manners
adan [adan] *adj* productive, profitable
adar [adar] *f* March
adem [adäm] *m* man
adet [adät] *m* rule, habit, tradition
adetî [adäti] *adj* regular, ordinary
adî [adi] *adj* maternal, relative
adîne [adineh] *adj* other
adrês [adres] *f* address
aferin [afäryn] *f* creation
afet [afät] *m* hero
afraz [afraz] *m* height, mountain
afret [afrät] *f* woman

agah [agah] *m* attention
agandar [agandar] *adj* attentive
agîtasî [agitasi] *f* propaganda
agir [agyr] *m* fire
agirdiz [agyrdyz] *m* volcano
agirperesî [agyrpäräsi] *f* Zoroastrism
aha [aha] *part, pron* here, here it is
aheng [ahäng] *m* melody, voice, sound
ahil [ahyl] *adj* knowlegeable, wise *m* old man
ahû [ahu] *m* wild goat
ah û zar [ah u zar] *m* cry
ax [agh] *f* earth; sole
axaftin [akhaftyn] *f* conversation; *v* speak, say
axawik [akhawyk] *f* word, expression
axeban [akhäban] *m* countryman
axir [akhyr] *f* end *part* isn't it?
axiret [akhyrät] *f* fate, destiny
axirî [akhyri] *f* end, outcome
axirîye [akhyriyä] *adj* finally
axivandin [akhyvandyn] *v* repeat, interpret, speak
axmax [akhmakh] *m* idiot, cretin
axmaxî [akhmakhi] *f* idiocy
axûnd [akhund] *m* educated person
aẍa [agha] *m* master
aẍu [aghu] *m* fish

axuş [aghush] *m* embrace
ajinî [azhyni] *f* habitation, living quarters, home
aktyabir [aktyabyr] *f* October
aqar [aqur] *m* relative
aquilmend [aqylmänd] *adj* intelligent, sensible, smart, understanding
aqûbet [aqubät] *f* fate, destiny
aqût [aqut] *m* hyacinth, ruby
al [al] *m* cunning, deceit
ala [ala] *adj* the best, the most outstanding
alan [alan] *f* announcement
alav [alav] *f* flame
alçax [alchakh] *adj* base, cruel, deceitful, quiet, weak
alçaxî [alchakhi] *f* baseness, cruelty, deceit, quietness, weakness
alem [aläm] *f* world, universe, people, humanity
alet [alät] *f* tool, instrument, weapon, machine
alî [ali] *m* side, area, direction
alîsor [alisor] *adj* red
alifba [alyfba] *m* alphabet
alişveriş [alyshverysh] *f* trade, market
alkan [alkan] Alkan (Kurdish tribe)
almas [almas] *m* pearl, diamond
aloz [aloz] *f* difficulty, obstacle, embarassment
altker [altkär] *m* winner, victor

altnebûyl [altnäbuyl] *m* unconquerable
alû [alu] *f* prune, plum
alvêr [alver] trade, market
am [am] *f* soul
am [am] *pl* common folks
amac [amadj] *m* aim, target
amade [amadä] *f* arrival, fulfilment of a task
aman [aman] *interj* oh sorrow, oh grief
amanet [amanät] *f* trust
ambûlatorîya [ambulatoriya] *f* ambulance
amin [amyn] *adj* true, trustworthy, safe, peaceful
amindarî [amyndari] *f* trust, trustworthiness, safety
aminî [amyni] *f* faith, trust, hope
anaxdar [anakhdar] *f* key (from a lock), lock
analîz [analiz] *f* analysis
anan [anan] *adj* egotistical, proud, haughty
anantî [ananti] *n* egoism, pride, haughtiness
anemetî [anämäti] *f* placement into storage
ango [ango] *conj* or, that is
angorî [angori] *adj* equal, similar
angortî [angorti] *f* equality, comparison, similarity
anîn [anin] *v* wear, bring, carry
anêka [aneka] *conj* as if

antîk [antik] *adj* antique, ancient, old, old
  fashioned

B

bednavî [bädnavi] *f* bad reputation
beg [bäg] *m* lord, feudal
begem [bägäm] *f* like, consider
begzade [bägzadä] *m* Kurdish tribe in Northern
  Iran
beha [bäha] *f* advance
behandin [bähandyn] *v* cut, split; *f* splitting
behane [bähanä] *f* excuse
behdînan [bähdinan] *m* (name of Kurdish Tribe
  in Southern Turkey) Behdinan
behistî [bähysti] *f* receptivity
behr [bähr] *f* see; part
behrî [bähri] *adj* see
behs [bähs] *f* narration, story; discussion,
  conversation
bext [bäkht] *m* success, happinness; honor
bextewar [bäkhtäwar] *adj* happy,
bextxirabî [bäkhtkhyrabi] *f* unhappinness
bextreş [bäkhträsh] *adj* unhappy, miserable;
  dishonorable
bextyar [bäkhtyar] *m* Kurdish tribe in Western Iran

bej [bäzh] *f* continent, earth
bejn [bäzhi] *f* growth, height
bejnbilind [bäzhnbylynd] *adj* tall
bejnkurt [bizhnkört] *adj* short
bekçî [bäkchi] *m* guard, doorman
beqa [bäka] *adj* constant
bela [bäla] *f* accident
bela-belayî [bäla-bälayi] *adj* dispersed, absent-minded
belaxet [bälakhät] *f* adventure
belalizk [bälalizk] *f* basil
belalûk [bälaluk] *f* cherry
belam [bälam] *conj* but
belaş [bälash] *adj* free of charge
belavker [bälavkär] *m* distributor
belçîm [bälchim] *m* leaf
belçik [bälchyk] *m* petal
beleban [bäläban] *m* rat
beled [bäläd] *adj* knowledgable
belek [bäläk] *adj* white, gray
belekpor [bäläkpor] *adj* gray-haired
belelerz [bälälärz] *f* earthquake
belengaz [bälängaz] *adj* poor
belengazî [bälängazi] *f* poverty
belg [bälg] *m* leaf

belê [bäleh] *part* yes
belêkirin [bälekyryn] *f* contract, affirmation, confirmation
belênî [bäleni] *f* agreement, affirmation, confirmation
belkî [bälki] *conj* in order to; maybe, possible
belqîtk [bälqitk] *f* infection, epidemic, paralysis
belqitandin [bälqytandyn] *vt* to infect, to paralyze
belor [bälor] *m* crystal *adj* crystal
belû [bälu] *adj* well known, visible, popular
belwa [bälwa] *f* temptation, trial
ben [bän] *m* rope, thread
bend [bänd] *m* slave, prisoner
bender [bändär] *f* port, haven, harbor
bendewarî [bändäwari] *f* slavery, plight
bendik [bändyk] *f* button; thread
beng [bäng] *f* appearance; mood
bengî [bängi] *adj* enamoured
bengîtî [bängiti] *f* passion, love
benî [bäni] *m* child, son
beniş [bänish] *m* cloak, gown
benişt [bänisht] *m* chewing gum
ber [bär] *prep* next, behind, before *m* face; fruit; stone *f* group, tribe; *adj* broad
bera [bära] *adv* before; okay
beraber [bärabär] *adj* equal

beraberbûn [bärabärbun] *f* equality
berade [bäradä] *m* bum, beggar
berahî [bärahi] *f* width
beran [bäran] *m* ram
berate [bäratä] *f* corpse, dead body
berav [bärav] *f* coast (of sea or lake)
beravan [bäravan] *m* direction, way
beraz [bäraz] *m* boar, pig; Kurdish tribe in
   Northeastern Iraq
berbang [bärbang] *f* early morning, dawn;
   morning bell
berbend [bärbänd] *f* belt, band; connection
berber [bärbär] *m* barber; barbarian; enemy, foe
berberxane [bärbärkhanä] *f* barber shop
berbiçav [bärbychav] *adj* visible, conspicuous;
   famous, well-known
berçavk [bärchavk] *m* glasses, pince-nez
berçem [bärchäm] *f* river bank
berda [bärda] *adv* near, nearby; in front of
berdax [bärdakh] *f* glass
berdan [bärdan] *v* set free, let go
berderek [bärdäräk] *m* threshold
berdestî [bärdästi] *m* helper, servant, apprentice
berdevk [bärdävk] *m* counselor, mentor, guide
berdîwar [bärdiwar] *adj* homeless *m* wanderer,
   tramp, beggar

berdêlvan [bärdelvan] *m* hostage

berdilk [bärdylk] *m* lover, beloved

bere-bere [bärä-bärä] *adv* gradually, little-by-little

berehne [bärähnä] *adj* naked

berek [bäräk] *f* tribe, clan, group *adj* wide

bereket [bäräkät] *f* blessing, mercy

berepaş [bäräpash] *adv* back, backwards, upside-down, inside-out

berf [bärf] *f* snow

berfende [bärfändä] *f* lie, falsehood, cunning

berx [bärkh] *f* lamb

berxweketî [bärkhwäkäti] *adj* sad, depressed

berxweketin [bärkhwäkätyn] *f* sadness, suffering

berxweneketî [bärkhwänäkäti] *adj* shameless *f* shamelessness

berxweş [bärkhwäsh] *f* fertile, fruitful, merry

berî [bäri] *adv* before *f* steppe, desert

berîdan [bäridan] *vt* repel, drive away

berîde [bäridä] *m* robbery, marauding

berîk [bärik] *f* bullet

berînî [bärini] *f* width, expanse

berîstan [bäristan] *f* desert; steppe

berîya [bäriya] *f* desire, wish

berê [bäreh] *adv* before, earlier

berêda [bäreda] *adv* in the beginning

berih [bäryh] *m* bush
beriştin [bäryshtyn] *vt* bake
berizandin [bärizandyn] *vt* lift
berjêr [bärdjer/ descent, slope
berjor [bärdjor] *f* ascent
berk [bärk] *adj* strong, hard, sturdy
berkbûn [bärkbun] *f* strength, hardness
berkî [bärki] *f* strength, hardness
berq [bärq] *f* lightning
bermal [bärmal] *f* façade
bermayî [bärmayi] *f* remains; heritage; result
bermîl [bärmil] *f* barrel
berneme [bärnämä] *f* program, aim
bernivîs [bärnyvis] *m* copyist
bernivîsarkirin [bärnyvisarkyryn] *v* copy
beropaşo [bäropasho] *adv* inside-out
berpal [bärpal] *f* side, slope
berpêş [bärpesh] *adv* forward
berpirsîyarî [bärpirsiyari] *f* responsibility
berra [bärra] *adv* in front of
bersîv [bärsiv] *f* answer; instruct
berteng [bärtäng] *m* belt
berû [bäru] *m* leaf
berûk [bäruk] *f* breast, stomach
bervanî [bärvani] *f* resistance
berwar [bärwar] *m* slope; (name of a Kurdish
    tribe) Berwar

besanî [bäsani] *adv* enough
best [bäst] *f* plain, steppe; battlefield
bestek [bästäk] *f* bed
bestem [bästäm] *f* aim, intention
beşer [bäshär] *f* appearance, mood, state of
   mind; people, humanity
beter [bätär] *adj* ugly, horrible; strange
betilîn [bätylin] *v* be tired
beyan [bäyan] *adj* clear, obvious
beyar [bäyar] *m* hill, mountain range
beyaz [bäyaz] *adj* white
beyt [bäyt] *f* couplet; religious hymn
bezav [bäzav] *v* move
bezaz [bäzaz] *m* merchant
bezgîr [bäzgir] *adj* fat
bezîn [bäzin] *v* run
bezm [bäzm] *m* feast
be'zî [bä'zi] *adv* except, except for
bîber [bibär] *f* pepper
bîhn [bihn] *f* scent, aroma
bîhnayî [bihnayi] *f* incense, scent, aroma
bîhnî [bihni] *f* smell, scent; nose
bîmar [bimar] *adj* sick, diseased, impotent
bîmarxane [bimarkhanä] *f* hospital
bîmarî [bimari] *f* sickness, disease
bîr [bir] *f* memory, remembrance

bîranî [birani] *adj* sensible, capable
bîrbir [birbyr] *adj* sensible, understanding, smart
bîrereş [biräräsh] *adj* forgetful
bîrkirî [birkyri] *adj* forgotten
bîst [bist] *num* twenty
bîşî [bishi] *f* pancake; pancakes
bêabrûyî [be'abruyi] *f* shame
bêaxir [be'akhyr] *adj* endless
bêaqil [be'aqyl] *adj* insane, crazy; stupid
bêaqilî [be'aqyli] *f* insanity; folly, stupidity
bêav [be'av] *adj* dry
bêbaranî [bebarani] *f* drought
bêbinî [bebyni] *adj* bottomless, deep
bêçar [bechar] *adj* helpless; unfortunate; poor
bêçarî [bechari] *f* helplessness; misfortune;
  poverty
bêdad [bedad] *adj* unfair, unlawful
bêdeng [bedäng] *adj* quiet, silent, still
bêdenganî [bedängani] *f* silence, stillness
bêdevan [bedävan] *adj* strange, odd, fantastic
bêemel [be'ämäl] *adj* idle, lazy
bêemelî [be'ämäli] *f* idleness, laziness
bêe'dalet [be'ädalät] *adj* unjust, restless
bêe'debî [be'ädäbi] *f* impudence
bêfesal [befäsal] *adj* inconvenient
bêfesalî [befäsali] *f* imprudence

bêfe'm [befä'm] *adj* stupid
bêfe'mî [befä'mi] *f* stupidity, ignorance
bêfitîya [befytiya] *adj* vain, useless, **adv** in vain
bêgan [began] *adj* strange, alien
bêganî [begani] *f* weakness
bêgavî [begavi] *f* hopelessness
bêguh [begöh] *adj* deaf
bêgune [begönä] *adj* innocent
bêgunehî [begönähi] *f* innocence
bêhasil [behasyl] *adj* unproductive
bêhavil [behavyl] *adj* fearless
bêheq [behäq] *adj* unfair; free, gratis
bêhemel [behämäl] *adj* careless
bêhemelî [behämäli] *f* carelessness
bêheval [behäval] *adj* lonely
bêhevta [behävta] *adj* magnificent
bêhewas [behäwas] *adj* indifferent
bêhewasî [behäwasi] *f* indifference
bêhal [behal] *adj* poor; weak; helpless; sick;
    vague
bêheya [beheya] *adj* sudden
bêheyam [beheyam] *adv* suddenly
bêhiş [behysh] *adj* unconscious; mad, foolish
bêhişî [behyshi] *f* madness
bêhunur [behönör] *adj* mediocre, unqualified
bêhurmet [behörmät] *adj* disgraceful, shameful

bêxatirî [bekhatyri] *f* disrespect
bêxebat [bekhäbat] *adj* unemployed
bêxebatî [bekhäbati] *f* unemployment
bêxeber [bekhäbär] *adj* ignorant; safe, secure
bêxederî [bekhädäri] *f* safety, security
bêxew [bekhäw] *adj* sleepless
bêxewî [bekhäwi] *f* insomnia
bêxêr [bekher] *adj* useless, unprofitable
bêxizmet [bekhizmät] *adj* idle
bêxwendî [bekhwändi] *adj* illiterate
bêxwenditî [bekhwändyti] *f* illiteracy
bêẍazende [beghazändä] *adj* quiet, calm, peaceful
bêẍur [beghör] *adj* unhappy
bêî ku [bei kö] *adv* instead of; for, in order to
bêîman [beiman] *adj* unscrupulous
bêîntîzamî [beintizami] *f* disorder
bêîtae't [beyitaä't] *adj* unruly, disobedient
bêîtbar [beyitbar] *adj* unreliable
bêjimar [bezhymar] *adj* countless *adv* a lot
bêjin [bezhyn] *adj* single, unmarried
bêkêf [bekef] *adj* sad, morose
bêkêfî [bekefi] *f* sadness, melancholy
bêkêmasî [bekemasi] *adj* flawless
bêqanûn [beqanun] *adj* unlawful
bêqîmet [beqimät] *adj* cheap, inexpensive *adv* cheap, inexpensive

bêlezet [beläzät] *adj* unpleasant
bêlûk [beluk] *f* region; regiment
bêmanî [bema'ni] *adj* absurd
bêmanîbûn [bema'nibun] *f* absurdity
bêmedenîyet [bemädäniyät] *adj* uncivilized
bêmerîfet [bemä'rifät] *adj* rude, impolite
bêminet [beminät] *adj* ungrateful
bêmiraz [bemiraz] *adj* unhappy, unfulfilled
bênav [benav] *adj* nameless, unknown
bênzîn [benzin] *f* gasoline
bêpergal [bepärgal] *adj* poor, helpless;
    impossible, unfeasible
bêr [ber] *f* oar
bêrabit [berabyt] *adj* huge, immense
bêresa [beräsa] *adj* strange, unusual
bêrîvan [berivan] *f* milkmaid
bêrim [berym] *m* basin, well
bêronahî [beronahi] *adj* dark, somber
bêsebir [besäbyr] *adj* impatient
bêsebirî [besäbyri] *f* impatience
bêserbêbînî [besärbebini] *adj* infinite, endless
bêş [besh] *f* tax; duty; forest
bêşerie't [beshäriä't] *adj* unfaithful
bêşîk [beshik] *f* cradle
bêşik [beshyk] *adj* undoubted, indubitable
bêşmêt [beshmet] *m* coat

bêşmêrt [beshmert] *m* coat
bêtab [betab] *adj* impatient; weak, impotent
bêtalaş [betalash] *adj* carefree
bêtalaşî [betalashi] *f* carelessness
bêteher [betähär] *adj* horrible, ugly; disordered
bêtexsîr [betäkhsi'r] *adj* merciless; innocent
bêteẍayûr [betäghayur] *adj* indifferent
bêter [betär] *adj* bad, terrible, awful
bêterbyet [betärbyät] *adj* unmannered, impolite,
    rude
bêteşkîl [betäshkil] *adj* unorganized
bêtewat [betäwat] *adj* anxious, alarmed, disturbed
bêtir [betyr] *adv* often; more; *adj* stronger
bêûmûd [be'umud] *adj* hopeless, desperate
bêûmûdî [be'umudyi] *f* hopelessness, despair
bêvece [bevädjä] *adj* simple, easy; cheap; free
bêvil [bevyl] *f* nose; nostrils
bêwar [bewar] *adj* homeless
bêwarî [bewari] *f* homelessness
bêwijdan [bewyzhdan] *adj* shameless
bêzehmet [bezähmät] *adj* easy, not difficult
    adv easily
bêziman [bezyman] *adj* dumb, mute
bêzuhum [bezöhöm] *adj* thin, skinny
bi [by] *prep* with
biçûk [bychuk] *m* baby, infant *adj* small; young

biçûktî [bychukti] *f* childhood
biha [byha] *m* price
bihabirîn [byhabyrin] *f* pricing, evaluation
bihakêm [byhakem] *adj* cheap
bihar [byhar] *f* spring
bihîstin [byhistyn] *v* listen, hear
bihnûnî [byhnuni] *f* lawn
bihok [byhok] *f* insect
bihur [byhör] m passage
bihurandin [byhörandyn] *v* spend; transfer;
   translate
bihurî [byhöri] *adj* past; past tense
bixok [bykhok] *adj* ugly
biînad [biyinad] *adj* fanatical
biînsaf [biyinsaf] *adj* just, fair
biînsafî [biyinsafi] *f* justice; **adv** fairly
bijang [byzhang] *f* eyelid; eyelash
bijar [byzhar] *f* choice
bijare [byzharä] *adj* better, the best
bijarkar [byzharkar] *m* elector, voter
bijartin [byzhartyn] *v* choose; select; elect
bijîşk [byzhishk] *m* doctor
bikêr [byker] *adj* necessary, indispensable;
   essential
bikirçî [bykyrchi] *m* customer, buyer
biqerz [byqärz] *v* borrow; lend

bila [byla] *adv* all right
bilezbûn [byläzbun] *v* hurry
bilîmet [bylimät] *adj* wise; well-known, prominent
bilêt [bylet] *f* ticket
bilind [bylynd] *adj* high
bilindayî [bylyndayi] *f* height
bilintir [bylyntyr] *adj* highest
bilûr [bylur] *f* flute
bimbarek [bymbaräk] *m* charity; congratulation
bin [byn] *prep* under
binçene [bynchänä] *f* chin
bindest [byndäst] *adj* subordinate
binecî [bynädzhi] *m* aborigene
binge [byngä] *f* basis
bingehîn [byngähin] *adj* basic
binî [byni] *m* bottom, basis
binîş [bynish] *m* underwear, lingerie
binpî [bynpi] *f* sole, step
binsol [bynsol] *f* sole (foot)
binûr [bynur] *adj* light (color)
bir [byr] *f* group, company; crowd
bira [byra] *m* brother; *part* okay
birajin [byrazhyn] *m* brother-in-law
birajtin [byrazhtyn] *v* fry, bake
biramakî [byramaki] *m* brother

biraştî [byrashti] *adj* fried
biraza [byraza] *m* nephew
birên [byren] *v* carry, lead, take away
birinc [byryndj] *m* rice, pilaf
birincî [byryndji] *num* first
birkan [byrkan] Kurdish tribe in Turkey
birkîyam [byrkiyam] *f* girl
birû [byru] *m* brow
birûsk [byrusk] *f* spark; lightning
birûskîn [byruskin] *adj* fast
biserxwe [bysärkhwä] *adj* independent
bisimil [bysymyl] *rel* in the name of Allah
bista [bysta] *adj* trausful
bistan [bystan] *f* breast
bist [byst] *m* stem
bisû [bysu] *adj* angry
bisûtî [bysuti] *f* anger, irritation
bişaret [bysharät] *f* humanity
bişav [byshav] *f* solution
bişavtin [byshavtyn] *v* dissolve
bişkoj [byshkozh] *f* bud
bişkorî [byshkori] *m* young man
bişûnva [byshunva] *adv* back, again
bitevayi [bytävayi] *adv* generally, totally
bite'm [bytä'm] *adj* tasty
bitirs [bytyrs] *adj* terrible

bitulge [bytölgä] *f* bottle
bizav [byzav] *f* zeal
bizdonek [byzdonäk] *m* coward
bizin [byzyn] *f* goat
bizinvan [byzynvan] *m* shepherd
bizir [byzyr] *m* oil
bizmar [byzmar] *m* nail
bizût [byzut] *pl* feet
bizûz [byzuz] *f* cigarette
bo [bo] *prep* for *inter.* why, for what
bobelat [bobälat] *f* punishment; disaster;
   whirlwind
bodelan [bodälan] *adj* creased; weak
boxçe [bokhchä] *m* packet, bundle
boïaz [boghaz] *f* throat
boïz [boghz] *f* hatred, malice
boke [bokä] *adj* mighty, huge
bor [bor] *m* horse *adj* grey
boran [boran] *f* crisis
borc [bordj] *m* debt, loan; honor
bostan [bostan] *m* garden
bostançî [bostanchi] *m* gardener
boş [bosh] *adj* futile *adv* a lot
boşahî [boshahi] *f* abundance
boşe [boshä] *m* drove, caravan
boşpîtal [boshpital] *f* hospital

bot [bot] *m* idol
boyax [boyakh] *f* color
bozbaş [bozbash] *f* meat bouillon
bozebelî [bozäbäli] *m* tramp
bozxane [bozkhanä] *f* brothel
boztî [bozti] *f* prostitution
buxari [bökhari] *f* fire-place, flue
buxtan [bökhtan] *f* slander; offence
bûcê [budjeh] *m* budget
bûk [buk] *f* bride; doll
bûlbûlk [bulbulk] *f* tap
bûlvar [bulvar] *f* boulevard
bûyer [buyär] *f* event, adventure
bûz [buz] *f* ice

C

ca [dja] *interj* well
cab [djab] *f* news; response
cabdar [djabdar] *m* executive *adj* responsible
cabdarî [djabdari] *f* responsibility
cacî [djadji] *f* farmer cheese
cade [djadä] *f* highway
cahil [djahyl] *adj* young
cahilî [djahyli] *f* innocence; youth
caẍ [djagh] *m* fence

cakêt [djaket] *m* jacket

cam [djam] *f* goblet, glass; church

camêr [djamer] *adj* noble, generous

camêrî [djameri] *f* nobility, generosity

can [djan] *m* body; soul *adj* young

candar [djandar] *adj* alive, living

candayî [djandayi] *adj* dead, deceased

canewar [djanäwar] *m* animal, beast, beast of prey

canêş [djanesh] *adj* sickly, diseased

cansaẍ [djansagh] *adj* healthy

cansaẍî [djansaghi] *f* heath

cara-carda [djara-djarda] *adv* immediately, on time

caran [djaran] *adv* sometimes, occasionally

carbûn [djarbun] *f* multiplication

cardin [djardyn] *adv* again, once again

carekêra [djaräkera] *adv* immediately, momentarily

carna [djarna] *adv* occasionally

cawbir [djawbyr] *f* scissors

cebhet [djäbhät] *f* forehead

cebir [djebyr] *f* force, strength

cebirxane [djäbyrkhanä] *f* arsenal, weapons

cebrî [djäbri] *f* force

cefa [djäfa] *m* labor, effort, worry

cehan [djäkhan] *f* world, universe
cehnem [djähnäm] *f* hell, nightmare, curse
ceẍrafî [djäghrafi] *f* geography
cejin [djäzhin] *f* holiday
celal [djälal] *m* robber, bandit *f* magnitude,
     glory, might; (name of Kurdish tribe) Jelal
celd [djäld] *m* volume, book
cemal [djämal] *adj* beautiful, splendid; *f* beauty
cemalî [djämali] *f* beauty
cemed [djämäd] *m* frost; ice
cemik [djämyk] *adj* little, small; narrow
cemmaş [djämmash] *adj* drunk, intoxicated
cenber [djänbär] *f* chain
cencele [djändjälä] *f* scandal
cendek [djändäk] *m* corpse
ceneral [djänäral] *m* general
cenet [djänät] *f* Paradise, heaven
ceng [djäng] *f* war, battle
cengçî [djängchi] *m* warrior
cengel [djängäl] *m* forest
cennet [djännät] *f* Paradise, heaven
cenûb [djänub] *f* South
ceres [djäräs] *m* bell
cesaret [djäsarät] *f* courage, fortitude
cesûr [djäsur] *adj* courageous, brave
cew [djäw] *f* river, stream

cewar [djäwar] *m* neighbor
cewaz [djäwaz] *f* permission
cewt [djäwt] *adj* empty
ceza [djäza] *f* punishment
cezbe [djäzbä] *f* ecstasy, exhaltation
cezbet [[djäzbät] *f* attraction
ce'dû [djä'du] *m* rival; magician
ce'dûgerî [djä'dugäri] *f* magic, sorcery
ce'rizî [djä'ryzi] *f* shame
cî [dji] *m* place
cîale [djialä] *conj* except for
cîanîn [djianin] *f* fullfilment, completion
cîda [djida] *adv* at once, immediately
cîdal [djidal] *f* quarrel with, argument; fight,
    battle
cîdalkirin [djydalkyryn] *v* argue, fight
cîderk [djidärk] *f* exit
cîgeh [djigäh] *m* stop
cîhgirtî [djihgyrti] *m* deputy, vice
cîmisken [djimyskän] *m* native land
cînav [djinav] *f gram* pronoun
cî-nivîn [dji-nyvin] *f* bed, linen
cêb [djeb] *f* pocket
cênîk [djenik] *f* temple
cêrb [djerb] *f* experience
cêribandin [djeribandyn] *v* experiment, try

cêwî [djewi] *m* twin, double
cibbe [djybbä] *f* mistake; argument
cidî [djydi] *adj* serious
cihade [djyhadä] *adj* separate
cihdaxwaz [djyhdakhwaz] *f* aim
cihê [djyheh] *adj* separate, different
cihêbûn [djyhebun] *f* separation, break-up
cihûd [djyhud] *m* Jew
cil [djyl] *f* clothes, suit
cilakî [djylaki] *adj* fast, speedy
cimaet [djymaä't] *f* society, people, public
cimcimî [djymdjymi] *adj* brave, courageous
cindî [djyndi] *adj* noble, decent, elegant
cindîtî [djynditi] *f* nobility, decency, elegance
cinêh [djyneh] *f* crime
cinûd [djynud] *m* army
cinyaz [djynyaz] *m* corpse
cirav [djyrav] *f* water
civandin [djyvandyn] *v* gather, collect, concentrate
civat [djyvat] *f* meeting, gathering, assembly
ciwanmêr [djywanmer] *adj* noble, generous, brave
cizîr [djyzir] *f* island
co [djo] *m* brook, stream, river
coher [djohär] *m* jewel

colan [djolan] *f* cradle
comerd [djomärd] *adj* brave, bold; noble, generous
comerdane [djomärdanä] *adv* bravely, boldly, nobly, generously
comerdî [djomärdi] *f* courage, boldness, nobility, generosity
commaş [djommash] *adj* merry, funny
commaşi [djommashi] *f* mirth
cot [djot] *m* pair
cotikî [djotyki] *f* jump
coybar [djoybar] *f* river
cuda [djöda] *adj* distinct, separate, different
cudabûn [djödabun] *f* distinction, separation, difference
cudayî [djödayi] *f* distinction, difference
cuhl [djöhl] *f* ignorance, illiteracy
culf [djölf] *adj* superficial, empty
cuma [djöma'] *f* Friday
curet [djörät] *f* courage, fortitude
cûd [djud] *m* generosity
cûm [djum] *m* gum
cûm cûtin [djum djutyn] *v* chew gum
cûmker [djumkär] *m* taylor
cûn [djun] *v* chew
cûrcûr [djurdjur] *f* turkey

cûre [djurä] *m* kind; quality; way
cûr-cûr [djur-djur] *adj* various
cûrekî [djuräki] *adv* somehow
cûtin [djutin] *v* chew

Ç

ça [cha] *conj* how, which *m* river
çadir [chadyr] *f* tent
çax [chakh] *m* time
çaxekê [chakhäkeh] *pron* once upon a time
çakî [chaki] *f* health; well being; kindness
çal [chal] *f* pit; ditch
çalkirin [chalkyryn] *v* bury
çalxane [chalkhanä] *f* grave, tomb
çamûr [chamur] *f* dirt; clay
çandin [chandyn] *v* sow
çap [chap] *f* measure
çapkirin [chapkyryn] *v* measure
çapxane [chapkhanä] *f* publishers
çapkirin [chapkryryn] *f* publication
çap û gûpkirdin [chap u gupkyrdyn] *v* lie, tell
   lies
çar [char] *num* four
çaranî [charani] *num* fourth
çarçik [charchyk] *f* square

çare [charä] *f* help
çarîn [charin] *f* cry, wail
çarme [charmä] *f* circle
çarmekirin [charmäkyryn] *v* surround; encircle
çarneçar [charnächar] *adj* helpless; weak-willed
çarneçarî [charnächari] *f* helplessnes
çarnical [charnycal] *adv* around, encircling, from all sides
çarsû [charsu] *f* market, fair
çarşem [charshäm] *f* Wednesday
çat-pat [chat-pat] *adv* inside-out; falsely
çav [chav] *m* eye
çavbelî [chavbäli] *f* envy
çavberk [chavbärk] *m* glasses
çavbestin [chavbästyn] *f* lie, falsehood
çavbirçî [chavbyrchi] *adj* miserly, greedy
çavfireh [chavfyräh] *adj* generous
çavxur [chavkhör] *adj* greedy
çavnêrîn [chavnerin] *f* expectation
çavreşî [chavräshi] *f* jealousy, envy
çavtêr [chavter] *adj* noble, generous
çavtêrî [chavteri] *f* nobility, generosity
çawabûn [chawabun] *f* quality
çawîş [chawish] *m* servant
çay [cha'y] *f* tea
çaynik [cha'ynik] *f* teapot, tea kettle

çayr [cha'yr] *f* meadow, field; grass
çehr [chähr] *m* face
çek [chäk] *f* weapon
çekme [chäkmä] *m* boot
çelebîtî [chäläbiti] *f* nobility; aristocracy
çelem [chäläm] *f* chains
çeleng [chäläng] *adj* fast, speedy
çelengkirin [chälängkyryn] *f* progress
çelq [chälq] *f* wave
çelte [chältä] *m* handbag
çem [chäm] *m* river
çemedan [chämädan] *m* suitcase
çend [chänd] *adv* how much
çendanî [chändanî] *f* quantity
çendî [chändi] *f* quantity
çene [chänä] *f* chin
çeng [chäng] *f* hand; handful; chin
çengene [chängänä] *m* Gipsy
çentîn [chäntin] *adj* ordinary
çep [chäp] *adj* left
çeper [chäpär] *f* fence
çephe [chäp'hä] *f* boundary, border
çepik [chäpyk] *m* hand
çepil [chäpyl] *m* hand
çer [chär] *adv* how, in what manner; what kind
çerçere [chärchärä] *f* difficulty

çerez [chäräz] *pl* fruit
çerx [chärkh] *f* wheel
çerm [chärm] *m* skin
çerpandin [chärpandyn] *v* throw
çeşm [chäshm] *m* eye *pl* eyes
çeşmek [chäshmäk] *m* eye *pl* eyes
çeşn [chäshn] *f* feast, banquet
çetin [chätyn] *adj* hard, difficult, complex
çetinayî [chätinayi] *f* difficulty
çetir [chätyr] *f* umbrella
çewender [chäwändär] *m* beet
çewt [chäwt] *adj* incorrect
çeyk [chäyk] *f* service
çîçek [chichäk] *f* flower
çîçîk [chichik] *adj* few
çîmange [chimängä] *m* flowerbed
çîmenzarîn [chimänzarin] *f* meadow
çîn [chin] *m* rank; layer; wrinkle; Chinaman
çînî [chini] *f* China *adj* Chinese
çîp [chip] *f* shin
çîredest [chirädäst] *m* architect
çîredestî [chirädästi] *f* architecture
çîrok [chirok] *f* fairy tale, story
çît [chit] *m* screen, fence
çîvanok [chivanok] *m* bird
çîya [chiya] *m* mountain

çîz [chiz] *m* thing; something
çê [cheh] *adj* good, best; slim
çêje [chezhä] *m* cub
çêk [chek] *f* bill
çêlek [cheläk] *f* cow
çêlî [cheli] *m* tribe
çêrmûk [chermuk] *m* warm spring
çêşme [cheshmä] *f* bathroom, toilet
çêştker [chestkär] *m* cook
çi [chi] *conj* that
çiçax [chychakh] *pron* when
çiçik [chychyk] *m* nipple
çik [chyk] *m* checkers
çikandin [chykandyn] *v* dig
çikil [chykyl] *m* branch; hand
çiko [chyko] *conj* then
çikûsî [chykusi] *f* avarice, greediness
çiqas [chyqas] *adv* how many, how much;
    as far as
çilape [chylapä] *f* jump
çilazok [chylazok] *adj* weak
çilçiçik [chylchychyk] *adj* flattering; *m* flatterer
çilmisîn [chylmysin] *v* wither, fade; die away, go
    out
çilo [chylo] *prep* in what way
çilpî [chylpi] *m* branch

çilû [chylu] *m* oak
çiman [chyman] *prep* why, what for
çimçim [chymchym] *m* coffee pot
çimkî [chymki] *conj* because
çir [chyr] *f* drop
çira [chyra] *f* lamp *prep* what for
çirî [chyri] *f* October
çirîya evel [chyriya äväl] *f* November
çirîya paşin [chyriya pashyn] *f* December
çirîn [chyrin] *f* cry; noise
çirîş [chyrish] *f* glue
çirik [chyryk] *f* waterfall; stream
çirmisîn [chyrmysin] *v* wither, dry up
çirpî [chyrpi] *m* branch, stem
çirûk [chyruk] *m* face; appearance; image
çist [chyst] *adj* fast; strict; sharp
çitewr [chytäwr] *adv* how, in what way
çivandin [chyvandyn] *vt* bend, turn
çivane [chyvanä] *m* curve, turn
çok [chok] *f* knee
çol [chol] *f* field, steppe, desert
çûçik [chuchyk] *m* child, baby, infant
çûk [chuk] *adj* small, little; younger, youngest
çûktî [chukti] *f* childhood
çûnkî [chunki] *conj* because
çûr [chur] *adj* red-haired, blonde

çûyîn [chuyin] *v* walk, go; flow

D

da [da] *f* mother
dabas [dabash] *f* gift
dabelandin [dabälandyn] *v* swallow
dabistan [dabystan] *f* school
daborîn [daborin] *v* pass by, pass over
daçûn [dachun] *v* walk down, descend
dad [dad] *f* mother; law, justice
dadan [dadan] *v* close; lock
dadge [dadgä] *f* court
dadvan [dadvan] *m* judge
dagerîn [dagärin] *v* turn; roll up
dagirtin [dagyrtyn] *v* fill
dahatin [dahatyn] *v* walk down, descend; fall
dahênan [dahenan] *v* invent; write, compose
dahilanîn [dahylanin] *v* lower; pick up
dahiştin [dahyshtyn] *v* lower; hang; insert, put
daxil [dakhyl] *adv* in, into; *adj* inside
daxwerin [dakhwäryn] *v* yield, give in; consent,
    agree
daxwez [daxwäz] *f* demand, request
daẍ [dagh] *f* brand, trade mark; bruise, scar;
daẍkirin [daghkyryn] *v* brand

daîre [da'irä] *f* circle; circumference
daîye [da'iyä] *f* cause, reason; occasion
daketin [dakätyn] *v* fall; go down
daqurtandin [daqörtandyn] *v* swallow
dakutan [dakötan] *v* beat off
dalan [dalan] *f* hall; corridor
daman [daman] *m* lease
damayî [damayi] *adj* sad
damirandin [damyrandyn] *v* put out, extinguish
dan [dan] *v* hit, beat
danavî [danavi] *f* suffering
dane [danä] *m* time
danezan [danäzan] *f* information
danî [dani] *m* founder
danîn [danin] *v* put, place
dawîn [dawin] *adj* last, final
dawîyê [dawiyeh] *adv* finally, at last
dawul [dawöl] *f* drum
dayîm [dayim] *adj* eternal, constant, continuous, everlasting
dayîmî [dayimi] *f* eternity, constancy, continuity
dayre [dayrä] *f* neighborhood
debar [däbar] *f* food; lie, deceit
dedirî [dädyri] *m* bum
define [däfinä] *f* treasure; treasury
degenek [dägänäk] *adj* sly, cunning, deceitful

deh [däh] *num* ten
dehbe [dähbä] *pl* animals, beasts
dehbetî [dähbäti] *f* cruelty, bestiality
dehfik [dähfyk] *f* trap
dehl [dähl] *f* valley
dehol [dähol] *f* continuation; drum
dexesî [däkhäsi] *f* envy
dexl [däkhl] *m* wage, earning
deẍel [däghäl] *adj* counterfeit, fraudulent; treac
   herous, deceitful
deẍs [däghs] *f* envy
dek [däk] *f* cunning, deceit, treachery; trap
dektor [däktor] *m* doctor
deq [däq] *f* spot, freckles
deqe [däqä] *f* minute, moment
delak [dälak] *m* barber
delakxane [dälak'khanä] *f* barber shop
delal [dälal] *adj* splendid, charming, wonderful
delalî [dälali] *f* splendor, charm, beauty
delav [dälav] *f* seashore, mouth of river; pail
delẍe [dälghä] *m* wave, dervish's clothes
delîl [dälil] *m* example, specimen, proof
delîr [dälir] *adj* brave, bold
delîrî [däliri] *f* courage, fortitude
delû [dälu] *adj* bitter, unpleasant; brave
dem [däm] *f* time, epoch, era

deman [däman] *adj* fast, speedy
dem-demî [däm-dämi] *adv* occasionally, now and
  then
den [dän] *m* color; beast
deng [däng] *m* voice, sound
denngîr [dänngir] *adj* famous, celebrated
dengiz [dängyz] *f* sea; wealth
depançe [däpanchä] *f* gun
der [där] *f* place, here
derav [därav] *m* bay, gulf; period of time
derd [därd] *m* pain, illness, suffering, grief
derdan [därdan] *f* dishware
derext [däräkht] *f* tree
derem [däräm] *f* loaf (of bread); vein
dereng [däräng] *adj* late, belated; slow
derengî [därängi] *f* lateness, delay
derew [däräw] *f* lie, falsehood
derewçî [däräwchi] *m* liar
derge [därgä] *m* gates, door
dergevan [därgävan] *m* doorman, waiter
dergûş [därgush] *f* child
derhal [därhal] *adj* huge; difficult; hopeless
derî [däri] *m* door; gate; entrance; exit
derince [därindjä] *f* ladder, staircase
dermal [därmal] *f* yard; street
derman [därman] *m* medicine, treatment

dermanxane [därmankhanä] *f* pharmacy
dermanivîs [därmanyvis] *m* perscription
ders [därs] *m* class, lesson
dersdar [därsdar] *m* teacher
dersxane [därskhanä] *f* school; classroom
derskom [därskom] *f* class
derva [därva] *adv* outside, on the street
dest [däst] *m* arm, hand
destanînî [dästanini] *f* success
destav [dästav] *f* bathroom, outhouse
destbend [dästbänd] *f* handcuffs
dest-dest [däst-däst] *adv* immediately, at once
destdirêjî [dästdirezhi] *f* robberry, theft
destek [dästäk] *f* group
desteng [dästäng] *adj* poor, needy
destengî [däständji] *f* poverty, need
destfireh [dästfiräh] *adj* generous
destgirî [dästgyri] *f* help, patronage
desthişk [däst'hyshk] *adj* cruel; miserly
desthişkî [däst'hyshki] *f* cruelty; avarice
destxweda [dästkhwäda] *adv* immediately
destî [dästi] *m* handle, handrail
destker [dästkär] *adj* fake, artificial
destmal [dästmal] *f* handkerchief, kerchief
destpêk [dästpek] *f* beginning
destsist [dästsyst] *adj* weak; miserly

destûr [dästur] *m* rule, order
destvekirî [dästväkyri] *adj* generous
deşwar [däshwar] *adj* hard, difficult
dev [däv] *m* mouth
deve [dävä] *f* camel
devgerm [dävgärm] *adj* brave, courageous
devkenî [dävkäni] *f* laugh, smile
dev û çav [däv u chav] *m* face
dewl [däwl] *f* plaza, place; field; drum; pail
dewlemend [däwlämänd] *m* rich person
dewlemendî [däwlämändi] *f* wealth, riches
dewlet [däwlät] *f* wealth, riches
dewr [däwr] *f* circle
dewrês [däwresh] *m* dervish; pauper
dews [däws] *f* place
deyn [däyn] *m* debt; voice
de'n [dä'n] *m* food
de'wat [dä'wat] *f* wedding
de'wet [dä'wät] *f* prayer
dîbace [dibadjä] *f* preface, foreword
dîhar [dihar] *adj* visible
dîhar [dihar] *m* gift, present
dîl [dil] *m* prisoner
dîlbend [dilbänd] *m* prisoner; slave; translator
dîn [din] *adj* crazy, insane
dîn [din] *m* faith

dînanî [dinani] *f* insanity, folly
dînîtî [diniti] *f* insanity, folly
dîplom [diplom] *f* diploma
dirêktor [direktor] *m* director
dîsa [disa] *adv* again
dîwan [diwan] *f* couch; collection of poems
dîwar [diwar] *f* wall
dîyarî [diyari] *f* present
dêmdur [demdör] *adj* unequalled (in beauty);
    innocent, chaste
dêmûrû [demuru] *m* face, visage
dêr [der] *f* church (Christian)
dêran [deran] *adj* unfortunate; homeless; lonely
dêris [derys] *adj* damaged, broken
därisandin [derysandin] *v* damage, break, de –
    stroy
dêw [dew] *m* demon, devil, monster
difn [dyfn] *m* nose; nostril
dixesî [dykhäsi] *adj* envious, jealous
dixesîn [dykhäsin] *v* envy, to be jealous
dijmin [dyzhmyn] *m* enemy
dijûn [dyzhun] *m* evil; curse
dejûnî [dyzhuni] *f* evil; wickedness, malice
dijwar [dyzhwar] *adj* hard, difficult
dil [dyl] *m* heart
dilawer [dylawär] *adj* courageous, brave

dilawerî [dylawäri] *f* courage, fortitude
dilbar [dylbar] *adj* splendid, gorgeous, magnifi
    cent
dilbarî [dylbari] *f* splendour
dilbirîn [dylbyrin] *adj* upset; sad
dildar [dyldar] *adj* courageous, brave; beloved
dildarî [dyldari] *f* courage; love
dildayî [dyldayi] *adj* beloved; in love
dileşq [dyläshq] *adj* joyous, happy
dileşqî [dyläshqi] *f* joy, happiness
dilfire [dylfirä] *adj* generous
dilgeş [dilgäsh] *adj* happy
dilgeşî [dilgäshi] *f* happiness
dilgîr [dilgyr] *adj* angry; sad; ravishing
dilgiran [dylgyran] *adj* sad, upset, gloomy, mo-
    rose
dilgiranî [dylgyrani] *f* sadness, sorrow
dilgirtî [dylgyrti] *adj* angry; insulted; sad; be
    loved
dilhebandî [dylhäbandi] *adj* in love; ravished
dilhişyar [dylhyshyar] *adj* compassionate
dilhişyarî [dylhyshyari] *f* compassion
dû [du] *m* steam *adv* after
dûxtmam [dukhtmam] *f* sister, cousin (female)
dûje [duzhä] *f* evil; hell
dûman [duman] *f* fog; darkness

dûmayî [dumayi] *f* leftovers, remnants
dûmeqesk [dumäqäsk] *f* lark
dûr [dur] *adj* distant
dûra [dura] *adj* after
dûranî [durani] *f* distance
dûrbîna [durbina] *adj* far-sighted
dûrbînayî [durbinayi] *f* far-sightedness
dûredûr [durädur] *adv* far away
dûrî [duri] *f* distance, parting
dû û derman [du u därman] *m* medicine, treat
    ment
dûv [duv] *f* tail
dûz [duz] *adj* straight; right, correct
dûzan [duzan] *m* razor blade
dûzbûn [duzbun] *f* improvement; truthfulness
dûzkirin [duzkyryn] *f* improvement; straighten-
    ing out; correction, repair

E

ebret [äbrät] *f* moral; lesson; example
ebrûhelal [äbruhälal] *adj* honest; sincere; pure
ebûr [äbur] *f* livelihood; shame
ebûrî [äburî] *f* life; livelihood; shame, scruples
ecnebî [ädjnäbi] *adj* foreign
eda [äda] *f* payment

efgan [äfgan] *m* Afghan (native of Afghanistan)
efxan [äfghan] *m* sigh, scream
eflak [äflak] *f* sky, heaven
efsene [äfsänä] *m* stupid person; fool
efser [äfsär] *m* crown; cup; officer
egle [äglä] *adj* late, belated
ehd [ähd] *m* agreement; act
ehl [ähl] *pl* people *adj* talented, gifted; experi
enced
ehmeq [ähmäq] *adj* stupid, foolish
ehsan [ähsan] *m* kindness
extîyar [äkhtiyar] *f* right, privelege
extîyarî [äghtiyari] *f* old age; poverty; right,
privelege
ejder [äzhdär] *m* tiger
ejmar [äzhmar] *f* date; number
Elah [älah] *m* Allah, God
elalet [älalät] *f* crowd
elbet [älbät] *adv* of course, certainly
eleqet [äläqät] *f* connection
elem [äläm] *f* pain; suffering; misfortune, unhap
piness
elfabe [älfäbä] *m* alphabet
elle [ällä] *adv* only
elm [älm] *m* knowledge, science

eman [äman] *f* pity, compassion; forgiveness, mercy

emek [ämäk] *m* food

emîn [ämin] *adj* calm; confident

emirkan [ämyrkan] *m* American

emirkanî [ämyrkani] *adj* American

emte'e [ämtä'ä] *f* goods; property

enbazî [änbazi] *f* society

enbî [änbi] *m* prophet

encam [ändjam] *m* end; result

encimen [ändjymän] *f* congress

enqest [änqäst] *adj* on purpose

enteqam [äntäqam] *f* vengeance

entikxane [äntik'khäne] *f* museum

erhemdula [ärhämdöla] *excl* Thank God! Thank Allah!

erẍewanî [ärghäwani] *adj* purple; red; scarlet

erqem [ärqäm] *m* number

ermenî [ärmäni] *m* Armenian

erzan [ärzan] *adj* cheap

erzeq [ärzäq] *adj* blue, azure *f* sky

esef [äsäf] *m* pity, compassion

eseh [äsäh] *v* look, watch

eshab [äs'hab] *m* companion, friend

esibil [äsybyl] *m* path, way; means

esker [äskär] *m* soldier

esmer [äsmär] *adj* brown

csna [äsna] *m* time, period of time

esrar [äsrar] *m* secret; secret thought; secret love

eşîya [äshiya] *m* thing, object

eşk [äshk] *m* appearance

eşq [äshk] *f* love, passion

eşqî [äshki] *adj* enamoured; happy

eşqlû [äshqlu] *adj* happy, joyous

eşref [äshräf] *adj* famous, well-known

eteb [ätäb] *f* discipline, order

etlahî [ätlähi] *f* fear

evez [äväz] *adv* instead of

evin [ävyn] *f* love

evindar [ävyndar] *adj* beloved; in love

evinî [ävyni] *f* love

ewha [äwha] *adv* this way, thus

ewqas [äwqas] *adv* that much

ewle [äwlä] *adj* first

ewlî [äwli] *f* floor, story; tier

eyredrom [äyrädrom] *f* airport

eywan [äywan] *f* terrace, balcony

ezel [äzäl] *m* fate; eternity *adj* eternal

ezelî [äzäli] *f* fate; eternity

ezep [äzäp] *m* servant

ezîr [äzir] *f* secret

ezibandîn [äzibandyn] *v* torture

ezibîn [äzibyn] *v* suffer

ezva [äzva] *f* juice; inflammable material; match

E'

e'bd [ä'bd] *m* person

e'bdal [ä'bdal] *adj* poor, needy; unhappy

e'bdî [ä'bdi] *adj* eternal, everlasting

e'bes [ä'bäs] *adj* vain, useless

e'cêb [ä'djeb] *f* wonder, amazement

e'cêbî [ä'djebi] *f* miracle, wonder

e'cêbokî [ä'djeboki] *adj* amazing, strange

e'cibandin [ä'djybandyn] *v* choose

e'cibîn [ä'djybin] *v* wonder

e'ciza [ä'djyza] *m* thing, object, material

e'cûze [ä'djuzä] *f* old lady

e'davet [ä'davät] *f* hatred; conflict; feud

e'deb [ä'däb] *f* shame, disgrace, humiliation; politeness

e'det [ä'dät] *m* custom, rule, habit

e'detî [ä'däti] *adj* usual, customary

e'dû [ä'du] *m* enemy, adversary

e'fîf [ä'fif] *adj* modest; chaste

e'firandin [ä'fyrandyn] *v* create, invent

e'firandkar [ä'fyrandkar] *m* creator, inventor

e'firandkarî [ä'fyrandkari] *f* creation, invention

e'fu [ä'fu] *m* forgiveness, pardon *v* forgive, pardon

e'gît [ä'git] *adj* brave, courageous

e'gîtî [ä'giti] *f* courage, boldness

e'kis [ä'kys] *m* reflection; depiction; photo

e'qilremîde [ä'qilrämidä] *adj* calm, composed, undisturbed

e'lalem [ä'laläm] *f* group

e'lem [ä'läm] *f* world

e'lîl [ä'lil] *adj* weak, sick

e'md [ä'md] *f* aim, purpose

e'mden [ä'mdän] *adv* purposely, on purpose

e'mel [ä'mäl] *m* work, job, assignment

e'melker [ä'mälkär] *m* worker

e'mir [ä'myr] *f* life *m* order

e'mirdar [ä'myrdar] *adj* alive, living *m* ruler; commander, chief

e'nadî [ä'nadi] *f* obstinacy

e'nayet [ä'nayät] *f* mercy, forgiveness, kindness

e'ne'ne [ä'nä'nä] *m* egoism, pride; legend, story

e'ngir [ä'ngyr] *adj* angry

e'ngirîn [ä'ngyrin] *v* be angry, sulk

e'nî [ä'ni] *f* forehead

e'nîn [ä'nin] *f* sigh

e'nir [ä'nyr] *f* anger

e'nirîn [ä'nyrin] *v* be angry

e'raz [ä'raz] *m* earth, land
e'rbab [ä'rbab] *m* aim, purpose, wish
e'rd [ä'rd] *m* earth
e'rdlerzîn [ä'rdlärzin] *f* earthquake
e'rif [ä'ryf] *adj* knowledgeable, wise
e'rifî [ä'ryfi] *n* wisdom, knowledge
e'rnokî [ä'rnoki] *f* threat, malice
e'rnûs [ä'rnus] *adj* envious
e'rnûsî [ä'rnusi] *f* envy
e'rş [ä'rsh] *m* throne *f* spear
e'rz [ä'rz] *f* width, honor
e'rze [ä'rzä] *f* complaint
e'sas [ä'sas] *m* basis
e'ser [ä'sär] *f* footprint, trace; result
e'sêba [ä'seba] *adv* as if
e'sil [ä'syl] *m* descent; family
e'sir [ä'syr] *f* age, epoch; dusk
e'sman [ä'sman] *m* sky, heaven
e'şar [ä'shar] *f* tax *pl* poems
e'vdal [ä'vdal] *m* beggar, pauper, slave
e'vdalî [ä'vdali] *f* poverty, slavery
e'wil [ä'wyl] *adj* first
e'wr [ä'wr] *m* cloud; sky
e'wrane [ä'wranä] *adj* cloudy
e'yal [ä'yal] *m* family
e'yan [ä'yan] *adj* visible, conspicuous

e'yb [ä'yb] *f* shame; dishonor
e'yd [ä'yd] *f* holiday, festivity
e'ynik [ä'ynyk] *f* source, spring; eyeglasses
e'zeb [ä'zäb] *m* torture, suffering; oppression
e'zelî [ä'zäli] *adj* eternal, everlasting
e'zîm [ä'zim] *adj* wonderful, amazing
e'zîmet [ä'zimät] *f* invitation
e'zîyet [ä'ziyät] *f* suffering, torture
e'zîz [ä'ziz] *adj* dear, beloved, respected
e'zra [ä'zra] *f* virgin

F

fabrîke [fabrikä] *f* factory
famîl [famil] *f* surname, family
fantazî [fantazi] *f* fantasy
fasiq [fasyq] *m* sinner, criminal
fars [fars] *f* Persian
farsî [farsi] *adj* Persian
fayîde [fayidä] *f* profit, use, value
fayîdekar [fayidäkar] *adj* profitable, valuable
fayiq [fayiq] *adj* highest, best; wonderful
fecaet [fädja'ät] *f* unexpected turn of events
fecar [fädjar] *m* lecher
feda [fàda] *f* victim
fedî [fädi] *f* chastity, shame; risk, courage

fehît [fähit] *adj* mean, base
fehm [fähm] *m* aptitude, intelligence
fehmdar [fähmdar] *adj* apt, astute, intelligent
fehmkor [fähmkor] *adj* inept, incompetent, stupid
fehmkorî [fähmkori] *f* ineptness, stupidy
feqet [fäqät] *conj* but
feqîr [fäqir] *adj* poor, needy
feqîrî [fäqiri] *f* poverty, need
felak [fälak] *f* misfortune; death
felat [fälat] *f* freedom, liberation
felek [fäläk] *f* heaven; fate, fortune; happiness
felekbaz [fäläkbaz] *adj* fortunate; happy
felekreş [fäläkräsh] *adj* unfortunate, unhappy
felsefî [fälsäfi] *f* philosophy
fen [fän] *m* cunning, treachery, deceit
fendar [fändar] *adj* sly, cunning, treacherous, deceitful
fendo [fändo] *m* dog
fener [fänär] *f* lamp, streetlamp, lantern
fepûle [fäpulä] *f* butterfly
ferange [färangä] *f* airport
feransiz [färansyz] *m* Frenchman
feransizî [färansyzi] *adj* French
ferec [färädj] *f* dawn

ferheng [färhäng] *f* science, knowledge; dictionary

ferx [färgh] *f* sun

ferih [färyh] *adj* clear, precision, definite

ferihî [färyhi] *f* clarity, precision

ferq [färq] *f* difference, distinction

ferqût [färqut] *f* parting, depart

ferman [färman] *f* order, command

fersend [färsänd] *f* anger, rage; lucky opportunity

ferwar [färwar] *adj* brilliant, splendid, exquisite

ferwarî [färwari] *f* brilliance, splendor

ferzan [färzan] *adj* important, significant; wise

ferzend [färzänd] *m* child; desdcendent

ferzî [färzi] *f* importance, significance, necessity

fesadî [fäsadi] *f* envy, provocation

fesil [fäsyl] *m* chapter, section; season

fetisandin [fätisandyn] *v* strangle, kill

fezilet [fäzilät] *f* goodness, honor, perfection

fezihet [fäzihät] *f* dishonor, shame

fikandin [fikandyn] *v* whistle

fîl [fil] *m* elephant

film [film] *f* film

filoloj [filolozh] *m* philologist

filolojî [filolozhi] *f* philology

filosof [filosof] *m* philosopher

filosofî [filosofi] *f* philosophy
fîncan [fincan] *f* goblet, wineglass
fînî [fini] *adj* Finnish
fîrme [firmä] *f* firm, company
fîte-fît [fitä-fit] *f* whistle, whistling sound
fîyat [fiyat] *m* price, cost
fîzîke [fizikä] *f* physics
fîzîkî [fiziki] *adj* physical
fêde [fedä] *f* courage, risk
fêdêrasî [federasi] *f* federation
fêkî [feki] *pl* fruit
fel [fäl] *f* action, deed; escapade, intrigue
fêldar [fäldar] *adj* sly, cunning
fêldarî [fäldari] *f* slyness, cunning
fêlnîş [felnish] *f gram* adverb
fêr [fer] *f* run
fêrbûn [ferbun] *f* study; aptitude
fêris [ferys] *m* hero, giant
fêrisî [ferysi] *f* courage, fortitude
fêrme [fermä] *f* farm
fêz [fez] *adv* above
fihêt [fyhet] *f* shame
fixan [fyghan] *m* cry
fikir [fykyr] *f* thought, contemplation, daydream
fikirdar [fykyrdar] *m* thinker, wise man, sage
fikirîn [fykyrin] *v* think, contemplate

fiqare [fyqarä] *adj* poor, needy

file [fylä] *m* Armenian

filekî [fyläki] *adj* Armenian

filfil [fylfyl] *f* pepper

finc [fyndj] *f* nostril; lie, deceit; cunning

find [fynd] *m* candle

fir [fyr] *f* flight

firavîn [fyravin] *f* lunch, dinner

firaz [fyraz] *f* phrase

firçak [fyrchak] *f* toothbrush

firebûn [fyräbun] *f* expansion, growth

firehî [fyrähi] *f* width, expanse; freedom

fireng [fyräng] *m* European; Frenchman

firengî [fyrängi] *adj* European; French

fireyî [fyräyi] *f* width, expanse; freedom

firîn [fyrin] *v* fly

firêqet [fyreqät] *adj* free; calm, safe

firêqetî [fyreqäti] *f* freedom; calmness, safety

firêz [fyrez] *f* height; altitude; ascent

firinçî [fyrynchi] *m* baker

firinde [fyryndä] *f* airplane

firindegah [fyryndägah] *f* airport

firindevan [fyryndävan] *m* pilot

firing [fyryng] *f, pl* nostril; nostrils

firk [fyrk] *f* drought

firkirin [fyrkyryn] *f* swallow; flight

firqandin [fyrqandyn] *v* pass through; throw
firqe [fyrqä] *f* political party, group; army unit
firqet [fyrqät] *f* parting, departure
firqî [fyrqi] *f* difference, distinction
firne [fyrnä] *f* bakery
firneçî [fyrnächi] *m* baker
firnik [fyrnyk] *f*, *pl* nostril; nostrils
firoşçî [fyroshchi] *m* salesman
firotan [fyrotan] *f* sale
firtone [fyrtonä] *f* storm, hurricane
fişe-fiş [fyshä-fysh] *f* hissing, whistle; sob
fîşîn [fyshyn] *f* hissing, whistle; sob
fişqe [fyshqä] *f* rocket; cherry
fitil [fytyl] *f* turn, turn of events
fitilandin [fytylandyn] *v* turn, turn around
fitin [fytyn] *f* dispute, quarrel
fitne [fytnä] *f* quarrel, feud, animosity
fitret [fyträt] *f* nature, character, temperament
fiyat [fiyat] *m* price
fize-fiz [fyzä-fyz] *f* scream; whistle; hissing
fizildûman [fyzylduman] *f* storm, hurricane
fola [fola] *m* quality
folk [folk] *f* ship
folklor [folklor] *f* folklore
fonêtîk [fonetik] *f* phonetics
form [form] *f* appearance

formûl [formul] *f* formula
fort [fort] *f* pomp, magnificence; beast
fortan [fortan] *f* pomp, splendor, magnificence
fotbal [fotbal] *f* football
fote [fotä] *f* death, end; loss
foto [foto] *m* photo, photograph
fotograf [fotograf] *m* photographer
fotografî [fotografi] *f* photographer
fûnksî [funksi] *f* function
fûre-fûr [furä-fur] *f* breath, gust of wind
fûtbol [futbol] *f* football
fûtbolçî [futbolchi] *m* football player

G

ga [ga] *m* bull, ox
gaajo [gaazho] *m* cowherd
gac [gadj] *f* strength
gak [gak] *conj* as if
gakûvî [gakuvi] *m* deer
gal [gal] *v* bring into order
gamboẍ [gambog] *f* ruins
gamêş [gamesh] *m* bull
garaj [garazh] *f* garage
garis [garys] *m* corn
garson [garson] *m* servant

gav [gav] *f* time, moment
gavekê [gaväkeh] *adv* afterward
gawir [gawyr] *m* non-Muslim
gaz [gaz] *f* gas
gazêt [gazet] *f* newspaper
geboz [gäboz] *f* precipice, ravine
gef [gäf] *m* threat
geh [gäh] *f* time
geh-geh [gäh-gäh] *adv* sometimes, occasionally
gehînek [gähinäk] *f* station
gele [gälä] *m* argument
gelek [gäläk] *adv* much, too much
gemar [gämar] *f* garbage, trash; filth
gemî [gämi] *f* ship; boat
gemîçî [gämichi] *m* sailor
gemîstan [gämistan] *f* harbor
genc [gändj] *f* argument; discussion; fight; war; treasure
gencîne [gändjinä] *f* treasure; treasury
gengaz [gängaz] *adj* easy
gep [gäp] *f* cheek; mouth
ger [gär] *f* circle; surroundings; plaza; arena
gerandîn [gärandin] *v* lead, direct
gerdan [gärdan] *m* beggar, pauper, bum
gerden [gärdän] *f* neck; throat
gerdenazadî [gärdänazadi] *adj* free, independent

gerdenkêş [gärdänkesh] *adj* obstinate
gerdenkêşî [gärdänkeshi] *n* obstinacy
gerdenkestî [gärdänkästi] *adj* downcast, despon
dent
gerek [gäräk] *adj* necessary, needed
gerekî [gäräki] *f* necessity
gerîn [gärin] *adj* walk; wander; stroll; meander
gerînendkar [gärinändkar] *m* director, chairman
gerîyayî [gäriyayi] *adj* experienced; knowledge
able
germ [gärm] *adj* warm, hot
germav [gärmav] *f* hot spring
germî [gärmi] *f* warmth, heat
germosarî [gärmosari] *adj* cool
germpîv [gärmpiv] *f* thermometer
gestin [gästyn] *v* bite
geş [gäsh] *adj* blooming, flowering; beautiful;
happy; brilliant *f* walk
geşan [gäshan] *v* sparkle; bloom
geveztî [gäväzti] *f* gossip
gewde [gäwdä] *adj* huge, corpulent
gewher [gäwhär] *m* pearl; jewel; image; appearance
gewr [gäwr] *adj* grey; light, white *f* beautiful
woman
gewrû [gäwru] *f* throat

gez [gäz] *f* bite
gezandin [gäzandyn] *v* bite; sting
gezîn [gäzin] *f* bite
gezme [gäzmä] *m* night guard
gî [gi] *pron* everything; everybody
gîha [giha] *m* grass, greenery
gîhandin [gihandyn] *v* finish; achieve
gîmin [gimyn] *f* hymn; national anthem
gêhan [gehan] *f* world; universe
gêj [gezh] *adj* defeated; bewildered; shocked
gêjbûn [gezhbun] *f* shock; bewilderment; insanity; loss of consciousness
gêl [ghel] *f* means, method
gêlaz [ghelaz] *f* cherry
gênêral [gheneral] *m* general
gêografî [gueografi] *f* geography
gêometrî [gueometri] *f* geometry
gêrmanî [guermani] *m, adj* German
gihanek [guihanäk] *f gram* conjunction
gihîştandin [ghyhishtandyn] *v* bring; grow up; bring up; gather
gihîştin [ghyihishtyn] *v* acchieve, reach; come
gilavî [ghylavi] *m* boss; chief; governor
gilî [ghyli] *m* word; speech; conversation
gilîbêj [ghylibezh] *m* narrator

gilîgotin [ghyligotyn] *f* story, narration; conversation

gimîn [ghymin] *f* thunder

gincirandîn [ghyndgyrandin] *v* tear

gincorî [ghyndjori] *adj* torn

gir [ghyr] *adj* big; sizeable; tall *m* hill

giramar [ghyramar] *f* grammar

giran [ghyran] *adj* heavy; sizeable; difficult

giranbiha [ghyranbyha] *adj* precious; costly; priceless

giranî [ghyrani] *f* heaviness; difficulty

girî [ghyri] *m* crying; sobbing

girîn [ghyrin] *v* cry, sob

girêdanî [ghyredani] *f* connection; union

girme-girm [ghyrmî-ghyrm] *f* thunder; racket

girtin [ghyrtyn] *v* take; grab

gişan [ghyshan] *pl* everything; everybody *adv* first of all

gişt [ghysht] *pl* everything; everybody *adv* totally

giva [ghyva] *adv* as if

givir [ghyvyr] *adj* fat

givirdar [ghyvyrdar] *adj* dead

givrik [ghyvryk] *adj* sizeable; big; huge

gol [gol] *f* lake; pond

gor [gor] *f* grave, coffin; obedience

gorandin [gorandyn] *v* change; trade

gore [gorä] *f* sock; stocking
gorxane [gorkhanä] *f* grave, coffin; cemetery
gorî [gori] *f* victim
gosirmat [gosyrmat] *adj* strange, amazing; funny;
　scandalous
gosirmatî [gosyrmati] *f* strangeness; silliness;
　scandal
goşe [goshe] *m* corner
goşt [gosht] *m* meat
gotar [gotar] *f* word; speech
gotin [gotyn] *v* talk, speak, say
govek [goväk] *f* circle; surroundings; orbit
grîp [grip] *f* flu
guh [göh] *m* ear; ears
guhan [göhan] *m* breast
guhartin [göhartyn] *v* change; replace
guhbel [göhbäl] *adj* cautious
guhbelî [göhbäli] *f* caution
guher [göhär] *m* pearl; jewel
guhêrandin [göherandyn] *v* change, trade
guhêrin [göheryn] *v* change, trade
guhmişk [göhmyshk] *adj* cautious
guje-guj [gözhä-gözh] *f* sound; noise
gul [göl] *f* flower; rose
gulak [gölak] *f* temple
gulan [gölan] *f* May

gulaş [gölash] *f* struggle

gulaşgirî [gölashghyri] *f* struggle

gulavgirî [gölavghyri] *f* eau de Cologne

guldan [göldan] *f* flower vase; flowering

gulgeş [gölgäsh] *adj* blooming, flowering

gulgulîn [gölgölin] *v* drip

gulistan [gölystan] *f* flower bed

gulking [gölkyng] *f* flower; rose

gulle [göllä] *f* bullet

gulleagirkirin [gölläagyrkyryn] *f* shot

gulol [gölol] *adj* round

gulover [gölovär] *adj* round; sphere-like

guman [göman] *f* hope; faith

gumgume [gömgömä] *f* thunder

gumreh [gömräh] *adj* big, large, sizeable

gumrehî [gömrähî] *f* big size; strength, might

gund [gönd] *m* country; village

gundî [göndi] *m* peasant

guneh [gönäh] *m* fault, guilt, crime; sin

gunehkar [gönähkar] *m* culprit, criminal; sinner

gupik [göpyk] *f* cheek; bud, sprout; edge

gur [gör] *m* wolf *adj* strong; expanding *f* threat

gurc [gördj] *m* Georgian

gurcikî [gördjyki] *adj* Georgian

gurdil [gördyl] *m* compassion; grief

gure-gur [görä-gör] *f* thunder; complaint

gurgure [görgörä] *f* waterfall
gurî [göri] *f* fierceness, savagery; greed
gurîn [görin] *f* thunder; racket; torrent of water
gustîl [göstil] *f* wedding ring
guya [göya] *adv* as if
gû [gu] *m* filth, dirt
gûc [gudj] *f* strength
gûzan [guzan] *m* razor blade

H

ha [ha] *interj* what? how? really? try it! *adj* such;
    in this way
ha-hanga [ha-hanga] *adv* in a hurry; suddenly
hacet [hadjet] *f* necessity, need
hadîs [hadis] *f* story, tale; legend
hacib [hadjyb] *m* doorman
haho [haho] *f* scream; cry
haj [hazh] *m* knowledge; information
hajxwe [hazhkhwä] *adj* cautious
hajxwehebûn [hazhkhwähäbun] *f* caution
hala [hala] *adv* now
halan [halan] *m* encouragement, approval
hana [hana] *f* time, period, epoch
har [har] *adj* mad; furious; hot
harî [hari] *f* fury; frenzy; seizure

hasarî [hasari] *f* gate
hased [hasäd] *m* envy, hatred
haşîtî [hashiti] *f* peace; freedom, liberty
havalkar [hävalkar] *m* colleague, partner
havîj [havizh] *f* envy
havîjîn [havizhin] *v* envy
havîn [havin] *f* summer
havil [havyl] *m* soul; spirit
hawa [ha'wa] *adj* futile; useless
hawak [ha'wak] *f* color
hawêr [ha'wer] *m* hill; heavens
hawûtin [haowutyn] *v* arouse, excite
hay [ha'y] *interj* oh! *f* knowledge
hazir [hazyr] *adj* ready
hazirbûn [hazyrbun] *f* readiness; presence
hebûn [häbun] *v* be, exist
hecac [hädjadj] *f* cloud
hedan [hädan] *m* border, boundary
hedimandin [hädymandyn] *v* destroy
heger [hägär] *conj* if
hejmar [häzhmar] *f* date; account
helaket [hälakät] *f* death, end
helbet [hälbät] *adv* certainly, of course
hele-hel [hälä-häl] *f* cry, wail
helecan [hälädjan] *f* worry, anxiety; cradle
helîm [hälim] *adj* soft, gentle

helqe [hälqä] *f* circle *m* wave
hemayet [hämayät] *f* protection, patronage
hemayetger [hämayätgär] *m* protector, patron
hember [hämbär] *adj* similar, alike
hemcivat [hämdjivat] *f* congress
hemd [hämd] *m* will
hemel [hämäl] *m* lamb
hemîn [hämin] *adv* still; exactly; already; but
hemil [hämyl] *adj* pregnant
hemkar [hämkar] *m* colleague, comrade
hemraz [hämraz] *m* friend, close friend
hemser [hämsär] *m* spouse
hemta [hämta] *adj* equal, similar, alike
hemwelat [hämwälat] *m* countryman
hemzik [hämzyk] *m* twin *pl* twins
henda [hända] *f* direction, side
hengam [hängam] *m* time, period, era
heq [häq] *m* right; will; truth; law
heqdest [häqdäst] *m* payment
heqî [häqi] *f* truth; reality
heqîq [häqiq] *adj* true
heqtî [häqti] *f* lawful action
heqxebat [häqkhäbat] *f* wage
heqyat [häqyat] *f* right; truth
her hal [här hal] *adv* of course; in any case
heravî [häravi] *f* destruction

hercar [härdjar] *adv* always, each time
herçax [härtchakh] *adv* always, constantly
herçend [härtchänd] *conj* because; to the extent of; despite, notwithstanding
hercîya [härdjiya] *adv* everywhere
herdem [härdäm] *adv* always
herder [härdär] *adv* everywhere
here [härä] *adv* most, the most
hereket [häräkät] *f* movement
hergav [härgav] *adv* always
herîs [häris] *adj* dull, boring
herikîn [härykin] *v* move; leak; shake
herir [häryr] *m* silk
herke [härkä] *conj* if
herkes [härkäs] *adj* every; any
herroj [härrozh] *adv* every day *adj* everyday, commonplace
hersim [härsym] *f* cold, flu
herze [härzä] *adj* futile
hesar [häsar] *m* fence, gate; blockade, siege
hesas [häsas] *m* feeling
hesincawî [häsyndjawi] *m* tool, instrument
hesp [häsp] *m* horse
hesret [häsrät] *f* grief, longing, sorrow
hestî [hästi] *m* bone
hestîçene [hästichänä] *f* jaw

heşifandin [häshyfandyn] *v* change
hev [häv] *adv* mutually
heval [häval] *m* comrade, friend
hevaltî [hävalti] *f* friendship
hevber [hävbär] *adj* alike, similar
hevçûn [hävchun] *f* argument
hevderdî [hävdärdi] *f* compassion, commiseration
hevdîn [hävdin] *f* meeting
hevgihandin [hävgihandyn] *v* connect
hevîr [hävir] *m* dough
hevkar [hävkar] *m* participant, companion
hevkarî [hävkari] *f* participation
hevkom [hävkom] *f* congress
hevo [hävo] *f* duck
hevok [hävok] *f* sentence
hevra [hävra] *adv* together, mutually
hevreng [hävräng] *adj* similar, alike; same color
hevrûbûn [hävrubun] *f* opposite; equality, similarity
hevşîn [hävshin] *m* mourning
hevta [hävta] *adj* equal, similar, alike
hevxistin [hävkhystyn] *v* fight; mix, unite
hew [häw] *adv* finally
hewa [häwa] *f* air, fresh air, weather; sound, melody
hewakî [häwaki] *adv* as; like

hewapîv [häwapiv] *f* barometer
hewesker [häwäskär] *adj* curious
hewil [häwyl] *m* help; profit
hewir [häwyr] *m* air, atmosphere, cloud *f* sponge
hewşek [häwshäk] *adv* little, a little
heye [häyä] *adv* maybe
heyîn [häyin] *v* be, exist
heyînî [häyini] *f* existence
heykel [häykäl] *m* statue, sculpture, monument
heywan [häywan] *f* balcony, verranda, terrace
hezêmet [häzemät] *f* defeat
hezerî [häzäri] *f* caution
hezret [häzrät] *m* presence; majesty
hê [heh] *adv* still, again; again and again
hêç [hech] *n* nothing *adj* insignificant; angry
hêçbûn [hechbun] *f* death, annihilation
hêdî [hedi] *adj* quietly; cautiously
hêja [hezha] *adv* now; recently; only *f* price
hêjayî [hezhayi] *f* price; cost
hêk [hek] *f* egg
hêl [hel] *f* top, height; country, province
hêlandin [helandyn] *v* leave, abandon
hêlekan [heläkan] *adj* highest; mightiest
hêlîn [helin] *f* nest
hênik [henyk] *adj* cool; fresh
hênikayî [henykayi] *f* coolness; freshness

hêrs [hers] *f* anger, rage
hêsa [hesa] *adj* calm, peaceful; light
hêsabûn [hesabun] *f* calm, peace, ease
hêsîr [hesir] *m* prisoner, captive
hêsîrî [hesiri] *f* captivity, slavery, poverty
hêstir [hestyr] *f* tear *pl* tears
hêşîn [heshin] *adj* green
hêwan [hewan] *adj* equal, alike, resembling
hêwirze [hewirzä] *f* noise; havoc
hêz [hez] *m* force, might, strength
hêzing [hezyng] *f* sigh
hîcret [hidjrät] *f* migration, emigration
hîjdeh [hizhdäh] *num* eighteen
hîn [hin] *v* learn, study
hînbûn [hinbun] *f* study, learning
hînker [hinkär] *m* teacher
hînxane [hinkhanä] *f* school
hîv [hiv] *f* moon, crescent
hîvî [hivi] *f* expectation, wait
hicran [hydjran] *f* parting, farewell
hikumet [hykömät] *f* government; rule, power
hilandin [hylandyn] *v* pick up, lift; take; hide
hilawet [hylawät] *f* sweets, pleasure
hilbet [hylbät] *adv* certainly, of course
hilbûn [hylbun] *v* rise, go up, ascend
hildan [hyldan] *v* pick up, raise

hilgirtin [hylgyrtyn] *v* pick up, raise
hilhatin [hylhatyn] *v* rise, go up, ascend
hilkês [hylkes] *f* ascent
hilneyî [hylnäyi] *adj* tall, high *adv* high
hilqetandin [hylqetandyn] *v* tear out, cut off
hilqeys [hylqäys] *adv* that much
hilşîn [hylshin] *v* fall, crumble
hilteqandin [hyltäqandyn] *v* blow up, explode
hilû [hylu] *adj* smooth, flat
himelî [hymäli] *f* amulet, talisman
hinarî [hynari] *f* sob, cry
hincas [hyndjas] *pl* almonds
hind [hynd] *f* side, direction *m* Indian
hindî [hyndi] *adv* after, later *adj* Indian
hindik [hyndyk] *adv* little, sparsely
hiner [hynär] *m* art, craft, talent; courage
hingam [hyngam] *m* time, period
hingî [hyngi] *adv* so much *prep* until
hingiv [hyngyv] *m* honey
hingor [hyngor] *m* comrade; equal *f* dawn; dusk
hira [hyra] *adv* here
his [hys] *m* feeling, emotion
hişbûn [hyshbun] *f* silence
hişmet [hyshmät] *f* respect; magnitude; modesty
hiştin [hyshtyn] *v* leave, abandon
hizin [hyzyn] *f* sorrow, sadness

hizir [hyzyr] *f* thought, sentence
hodax [hodakh] *m* worker, servant
hoker [hokär] *f* adverb
hol [hol] *f* circle, sphere, ball
holandî [holandi] *M* Dutchman
holê [holeh] *adv* this way, in this manner
horîzon [horizon] *f* horizon
hostakar [hostakar] *m* master, craftsman
hosûd [hosud] *adj* envious, jealous
hov [hov] *m* wild man; beast
hucir [hödjir] *f* classroom
hucret [hödjrät] *f* reward
hucur [hödjör] *m* stone, rock
hulmgulm [hölmgölm] *f* steam, evaporation
hundur [höndör] *m* inside, inner part
hurmet [hörmät] *f* respect, honor; woman, wife
hurmîn [hörmin] *f* noise, scream, havoc
hurum [höröm] *m* Greek, Greek language
hurumî [hörömi] *adj* Greek
husin [hösyn] *m* beauty, splendor
hûnandin [hunandyn] *v* weave
hûncarî [hundjari] *adj* Hungarian
hûr [hur] *adj* little, tiny
hûr [hur] *f* stomach
hûrayî [hurayi] *f* small change, trifle
hûrgilî [hurgyli] *adj* in detail *f* detail

hûrmûr [hurmur] *pl* things, household ware
hûrxaş [hurghash] *adj* broken
hûzan [huzan] *m* razor

Ḧ

ḧadîse [hadisä] *f* incident
ḧaf [haf] *f* side
ḧebs [häbs] *f* prison; confinement
ḧed [häd] *m* boundary, borderline
ḧefs [häfs] *f* caution
ḧeftê [häfteh] *f* week *num* seventy
ḧelal [hälal] *adj* chaste, pure
ḧelalî [hälali] *f* chastity
ḧemêz [hämez] *f* embrace
ḧenek [hänäk] *f* joke
ḧeram [häram] *adj* dirty, unclean
ḧerambaz [härambaz] *m* criminal
ḧerf [härf] *f* letter
ḧerî [häri] *f* clay, dirt
ḧerimandin [härimandyn] *v* pollute
ḧesab [häsab] *m* account
ḧesabê [häsabeh] *adv* as if
ḧesen [häsän] *f* kindness
ḧesin [häsyn] *m* iron
ḧesûdî [häsudi] *f* envy

heta [häta] *prep* before
hetk [hätk] *f* caution
hevekî [häväki] *adv* a little
hevtsed [hävtsäd] *num* seven hundred
hewal [häwal] *m* condition
hewas [häwas] *f* feeling; interest; wish
hewce [häwdjä] *m* need, necessity
hewîn [häwin] *v* calm
hewînî [häwini] *f* calm
hewle [häwlä] *f* halvah
heya [häya] *f* shame
heyr [häyr] *f* care
heyran [häyran] *f* victim *adj* amazing
heyret [häyrät] *f* wonder, amazement
heyşt [häysht] *num* eight
heyştê [häyshteh] *num* eighty
heywan [häywan] *f* beast
hezar [häzar] *num* thousand
hezîn [häzin] *adj* sad
hezîne [häzinä] *f* sadness
heziran [häzyran] *f* June
hezkirî [häzkyri] *adj* beloved
hezmekar [häzmäkar] *adj* sensitive
hezmekarî [häzmäkari] *f* sensitivity
hîle [hilä] *f* cunning; deceit
hîm [him] *m* base, foundation

ḧinarik [hynaryk] *f* cheek
ḧir [hyr] *adj* bold, obstinate
ḧiş [hysh] *m* mind, intellect
ḧişk [hyshk] *adj* dry, hard
ḧişkayî [hyshkayi] *f* dryness
ḧişker [hyshkär] *m* thinker
ḧişyar [hyshyar] *adj* awake
ḧubandin [höbandyn] *v* love *n* love
ḧucir [hödjyr] *m* room; pavillon
ḧucûm [hödjum] *f* attack
ḧukum [hököm] *m* rule, power; order
ḧukumdar [hökömdar] *m* ruler, monarch
ḧur [hör] *adj* strong, powerful
ḧusin [hösyn] *m* beauty
ḧûr [hur] *m* stomach

X

xaçparêz [khatchparez] *m* Christian
xaçparêzî [khatchparezi] *f* Christianity
xalî [khali] *adj* empty
xalîçe [khalitchä] *f* rug
xalis [khalys] *adj* useful
xalojn [khalozhn] *f* aunt
xaloza [khaloza] *m* cousin
xam [kham] *adj* raw

xame [khamä] *m* pencil
xan [khan] *f* room; house, building
xaneban [khaneban] *m* roof; terrace
xanim [khanym] *f* Mrs., madam, dame
xanî [khani] *m* house, building
xap [khap] *f* lie, deceit
xar [khar] *adj* crooked; wrong
xarite [kharitä] *f* map
xarû [kharu] *adj* pure, undiluted; typical
xas [khas] *adj* naked
xasmêr [khasmer] *adj* brave, courageous
xasmêrî [khasmeri] *f* courage
xastî [khasti] *f* quality
xatim [khatym] *f* ring
xatirgirtin [khatyrgyrtyn] *f* respect, esteem
xatirnas [khatyrnas] *adj* respectful
xavî [khavi] *adj* raw, unripe
xayînî [khayini] *f* treason
xaz [khaz] *f* line
xebat [khäbat] *f* work
xebatgeh [khäbatgäh] *f* center
xebatker [khäbatkär] *m* worker
xeber [khäbär] *f* word; speech
xeberdan [khäbärdan] *f* conversation, speech
xeberdar [khäbärdar] *m* speaker, orator
xebernivîs [khäbärnyvis] *f* dictionary

xeder [khädär] *adj* dangerous, fatal, uncurable
xelayî [khälayi] *f* hunger
xeleq [khäläq] *f* ring, circle
xelic [khälydj] *f* bay, harbor
xelq [khälq] *m* people, population
xem [khäm] *f* misfortune, grief, sadness
xemgîn [khämgin] *adj* upset, sad
xemil [khämyl] *f* ornament, decoration
xendan [khändan] *adj* laughing, smiling, happy
xeneq [khänäq] *f* throat
xeniqin [khänyqyn] *v* choke; drown
xepe-xep [khäpä-khäp] *adv* suddenly
xerc [khärdj] *m* expense, cost
xerçeng [khärdjäng] *m* lobster, crab
xerez [khäräz] *f* swiftness; aim
xerîdar [khäridär] *m* buyer
xerêq [khäreq] *f* care, worry
xeriqîn [khäryqin] *v* drown
xerz [khärz] *m* caviar
xesirîn [khäsyrin] *v* try, make an effort
xesle [khäslä] *adj* sick, ill; tired
xesterane [khästäranä] *f* hospital
xeşîm [khäshim] *adj* naïve, unexperienced
xeşm [khäsm] *f* anger, rage
xet [khät] *f* line
xeta [khäta] *f* fault, guilt

xetabela [khätabäla] *f* misfortune
xew [khäw] *f* sleep; dream
xewer [khäwär] *m* sun
xewf [khäwf] *f* fear, terror
xewle [khäwlä] *adj* secret, hidden
xewlet [khäwlät] *f* secret
xeyal [khäyal] *m* thought; specter
xeylî [khäyli] *adv* much, very
xezan [khäzan] *f* autumn
xezeb [khäzäb] *f* rage
xesne [khäznä] *f* treasure
xirab [khyrab] *adj* destroyed, ruined
xirêt [khyret] *f* effort
xistin [khystyn] *adj* beaten, struck, hit
xiyanet [khiyanät] *f* treason
xiyar [khiyar] *m* cucumber
xizan [khyzan] *adj* naïve, unexperienced
xizmet [khyzmät] *f* business, work, duty
xort [khort] *m* youth, young man
xortanî [khortani] *f* youth
xubar [khöbar] *f* dust; smoke; darkness
Xuda [khöda] *m* God, Lord; lord, ruler
xudan [khödan] *m* master, lord; patron
xudanbext [khödanbäkht] *adj* honest, sincere
xudantî [khödanti] *f* patronage
xufye [khöfyä] *m* spy

xulam [khölam] *m* slave

xulî [khöli] *f* dream, illusion; ecstasy

xumam [khömam] *f* heat

xumîn [khömin] *f* noise, sound

xumrî [khömri] *adj* red

xunav [khönav] *f* dampness; dew

xurekxane [khöräkkhanä] *f* kitchen

xurekpêj [khöräkpezh] *m* chef, cook

xurîn [khörin] *v* scold, yell, reproach

xurt [khört] *adj* fat, obese, plump

xurtebarî [khörtäbari] *f* courage, boldness

xusûs [khösus] *adj* essential; material; special

xuya [khöya] *adj* visible *f* quality

xûdan [khudan] *v* sweat

xûn [khun] *f* blood

xûnçe [khunchä] *f* tray

xûnxur [khunkhör] *m* exploiter *adj* bloodthirsty

xûnkar [khunkar] *m* murderer

xûnkêş [khunkesh] *adj* appealing, attractive, splendid

xûnkêşî [khunkeshi] *f* appeal, splendor

xûsran [khusran] *f* loss; death; accident

xûsk [khushk] *f* sister

xût [khut] *adv* exactly *pron* that one; the same

xwarzî [khwarzi] *m* nephew *f* niece

xwe [khwä] *pron* himself, herself, itself

xweberajo [khwäbärazho] *m* machine-gun

xwebergirî [khwäbärgyri] *f* restraint

xwedan [khwädan] *m* master; patron; creator

xwedanterîqet [khwädantäriqät] *adj* religious

xwedî [khwädi] *v* guard, protect

xwedîbext [khwädibäkht] *adj* happy

xwediehmîyet [khwädiäkhmiyät] *adj* important, serious

xwedînamûs [khwädinamus] *adj* honest

xwedîtî [khwäditi] *f* protection; patronage

Xwedê [khwädeh] *m* God, Lord

xwedêdan [khwädedan] *f* possession

xwedêgiravî [khwädegyravi] *adv* as if

xwedênenas [khwädenänas] *m* atheist

xwehebîn [khwähäbin] *m* egoist *adj* egotistical

xwexwetî [khwäkhwäti] *f* independence

xweltik [khwältyk] *f* aunt

xwendevan [khwändävan] *m* reader; student

xwendîn [khwändin] *v* read

xwendînxanî [khwändinkhani] *f* school

xwer [khwär] *m* food; fate

xwerin [khwäryn] *v* eat; drink *f* food

xwest [khwäst] *f* longing

xwestek [khwästäk] *f* wish; aim; favor

xwestik [khwästyk] *f* bride, fiancée
xweş [khwäsh] *adj* good; beautiful; happy; good-tasting
xweşbang [khwäshbang] *adj* harmonious
xweşbangî [khwäshbangi] *f* harmony
xweşbîn [khwäshbin] *f* aroma
xweşdîl [khwäshdil] *adj* merry, happy
xweşdîlî [khwäshdili] *f* happiness
xweşhal [khwäshhal] *adj* healthy
xweş-xweş [khwäsh-khwäsh] *adv* pleasingly
xweyan [khwäyan] *adj* famous; conspicuous
xweydan [khwäydan] *f* sweat
xweyguneh [khwäygönäh] *adj* guilty, sinful
xweyhiş [khwäyhysh] *adj* smart; wise
xweyî [khwäyi] *m* patron; owner, master
xweyês [khwäyes] *adj* sick, ill
xweykemal [khwäykämal] *adj* talented
xweykeremî [khwäykärämi] *f* goodness
xweykulfet [khwäykölfät] *adj* married
xwezî [khwäzi] *adv* necessarily
xwezok [khwäzok] *m* pauper, beggar
xwê [khweh] *v* salt
xwêndewarî [khwendäwari] *f* studies

Ẍ

ẍafil [ghafyl] *adv* carelessly, suddenly
ẍaret [gharät] *f* robbery, destruction *v* rob,
  destroy
ẍaze [ghazä] *f* noise, clamor, scream *v* scream
ẍelet [ghälät] *f* mistake
ẍeltan [ghältan] *adj* round
ẍenî [ghäni] *adj* rich
ẍerb [ghärb] *f* West
ẍerbî [ghärbi] *adj* Western
ẍerez [ghäräz] *prep* except
ẍeyb [ghäyb] *adj* secret, mysterious
ẍezibîn [ghäzybin] *v* be angry, rage
ẍorfe [ghorfä] *f* veranda
ẍurbet [ghörbät] *f* exile
ẍusse [ghössä] *f* grief, saddness

Î

îbahat [ibahat] *f* permission
îblîs [iblis] *m* devil
îbra [ibra] *f* receipt
îbtîda [ibtida] *f* beginning

îcabet [idjabät] *f* acceptance

îcar [idjar] *adv* this time

îcare [idjarä] *f* hire, rent

îcat [idjat] *f* invention, creation

îcatkar [idjatkar] *m* inventor

îcgar [idjgar] *adv* too

îcret [idjrät] *f* payment

îctime [idjtimä] *f* collection

îda [ida] *adv* more; then, in that case; consequently

îdam [idam] *f* rage, anger

îdêal [ideal] *f* ideal

îdêalî [ideali] *adj* ideal

îdêalîst [idealist] *m* idealist

îdêya [ideya] *f* idea

îdqat [idqat] *f* faith; hope

îhtîmal [ikhtimal] *adv* likely

îkram [ikram] *f* generosity, hospitality, honor

îqin [iqyn] *adj* necessary

îlac [iladj] *f* help; means

îlahî [ilahi] *adv* especially

Îlahî [ilahi] *m* Allah, God

îlan [ilan] *f* announcement, advertisement

îlet [ilät] *f* family, heredity

îlon [ilon] *f* September

îmam [imam] *m* Imam *f* obedience
îmza [imza] *f* signature
înandin [inandyn] *v* convince *f* conviction
înanî [inani] *f* trust
Încîl [indjil] *f* Gospel
îndûstrî [industri] *f* industry
înglîzî [inglizi] *adj* English
înî [ini] *f* Friday
înkar [inkar] *f* refusal
însan [insan] *m* human being, humanity
întîxab [intikhab] *f* choice; election
înşala [inshala] *excl* God grant it!
întîzam [intizam] *f* order, discipline
îrad [irad] *f* income; tax
îreda [iräda] *adv* here
îrq [irq] *m* race, descent
îsaf [isaf] *f* justice
îskela [iskäla] *f* port
Îslamiyet [islamiyät] *f* Islam
îsm [ism] *m* name
îspenax [ispänakh] *f* spinach
îstasîon [istassion] *f* station
îstekan [istäkan] *f* glass
îstîlah [istilah] *f* phrase, idiom
îş [ish] *m* business, work, profession

îşkav [ishkav] *f* wardrobe, shelf, cupboard
îşker [ishkär] *m* worker
îşkol [ishkol] *f* school
îşq [ishq] *f* light, ray; love, passion
îtbar [itbar] *f* trust, faith
îtîraz [itiraz] *f* objection, protest
îyûl [iyul] *f* July
îyûn [iyun] *f* June
îza [iza] *f* punishment; suffering
îzin [izyn] *f* right; permission

Ê

ê [eh] *part* yes
êcgar [edjgar] *adv* also
êdin [edyn] *adj* other
êẍbal [eghbal] *m* happiness; fortune
êẍlî [eghli] *m* group
êlat [elat] *f* confederation; people
êm [em] *m* food
êmanê [emaneh] *adv* near
êmîş [emish] *m* fruit; vegetable
êramûk [eramuk] *f* hook
êrîşbir [erishbir] *m* robber
êrîşkirin [erishkirin] *f* robbery

êris [erys] *m* monk, priest
êrmenî [ermäni] *m* Armenian
êş [esh] *f* pain; illness
êşayî [eshayi] *f* illness
êşîn [eshin] *v* be ill
êvar [evar] *f* evening
Êzdan [ezdan] *m* God
êzid [ezyd] *m* Ezid (kurdish tribe)
êzing [ezing] *m* wood *f* sigh

I

ibadet [ybadät] *f* prayer
ibadetgeh [ybadätgäh] *f* temple
ifad [yfad] *f* guilt; punishment
ifaet [yfaät] *f* danger; calamity
ixtîyar [ykhtiyar] *adj* old, weak, poor
iqlîm [yqlim] *m* country
ilm [ylm] *m* science, learning
ilmî [ylmi] *adj* scientific
imaret [ymarät] *m* building
imkan [ymkan] *f* possibility
in [yn] *f* mommy, mom
ins [yns] *m* habit
inwan [ynwan] *m* title, name

irfan [yrfan] *m* culture
irin [yryn] *f* hatred, rage
işaret [ysharät] *f* sign, symbol
iştehawer [yshtähawär] *adj* appetizing
itham [yt'ham] *f* food
izb [yzb] *m* bachelor

J

jakêt [zhaket] *m* jacket
jan [zhan] *f* pain, illness
japon [zhapon] *m* Japanese
japonî [zhaponi] *adj* Japanese
jar [zhar] *adj* thin, skinny
jehr [zhähr] *f* poison
jehrdar [zhährdar] *adj* poisonous
jeneral [zhänäral] *m* general
jîndar [zhindar] *adj* alive
jîr [zhir] *adj* sensible
jîyîn [zhiyin] *v* live
jêbirîn [zhebirin] *v* cut off
jêderketin [zhedärkätyn] *v* go out, go away
jêmexesîn [zhemäxäsyn] *v* envy
jêr [zher] *f* bottom

jêrejorbûn [zheräzhorbun] *f* ascent
jêrmal [zhermal] *f* basement
jêrmen [zhermen] *m* German
jêrmenî [zhermeni] *adj* German
jêveqetandin [zheväqätandyn] *v* disconnect
ji [zhy] *prep* from
jibergirtin [zhybärgyrtyn] *v* make a copy
jihevbela [zhyhävbäla] *adj* dispersed
jihevcudakirin [zhyhävdjödakyryn] *v* divide
jihevvekirin [zhyhävväkyryn] *v* open, open up
jimar [zhymar] *f* account; number, numeral
jimartin [zhymartyn] *v* count
jin [zhyn] *f* wife, woman
jinbav [zhynbav] *f* stepmother
jindar [zhyndar] *adj* married
jinebî [zhynäbi] *f* widow
jinepîr [zhynäpir] *f* old woman
jinxwestin [zhynkhwästyn] *f* marriage
jinmirî [zhynmyri] *m* widower
jinû [zhynu] *adv* again
jor [zhor] *f* top
jorê [zhoreh] *adv* above, on top
jwan [zhwan] *f* meeting

K

kabûs [kabus] *m* demon, nightmare
kaxet [kakhät] *f* letter; paper
kak [kak] *m* older brother; uncle
kal [kal] *adj* old; unripe *m* old man; watermelon
kala [kala] *pl* goods, ware
kambax [kambakh] *f* ruins; curse
kanfêt [kanfet] *f* candy *pl* candy
kanûn [kanun] *f* January
kanyak [kanyak] *f* cognac
kapek [kapäk] *f* bran
kar [kar] *f* profit, gain; work; earnings
karçin [karchyn] *f* pear
kardar [kardar] *adj* useful, profitable
karxane [karkhanä] *f* factory
karî [kari] *f* mushroom
kart [kart] *f* map; cards
kartol [kartol] *f* potato
kas [kas] *f* cup; glass; goblet
kasib [kasyb] *adj* poor *m* pauper
kastûm [kastum] *m* suit
katib [katyb] *m* secretary
kavran [kavran] *m* cattle
kaw [ka'w] *adj* proud, haughty
kawî [ka'wi] *f* pride

kayser [kaysär] *m* king, emperor
keç [käch] *f* daughter, girl, maiden
keçel [kächäl] *adj* bald
ked [käd] *f* work, toil; earnings
keder [kädär] *f* suffering, pain
kej [käzh] *adj* red, red-haired; white, light
kel [käl] *m* thing *f* heat, boil
kelax [kälakh] *adj* thin
kelam [kälam] *f* word, speech
kelb [kälb] *m* dog
kele [kälä] *m* head; top
kelem [käläm] *f* cabbage
keleş [käläsh] *adj* beautiful; noble
kelişo [kälysho] *f* laundry
kelle [källä] *m* head
kemal [kämal] *f* maturity, talent
kember [kämbär] *f* belt
ken [kän] *m* laugh, smile
kenandin [känandyn] *v* make laugh
kengê [kängeh] *conj* when
kep [käp] *f* nose
ker [kär] *adj* deaf
kerb [kärb] *f* sadness, depression
kerem [käräm] *f* good, kindness
kerî [käri] *m* piece, part
kerîgêj [kärigezh] *adj* silly

kerîm [kärim] *adj* generous, merciful *f* generosity
kero [käro] *adj* deaf
kevej [käväzh] *adj* white
kevir [kävyr] *m* stone
kevjal [kävzhal] *f* duck
kevn [kävn] *adj* old, worn
kevnahî [kävnahi] *f* old age
kew [käw] *f* pigeon; wound *adj* blue
kewandin [käwandyn] *v* cure, treat
kîderê [kidäreh] *pron* where
kîka [kika] *pl* (name of Kurdish tribe) Kika
kîn [kin] *f* malice
kîp [kip] *adj* vertical
kîs [kis] *m* purse
kêf [kef] *f* mood
kêfxweş [kefkhwäsh] *adj* happy, merry
kêlm [kelm] *f* word, speech
kêm [kem] *adv* little, scantily
kêmaqil [kemaqyli] *adj* stupid, silly
kêmasî [kemasi] *f* lack, scarcity
kêmî [kemi] *f* grudge
kêr [ker] *adj* useful, needed *f* knife
kêşan [keshan] *f* measure; weights
kifte [kyftä] *m* dish of meatballs
kilam [kylam] *f* song
kilîma [kylima] *f* climate

kilît [kylit] *f* lock; key
kilûb [kylub] *f* club
kin [kyn] *adj* short, small
kinc [kyndj] *m* clothes, dress
kineşo [kynäsho] *f* laundry
kinêz [kynez] *m* relative *adj* sociable
kip [kyp] *adj* calm, quiet
kir [kyr] *m* business, deed; worry
kiras [kyras] *m* shirt
kirîzîs [kyrizis] *f* crisis
kirê [kyreh] *f* rent
kirin [kyryn] *v* do, act
kişik [kyshyk] *f* slippers, sandals *f* chess
kitêbxane [kytebkhanä] *f* library
kitêbnasî [kytebnasi] *f* bibliography
kitêbok [kytebok] *f* book
kitik [kytyk] *f* cat
kit-kit [kyt-kyt] *adj* detailed
kivş [kyvsh] *adj* definite, clear
kivşkirin [kyvshkyryn] *f* definition
ko [ko] *adj* bent, curved, crooked
koçek [kochäk] *m* hermit
kok [kok] *f* root *adj* fat
kokhatin [kokhatyn] *f* disappearance; death
kol [kol] *m* slave *f* hole
kolan [kolan] *v* dig

kolonî [koloni] *f* colony
komek [komäk] *f* help
komîtê [komiteh] *f* committee
komêdî [komedi] *f* comedy
konfêrênsî [konferensi] *f* conference
kongirê [kongyreh] *f* congress
konsêrt [konsert] *f* concert
konstîtûsî [konstitusi] *f* constitution
konsûltî [konsulti] *f* consulate
kopal [kopal] *m* stick
kor [kor] *adj* blind *f* field, plain
koranî [korani] *f* blindness
korê [koreh] *m* Korean
kovar [kovar] *f* journal, magazine; newspaper
ku [kö] *conj* what, that
kubar-kubar [köbar-köbar] *adv* proudly, haughtily
kuç [köch] *m* stone
kuda [köda] *adv* where (to)
kuder [ködär] *adv* where (at)
kuxik [kökhik] *f* cough
kul [köl] *f* pain; illness
kulek [köläk] *adj* sick, ill; lame
kulfet [kölfät] *f* wife; woman
kulîlk [kölilk] *f* flower
kulmal [kölmal] *adj* unhappy, unfortunate

kum [köm] *f* hat
kur [kör] *m* son, boy
kura [köra] *adv* through
kurd [körd] *m* Kurd
kurdî [kördi] *adj* Kurdish
kurm [körm] *m* worm
kurmancî [körmandji] *adj* Kurdish *f* Kurdish
    language, Kurmandji (North-Western Kur-
    dish dialect)
kursî [körsi] *m* chair; armchair
kurt [kört] *adj* short
kurtbûn [körtbun] *f* shortness
kuştin [köshtyn] *v* kill
kuta [köta] *v* finish, end
kutan [kötan] *v* beat; hit
kutasî [kötasi] *f* end, ending, outcome
kuva [köva] *adv* (from) where; (to) where
kûçe [kuchä] *f* street
kûçik [kuchyk] *m* dog
kûxnî [kukhni] *f* kitchen
kûltûr [kultur] *f* culture
kûn [kun] *f* behind, buttocks
kûr [kur] *adj* deep
kûranî [kurani] *f* depth, center
kûrs [kurs] *f* course
kûtxur [kutkhör] *m* beggar, pauper

Q

qab [qab] *f* box
qabî [qabi] *f* lechery, prostitution
qabil [qabyl] *adv* against
qabilbêjî [qabylbezhi] *f* disagreement, contradiction
qacqicandin [qadjqydjandyn] *v* torture
qacqicîn [qadjqydjin] *v* suffer
qad [qad] *f* borderline, boundary
qaf [qaf] *m* head
qahîm [qahim] *adj* hard, sturdy, strong
qaid [qayd] *m* leader
qal [qal] *f* argument; quarrel
qalme-qalm [qalmä-qalm] *f* noise, scream, racket
qan [qan] *f* blood
qane [qanä] *f* faith, trust, conviction
qanûn [qanun] *f* law
qanûntî [qanunti] *f* lawful action; lawfulness
qar [qar] *f* lack, fault; scream
qarîn [qarin] *v* scream, yell
qarpûz [qarpuz] *m* watermelon
qasid [qasyd] *m* messenger
qaş [qash] *f* eyebrow
qatolîk [qatolik] *m* Catholic
qawexane [qawäkhanä] *f* café

qayîlî [qayili] *f* agreement
qayîm [qayim] *adj* strong, sturdy
qayîme [qayimä] *f* contract, pact
qayîmî [qayimi] *f* strength, sturdiness
qazî [qazi] *m* judge; fighter for Islam
qazîk [qazik] *adv* purposely, on purpose
qebe [qäbä] *adj* ugly, disgusting
qebir [qäbyr] *f* grave
qebiristan [qäbyrystan] *f* cemetery
qebûlbûn [qäbulbun] *f* approval
qeda [qäda] *f* misfortune
qedeh [qädäh] *f* cup; misfortune
qedem [qädäm] *m* leg, foot
qeder [qädär] *f* fate, fortune
qedîm [qädim] *adj* old, ancient
qedir [qädyr] *m* respect, honor
qedirgiran [qädyrgyran] *adj* important, respectable; precious
qefes [qäfäs] *f* cage
qefil [qäfyl] *f* group
qefilîn [qäfylin] *v* freeze
qehf [qähf] *m* head
qehir [qähyr] *f* anger, rage
qehirîn [qähyrin] *v* be angry, rage
qehreman [qähräman] *m* champion
qela [qäla] *f* tin

qelandin [qälandyn] *v* fry
qelaştin [qälashtyn] *v* tear
qelb [qälb] *m* heart; soul
qelem [qäläm] *f* pencil
qelemzirêç [qälämzyrech] *f* pencil
qelet [qälät] *f* mistake
qelf [qälf] *f* group; row
qeliqandin [qälyqandyn] *v* shake, rock
qelişandin [qälyshandyn] *v* tear; dig
qeliştek [qälyshtäk] *f* crack
qelp [qälp] *m* falsehood; fake; distortion
qelpkirin [qälpkyryn] *f* falsification
qels [qäls] *adj* weak, useless
qember [qämbär] *f* bomb, bullet
qenaet [qänaät] *m* pleasure
qenc [qändj] *adj* good, best
qencî [qändji] *f* good, goodness
qend [qänd] *m* sweets, sugar
qene [qänä] *adv* somehow
qeneyî [qänäyi] *f* debt, duty
qenter [qäntär] *f* chain; pail
qeptan [qäptan] *m* captain
qer [qär] *adj* black, dark
qeraçî [qärachi] *m* Gypsy
qeratû [qäratu] *m* specter, ghost
qerd [qärd] *adj* big, huge, sizeable

qerebaşî [qäräbashi] *m* servant, slave
qereh [qäräh] *f* wound, scar
qereqot [qäräqot] *f* blackcurrant
qeresî [qäräsi] *m* cherry
qerez [qäräz] *prep* except
qerimîn [qärymin] *v* freeze
qerqaş [qärqash] *adj* white
qermiçî [qärmychi] *adj* disgusting
qesas [qäsas] *m* vengeance; executioner
qesd [qäsd] *f* intention
qeseb [qäsäb] *m* oath *f* bouquet
qesirbend [qäsyrbänd] *f* fortress, castle, citadel
qestana [qästana] *adv* intentionally, purposely
qeşeng [qäshäng] *adj* beautiful, handsome
qeşîrandin [qäshirandyn] *v* discern
qet [qät] *adv* totally, completely
qeter [qätär] *f* chain, row
qetil [qätyl] *f* murder; death
qewat [qäwat] *f* strength, force
qewî [qäwi] *adj* strong; loud
qewl [qäwl] *m* word, speech
qewrandin [qäwrandyn] *v* banish
qey [qäy] *adv* maybe; totally
qeyk [qäyk] *f* boat
qeys [qäys] *pron* someone
qeyser [qäysär] *m* king, emperor

qeysî [qäysi] *pl* apricots

qezîya [qäziya] *f* unfortunate incident, misfortune

qîçik [qichyk] *adj* yellow

qîçolek [qicholäk] *adj* pale

qîçolekî [qicholäki] *f* paleness

qîj [qizh] *f* scream, noise

qîjandin [qizhandyn] *v* scream, yell

qîloqaç [qiloqach] *adj* crooked

qîmet [qimät] *m* price

qîmetdar [qimätdar] *adj* valuable

qîr [qir] *f* soot; scream; calumny

qîrîn [qirin] *v* scream

qîyafet [qiyafät] *f* face, appearance

qîz [qiz] *f* daughter, young woman

qîzik [qizyk] *f* girl

qêmîş [qemish] *m* mercy

qiç [qych] *f* minute

qidîk [qydik] *m* misfortune; evil

qifil [qyfyl] *f* lock

qijavî [qyzhavi] *f* heat, hot summer

qijilandin [qyzhylandyn] *v* fry

qilafet [qylafät] *m* appearance, figure; height

qilêr [qyler] *f* dirt, rubbish

qilêrkirin [qylerkyryn] *f* pollution

qinyat [qynyat] *m* essence, meaning

qir [qyr] *f* death, destruction
qirar [qyrar] *m* decision
qirbûn [qyrbun] *f* death
qirçimandin [qyrchimandyn] *v* wink
qird [qyrd] *m* monkey
qirêj [qyrezh] *f* dirt, rubbish
qirinte [qyryntä] *adj* big
qisaret [qysarät] *f* compulsion
qism [qysm] *m* type, sort
qişirandin [qyshyrandyn] *v* discern
qişûn [qyshun] *m* army
qiyas [qiyas] *m* comparison
qoç [qoch] *m* horn
qoçax [qochakh] *adj* brave, bold
qol [qol] *m* hand *adj* short
qola [qola] *adj* sick, ill; easy
qonax [qonakh] *f* lodge, dwelling
qonsûl [qonsul] *m* consul
qor [qor] *adj* thin, skinny
qorede [qorädä] *adj* thin, skinny
qorî [qori] *adj* bent
qorîn [qorin] *v* scream
qubale [qöbalä] *f* direction
qubet [qöbät] *adj* rude, vulgar
qubetî [qöbäti] *f* rudeness, vulgarity
qude [qödä] *adj* proud, haughty

qude-qude [qödä-qödä] *adv* proudly, haughtily
qudetî [qödäti] *f* pride, haughtiness
qudret [qödrät] *f* strength, power; mercy
qudûm [qödum] *pl* legs
quflik [qöflyk] *f* lock
qulç [qölch] *m* corner
qulibandin [qölybandyn] *v* destroy, annihilate
qulibîn [qölybin] *v* disappear, hide
qulix [qölykh] *f* job, work, occupation
qulixçî [qölykhchi] *m* employee
qulqulk [qölqölk] *f* hole
quloz [qöloz] *f* jump
qulteyn [qöltäyn] *f* fountain
qumar [qömar] *f* gambling
qumber [qömbär] *f* bomb
quncirandin [qöndjyrandyn] *v* pinch, scratch
qunî [qöni] *f* spring, source
quran [qöran] *f* Koran
qurban [qörban] *f* victim, sacrifice
qurçimandin [qörchymandyn] *v* break
qure [qörä] *adj* proud
qutetî [qöräti] *f* pride
qurijîn [qöryzhin] *v* surround
qurn [qörn] *f* century, age, epoch
qurtandin [qörtandyn] *v* swallow
qut [qöt] *m* piece

qutb [qötb] *m* pole
qûjîn [quzhin] *v* scream, yell
qûjînî [quzhini] *f* scream, cry
qûl [qul] *m* slave
qûltî [qulti] *f* slavery
qûm [qum] *f* sand
qûn [qun] *f* behind
qûz [quz] *adj* hunchbacked
qûzo [quzo] *m* hunchback

L

labod [labod] *adj* necessary
laboratorî [laboratori] *f* laboratory
laq [laq] *m* leg
lal [lal] *adj* mute
lap [lap] *adv* totally, completely
lastîk [lastik] *m* eraser
lat [lat] *f* cliff
lava [lava] *f* request
law [la'w] *m* child
lawanî [la'wani] *f* youth
lawko [la'wko] *m* young man
lay [la'y] *prep* through
lazim [lazym] *adj* necessary, needed
lazimayî [lazymayi] *f* necessity

lebaleb [läbaläb] *adj* full, filled
lec [lädj] *f* competition, race
lehane [lähanä] *m* neck
lehî [lähi] *f* stream, torrent
lehze [lähzä] *m* moment; dialect
leqandin [läqandyn] *v* rock, shake
lema [läma] *conj* because *adv* thus
lepitandin [läpytandyn] *v* move
lerizîn [läryzin] *v* tremble
lesan [läsan] *m* language, dialect
leşker [läskär] *m* army
letîf [lätif] *m* joker *adj* beautiful, handsome
lewand [läwand] *adj* beautiful; unruly
lewandî [läwand] *f* beauty; disorder
lewm [läwm] *f* form
leylan [läylan] *f* song; mirage
lez [läz] *adj* fast, swift
lezet [läzät] *f* pleasure
leztî [läzti] *f* swiftness
le'z [lä'z] *f* moment
lîbêral [liberal] *m* liberal
lîqa [liqa] *f* meeting
lîl [lil] *f* swamp
lîmon [limon] *f* lemon
lîmoned [limonäd] *f* lemonade
lîst [list] *m* leaf

lîstîk [listik] *f* game
lîtêratûr [literatur] *f* literature
lîtir [lityr] *f* liter
lîzk [lizk] *f* game
lêdan [ledan] *v* beat, hit
lêgerîn [legärin] *v* look for, seek
lêh [leh] *m* Pole (native of Poland)
lêxistin [lekhistin] *v* beat, hit
lêk [lek] *m* group
lêmişt [lemysht] *f* flood
lêpok [lepok] *m* comedy, joke
lêvegerandin [levägärandyn] *v* answer
li [ly] *prep* on; in
lib [lyb] *f* seed, grain
libas [lybas] *f* clothes, dress
liber [lybär] *adv* on the other side of; ahead of; near
lidû [lydu] *adv* behind
lihevdan [lyhävdan] *v* fight
lihvan [lyhvan] *f* enjoyment
liku [lykö] *adv* where; when
liq [lyq] *m* branch
ling [lyng] *m* leg
lipaş [lypash] *adv* behind, in back of
lipat [lypat] *f* movement
lipêş [lypesh] *adv* in front of; opposite to

livêderê [lyvedäreh] *adv* here; there
liwê [lyweh] *adv* there
lobî [lobi] *pl* beans
loxet [loghät] *m* word, expression; speech, conversation; dictionary
loq [loq] *m* piece
lome [lomä] *f* reproach
lora [lora] *adv* here
lot [lot] *f* jump
lotin [lotyn] *v* jump, hop
lotke [lotkä] *f* boat
lûce [ludjä] *f* sky; horizon
lûle [lulä] *f* trumpet
lûrî [luri] *f* lullaby
lûtf [lutf] *f* compassion

M

macar [madjar] *m* Hungarian
macarî [madjari] *adj* Hungarian
macira [madjyra] *f* event
madam [madam] *conj* because, since *f* madam
made [madä] *f* paragraph; material
maden [madän] *conj* as; similarly to
mafir [mafir] *m* circle, society *conj* if
mak [mak] *f* mother

maqûl [maqul] *adj* respectable, noble
mal [mal] *f* house; family
malbat [malbat] *f* family, relatives
malbend [malbänd] *f* region, area
malbûs [malbus] *m* clothes
maldar [maldar] *adj* wealthy
maldarî [maldari] *f* wealth
malkavil [malkavyl] *adj* ruined
mana [mana] *f* meaning, reason
manarx [manarkh] *m* monarch
manawira [manawyra] *f* maneuver
mange [mangä] *f* cow
manîfest [manifest] *f* manifesto
mar [mar] *m* snake; marriage
marş [marsh] *f* march
mart [mart] *f* March
marûf [maruf] *adj* famous
mase [masä] *f* table
masî [masi] *m* fish
masîvan [masivan] *f* fisherman
masowa [masowa] *prep* except
maşoq [mashoq] *m* beloved
mat [mat] *adj* smooth, polished
matêryal [materyal] *m* material
mator [mator] *f* motor
mayî [mayi] *f* egoism *adj* remaining

mazeret [mazärät] *f* damage, danger
mazûban [mazuban] *m* master
meal [mä'al] *m* meaning, essence
mebna [mäbna] *f* basis, foundation
mecal [mädjal] *f* force, might
mecar [mädjar] *f* tear
mecît [mädjit] *adj* true
mecîtî [mädjiti] *f* truth
mecnûn [mädjnun] *adj* crazy
meçit [mächit] *f* Mosque
medam [mädam] *adj* permanent
medar [mädar] *f* basis, foundation
medekirî [mädäkyri] *adj* sad
medet [mädät] *f* misfortune, grief
medhet [mädhät] *f* praise
meftûh [mäftuh] *adj* open
meh [mäh] *f* crescent, moon; month
mehbûb [mähbub] *f* love; beloved
mehef [mähäf] *f* coffin
mehfî [mähfi] *adj* secret; secretive
mehkem [mähkäm] *adj* strong, sturdy
mehkeme [mähkämä] *f* court
mehne [mähnä] *f* reason
mehrûm [mährum] *adj* poor
mehrûmî [mährumi] *f* poverty
mehsûl [mähsul] *m* product

mehûj [mähuzh] *f* raisin
mehw [mähw] *f* destruction, annihilation
mehza [mähza] *adv* only
mexab [mäkhab] *f* grief, sadness
mexer [mäkhäb] *f* ruins
mexlûqet [mäkhluqät] *f* people
mexmûr [mäkhmur] *adj* drunk
mexber [mäghbär] *m* grave
mexlubîyet [mäghlöbiyät] *f* defeat
mexrîb [mäghryb] *m* sunset; West; dusk
mejû [mäzhu] *m* brain
mejvema [mäzhväma] *f* legend
mekan [mäkan] *m* place
mekr [mäkr] *f* cunning
mekranî [mäkrani] *adj* shrewd
mekteb [mäktäb] *f* school
mektûb [mäktub] *f* letter
meqam [mäqam] *m* motive; melody; cave
meqes [mäqäs] *f* scissors
meqletûz [mäqlätuz] *m* magnet
meqsed [mäqsäd] *f* aim
meqyas [mäqyas] *f* size
melamet [mälamät] *f* reproach
melîk [mälik] *m* king, ruler
melûl [mälul] *adj* sad, mournful
melûlî [mäluli] *f* sadness

melûm [mälum] *adj* obvious, apparent *n* teacher
mcmnûn [mämnun] *adj* content, pleased
menc [mändj] *f* wish, desire, passion
menfehet [mänfähät] *adj* open
mentîq [mäntiq] *f* logic
menzûr [mänzur] *m* aim; hope
meraq [märaq] *f* care
merekat [märäkat] *f* curiosity
meremet [märämät] *f* intention
merh [märh] *f* happiness
merhemet [märhämät] *f* mercy
merî [märi] *m* person *pl* people
merqed [märqäd] *f* grave
mermer [märmär] *m* marble, rock
merov [märov] *m* person
merş [märsh] *m* rug
merziq [märzyq] *f* swamp
mesafe [mäsafä] *f* distance
mesele [mäsälä] *f* question, problem
meseret [mäsärät] *f* happiness
mesilkhet [mäsilhät] *f* conversation
mesref [mäsräf] *f* expense
mest [mäst] *adj* drunk
mestir [mästyr] *adj* bigger, older
meşam [mäsham] *f* nose; scent
meşfûf [mäshfuf] *adj* bright, light

meşhûr [mäsh'hur] *adj* famous
meşîn [mäshin] *v* walk; go
meşq [mäshq] *f* excercise *v* write
mesveret [mäshvärät] *f* advice, council
metel [mätäl] *adj* upset *f* riddle
metne [mätnä] *f* text; original
mewcan [mäwdjän] *f* wave
mewcûd [mäwdjud] *f* existence; presence
mewlûd [mäwlud] *f* birth; descent
mewsim [mäwsym] *f* season
mewuj [mäwözh] *m* raisin
meya [mäya] *f* wine; liquid
meydan [mäydan] *f* plaza
meyxane [mäykhanä] *f* inn, bar, pub
meyl [mäyl] *f* inclination, tendency
meywe [mäywä] *m* fruit
mezheb [mäz'häb] *m* faith, religion; throne
mezintir [mäzyntyr] *adv* more
mezmûn [mäzmun] *f* content; essence
me'lûl [mä'lul] *adj* sick, ill
me'sûm [mä'sum] *adj* innocent
me'zûl [mä'zul] *adj* abandoned
mî [mi] *f* sheep
mîl [mil] *f* mile
mîlyard [milyard] *f* billion, milliard
mîlyon [milyon] *f* million

mîlyondar [milyondar] *m* millionaire
mîna [mina] *adv* as if
mînîstir [misistyr] *m* minister
mîrat [mirat] *f* inheritance, heritage
mîs [mis] *m* copper
mê [meh] *f* female
mêdal [medal] *f* medal
mêxûlî [mekhuli] *f* fantasy, imagination; raving
mêr [mer] *m* man; husband
mêranî [merani] *f* manliness, courage
mêrg [merg] *f* meadow
mêrxas [merkhas] *m* hero
mêş [mesh] *f* fly
mêtir [metyr] *f* meter
mêtod [metod] *f* method
mêtro [metro] *f* metro, subway
mêvanxane [mevankhanä] *f* hotel
mêzek [mezäk] *f* glance, gaze
mêzîn [mezin] *f* weight
micewherat [midjäwhärat] *pl* jewels, jewelry
midafe [midafä] *f* defense
midas [mydas] *m* shoes
midet [mydät] *m* time, period
mifade [myfadä] *adj* useful, profitable
mifsid [myfsyd] *adj* evil, wicked; nasty
mifte [myftä] *f* key

mihaceret [myhadjärät] *f* emigration, migration
mihacir [myhadjyr] *m* emigrant
mihafize [myhafizä] *f* defense, security
mihendiz [myhändyz] *m* master, craftsman
mihr [myhr] *m* sun *f* love
mihrecan [myhrädjan] *f* festival
mihwer [myhwär] *f* axis; connection
mix [myx] *m* nail
mixenet [mykhänät] *m* traitor
mixaze [myghasä] *f* store, shop
mij [myzh] *m* mist
mijûl [myzhul] *f* hobby, pastime; pleasure
mikafat [mykafat] *f* reward
mikûn [mykun] *f* hope
mikurî [myköri] *f* boredom
miqale [myqalä] *f* article
miqaledar [myqalädar] *m* reporter
miqat [myqat] *adj* careful, cautious
miqur [myqör] *f* despair
mil [myl] *m* shoulder; neck
milahîm [mylahim] *adj* calm, peaceful
milet [mylät] *m* people; nationality
milyaket [mylyakät] *m* angel
mimkûn [mymkun] *f* possibility, probability
min [myn] *pron* me; I
mina [myna] *v* disappear

minabûn [mynabun] *f* disappearance
minet [myrät] *f* kindness, good will
minêkarî [mynekari] *f* wish
minnî [mynni] *f* butterfly
miraz [myraz] *m* wish, desire
mirî [myri] *adj* dead
mirîşk [myrishk] *f* chicken
mirês [myres] *m* inheritance
mirtib [myrtyb] *m* Gypsy
mirtoxe [myrtokhä] *f* halvah
misafir [mysafyr] *m* traveller
misîbet [mysibät] *f* misfortune
misilman [mysylman] *m* Muslim
misilmanî [mysylmani] *adj* Muslim
misirî [mysyri] *m* Egyptian *adj* Egyptian
miskîn [myskin] *adj* poor, impoverished
miskînî [myskini] *f* poverty
mişabih [myshabih] *f* similarity, likeness
mişar [myshar] *f* saw
mişirîk [myshyrik] *m* neighbor
mişk [myshk] *m* mouse; rat
mişkil [myshkil] *adj* difficult
mişko [myshko] *m* rat
mişterek [myshtäräk] *m* companion
mişterî [myshtäri] *m* customer, buyer
mitexesîs [mytäkhäsis] *m* profession

miteyî [mytäyi] *f* submission
mitîn [mytin] *adj* strong, sturdy
mizeferîyet [myzäfäriyät] *f* victory, triumph,
    success
mod [mod] *f* fashion, mode
modet [modät] *f* time
modêl [model] *f* model
mohenna [mohänna] *adj* crooked; content, happy
mohib [mohyb] *m* lover
mohlet [mohlät] *f* patience
moxetet [mokhätät] *adj* striped
mokafat [mokafat] *f* reward
moqteza [moqtäza] *f* necessity
moldav [moldav] *m* Moldavian
moldavî [moldavi] *adj* Moldavian
monim [mony'm] *adj* generous *m* benefactor
monopolî [monopoli] *f* monopoly
morewir [moräwyr] *m* liar
mostemere [mostämärä] *f* colony
moşk [moshk] *f* darkness
motosîkil [motosikyl] *f* motorcycle
mowacib [mowadjyb] *f* result
mudbir [mödbyr] *adj* careful, cautious; unfortu-
    nate
muferdat [möfärdat] *f* seclusion
muhafiz [möhafyz] *f* defense

muhb [möhb] *f* love
muxabere [mökhabärä] *m* message; correspondence
muẍdar [mökhdar] *m* time, period
murẍ [mörkh] *m* bird
muta [möta] *f* glory, honor
mû [mu] *m* fur; hair
mûcize [mudjyzä] *f* miracle, wonder
mûm [mum] *f* candle
mûrabe [murabä] *f* jam, preserves
mûrî [muri] *f* ant
mûtî [muti] *adj* obedient, compliant
mûzîk [muzik] *f* music, orchestra
mûzê [muzeh] *f* museum

N

na [na] *conj* no; not
nab [nab] *adj* clean, pure
nagah [nagah] *adv* suddenly
naka [naka] *adv* now, presently
nakes [nakäs] *adv* nobody
naqos [naqos] *f* shortcoming, mistake
nalet [nalät] *f* curse
name [namä] *f* letter; contract, pact
namenasî [namänasi] *f* instruction

namûs [namus] *f* honor, reputation
namzed [namzäd] *m* candidate
nan [nan] *m* bread; food
nana [nana] *adv* no
nanayî [nanayi] *f* rejection
nanpêj [nanpezh] *m* baker
nar [nar] *m* fire
narîn [narin] *f* roar; laughter
nas [nas] *adj* familiar
nasbûn [nasbun] *f* acquaintance, familiarity
nasî [nasi] *f* knowledge; acquaintance
nasîn [nasin] *v* know; recognize; acquaint oneself
nask [nask] *adj* frail, gentle *m* deer
nav [nav] *m* name *prep* in, inside
navbang [navbang] *m* glory, fame
navbend [navbänd] *f* belt
navbir [navbyr] *f* intermission, break
navçav [navchav] *m* forehead
navdar [navdar] *adj* famous
navdarî [navdari] *f* fame
navend [navänd] *f* center, middle
navlep [navläp] *m* palm (of hand)
navra [navra] *adv* through
naz [naz] *adj* gentle, frail
nazî [nazi] *f* gentleness, frailty *n* Nazi
ne [nä] *adv* not; do not

nebawar [näbawar] *adj* distrustful
nebî [näbi] *m* prophet
nebindest [näbyndäst] *adj* independent
nebindestî [näbyndästi] *f* independence
necat [nädjat] *f* aim
necîb [nädjib] *adj* noble
necis [nädjys] *adj* dirty, unclean
necm [nädjm] *f* star
neçê [nächeh] *adj* bad, mean, wicked
neçêyî [nächeyi] *f* evil, wickedness
neder [nädär] *f* appearance
nedîncî [nädindji] *f* unrest
neeşkela [nä'äshkäla] *adj* mysterious, hidden
neeşkelayî [nä'äshkälayi] *f* mystery, secret
nefer [näfär] *f* face
nefes [näfäs] *f* breath, sigh; soul
nefî [näfi] *f* exile
nefretî [näfräti] *f* curse
nefsmezin [näfsmäzyn] *adj* greedy
negîn [nägin] *m* ring
neh [näh] *num* nine
neheng [nähäng] *m* whale
nehin [nähyn] *f* non-existence, nothing *adj* non-existant
nehriz [nähryz] *adj* sharp
nehwêd [nähwed] *num* ninety

nexme [näkhmä] *f* melody
nexşkar [näkhshkar] *m* painter, artist
nextî [näkhti] *adv* a little, a bit
nexweş [näkhwäsh] *adj* sick, ill
nexweşge [näkhwäshgä] *f* hospital
nejîyandin [näzhiyandyn] *v* kill
nekes [näkäs] *pron* nobody *m* insignificant person
neqil [näqyl] *f* story, short story, narrative
neqiş [näqysh] *m* picture, drawing, painting
neqişandin [näqyshandyn] *v* draw, paint
neqşbendî [näqshbändi] *f* visual art
nemayî [nämayi] *f* dampness, humidity
nemerd [nämärd] *adj* mean, base, cruel
nemêr [nämer] *m* coward
nemêrî [nämeri] *f* cowardice
nerdewan [närdäwan] *f* step; staircase, ladder
nerx [närkh] *adj* precious, valuable, expensive
nerm [närm] *adj* soft
nerwêc [närwedj] *m* Norwegian
nerwêcî [närwedji] *adj* Norwegian
nesxe [näskhä] *f* copy
nesîhet [näsihät] *f* instruction
nesl [näsl] *f* generation
nestêl [nästel] *adj* young; fresh; naïve
neşir [näshyr] *f* publication, edition
neşirkar [näshyrkar] *m* publisher, editor

netevitî [nätävyti] *adj* impatient, restless *f* impatience, restlessness
netutişt [nätötysht] *prep* nothing
newa [näwa] *m* melody, song *f* need
neyar [näyar] *m* enemy, foe
neyîn [näyin] *f* nothing
nezam [näzam] *m* soldier
nezer [näzär] *f* glance, gaze
ne'tik [nä'tyk] *f* forehead
nî [ni] *conj* not
nîsa [nisa] *f* woman
nîsan [nisan] *f* April
nîşan [nishan] *f* sign, symbol
nîvek [niväk] *f* half; middle
nîverast [nivärast] *f* middle, center
nîvro [nivro] *f* midday, noon; south
nîvroyî [nivroyi] *adj* central
nîvşev [nivshäv] *f* midnight
nîyet [niyät] *f* intention, aim
nêr [ner] *m* male
nêrevan [nerävan] *f* fleet
nêrîn [nerin] *v* look *f* look
nêt [net] *f* sense; thought; opinion
nêz [nez] *f* hunger
nêzîk [nezik] *adj* close; intimate
nêzîkva [nezikva] *adv* closely

niçandin [nychandyn] *v* beat
nifir [nyfyr] *f* curse
nifûs [nyfus] *f* influence; personality
hina [nyha] *adv* now, presently
nihad [nyhad] *m* nature
nihêrandin [nyherandyn] *v* look
nihêt [nyhet] *m* marble, granite *f* essence
nijad [nyzhad] *m* descent; generation; nationality
nikeh [nykäh] *f* wedding, marriage
niqam [nyqam] *m* melody
niqar [nyqar] *m* silver
niqboq [nyqboq] *f* boat
niqis [nyqys] *f* loss, damage
niqitandin [nyqytandyn] *v* drop, leak
niqitk [nyqytk] *f* drop
nimûş [nymush] *m* image, appearance
nişkêva [nyshkeva] *adj* sudden *adv* suddenly
niştir [nyshtyr] *f* needle
nitrandin [nytrandyn] *v* describe, depict
nivîsandin [nyvisandyn] *v* write
nivîsar [nyvisar] *f* letter; writing
nivîsevan [nyvisävan] *m* writer
nivistin [nyvvystyn] *v* dream, sleep
nizm [nyzm] *adj* short
nizmbûn [nyzmbun] *f* descent
nobe [nobä] *f* turn, bend

nobet [nobät] *f* line, turn
nod [nod] *num* nine hundred
noker [nokär] *m* servant
nomêr [nomer] *f* number
normal [normal] *adj* normal
note [notä] *f* note; melody
notlanî [notlani] *adv* as if, similarly to
nozdeh [nozdäh] *num* nineteen
nuqte [nöqtä] *f* point, dot; drop
nû [nu] *adj* new
nûber [nubär] *adj* blooming, blossoming, young
nûjen [nuzhän] *f* knee
nûr [nur] *f* light
nûva [nuva] *adv* again
nûwînî [nuwini] *f* news

O

objêkt [obzhekt] *m* object
objêktîv [obzhektiv] *adj* objective
objêktîvî [obzhektivi] *f* objectivity
ocax [odjakh] *f* furnace, stove
ocaxzade [odjakhzadä] *adj* famous
ofîsêr [ofiser] *m* officer
oho [oho] *interj* Oh! Aha!
oẍir [oghyr] *f* happiness; fortune, fate

oẍirxêr [oghyrkher] *adj* happy, lucky, prosperous
oẍirme [oghyrmä] *f* way
okîan [okian] *f* ocean
ol [ol] *f* group; religion, faith
olan [olan] *m* intellect, consciousness
olfet [olfät] *f* friendship
olk [olk] *f* province
oltîmatom [oltimatom] *f* ultimatum
opêra [opera] *f* opera
opêrasîon [operasion] *f* operation
oportûnîst [oportunist] *m* opportunist
opozîsî [opozisi] *f* opposition
opozîsîonêr [opozisioner] *m* oppositionist
ordek [ordäk] *f* duck
ordî [ordi] *f* army
organ [organ] *m* department; organization
organîzasî [organizasi] *f* organization
orket [orkät] *f* empire, monarchy
ors [o'rs] *f* wedding
orte [ortä] *f* middle, center
ortemiletî [ortämyläti] *adj* international
osaf [osaf] *m* quality; element
otax [otakh] *f* room
otarbêj [otarbej] *m* orator
otêl [otel] *f* hotel
otomobîl [otomobil] *f* automobile

owlî [owli] *f* balcony
oyîn [oyin] *f* queue, line *adj* funny
oyînbaz [oyinbaz] *m* jester; acrobat

P

paç [pach] *f* kiss
paçkirin [pachkyryn] *v* kiss
padşah [padshah] *m* king
padşahî [padshahi] *m* kingdom
paxir [pakhyr] *m* copper
pak [pak] *adj* clean
pal [pal] *f* side
palançî [palanchi] *m* mover
pale [palä] *m* worker
palto [palto] *m* coat
palûd [palud] *f* oak
pamîdor [pamidor] *f* tomato
panzde [panzdä] *num* fifteen
par [par] *f* fate, lot
para [para] *adv* in back of
parad [parad] *f* parade
paragraf [paragraf] *f* paragraph
parbûn [parbun] *f* division
parçe [parchä] *m* piece
parxan [parkhan] *f* rib

parî [pari] *m* piece, part
parîz [pariz] *f* garden, park
parlamênt [parlament] *f* parliament
parone [paronä] *f* trace, footprint
pasajîr [pasazhir] *m* passenger
pasport [pasport] *f* passport
paş [pash] *prep* behind
paşda [pashda] *adv* back
paşdahatin [pashdahatyn] *v* return
paşdawî [pashdawi] *f* future
paşîn [pashin] *adj* last, final
paşê [pasheh] *adv* after; afterwards
paşmer [pasmär] *m* defender; follower
paşpartik [pashpartik] *f* suffix
paşport [pashport] *f* passport
paşwextî [pashwäkhti] *f* future *adv* finally
patrîot [patriot] *m* patriot
patron [patron] *f* patron
pawtandin [pa'wandyn] *v* guard; patronize
pawanî [pa'wani] *f* defense, security
pay [pa'y] *m* degree; rank *f* lot, fate
payî [pa'yi] *m* praise
payîdan [pa'yidan] *v* praise, extoll
payîz [pa'yiz] *f* autumn
paytext [pa'ytäkht] *m* capital (city)
pehn [pähn] *adj* broad, wide

pehnayî [pähnayi] *f* width, breadth
pehnî [pähni] *f* heel
pej [päzh] *m* thorn
pejî [päzhi] *m* shoelace
pel [päl] *m* leaf, petal
pelemîşk [pälämishk] *f* stream
peleseng [päläsäng] *m* abundance
penah [pänah] *m* refuge
pencere [pändjärä] *f* window
pend [pänd] *m* studies *f* advice
pene [pänä] *f* secret, mystery
penêr [päner] *m* cheese
pepûk [päpuk] *m* beggar, pauper
perav [pärav] *f* wave
perdaq [pärdaq] *f* politeness
perde [pärdä] *f* curtain
pere [pärä] *pl* money
perest [päräst] *f* defense; patronage
perxandin [pärkhandyn] *v* rub
perîn [pärin] *v* fly; go
perîşan [pärishan] *adj* poor; unhappy, sad;
    confused; tired
peritandin [päritandyn] *v* tear apart
parsim [pärsym] *f* cold; running nose
pertab [pärtab] *f* ray of light; brightness; trem-
    bling

pertew [pärtäw] *f* brightness, dazzle
perwane [pärwanä] *f* butterfly; bird
pesin [päsyn] *m* praise; dream
pesnevedan [päsnävädan] *f* praise, appraisal
peşk [päshk] *f* destiny
pevçûn [pävchun] *v* quarrel, argue, fight
pevgirêk [pävgyrek] *f* connection, tie; conjunction
pey [päy] *prep* after *m* praise, appraisal
peyal [päyal] *f* cup
peyẍam [päykham] *m* news, message
pez [päz] *f* sheep
pe'nî [pä'ni] *adj* obvious, apparent *f* heel
pî [pi] *adj* wealthy *m* dependence
pîçke [pichkä] *f* matches
pîj [pizh] *adj* sharp
pîr [pir] *adj* old *m* old man
pîrayî [pira'yi] *f* old age
pîrebî [piräbi] *f* widow
pîrek [piräk] *f* old lady
pîrq [pirq] *f* laughter
pîroz [piroz] *adj* triumphant, heroic
pîrozî [pirozi] *f* triumph
pîs [pis] *adj* dirty
pîşto [pishto] *f* gun
pîvan [pivan] *v* weigh, measure

pîvaz [pivaz] *f* onion
pîyês [piyes] *f* play; theatre
pê [peh] *m* leg
pêçandin [pechandin] *v* wrap
pêçat [pechat] *f* stamp, seal
pêdagog [pedagog] *m* pedagogue
pêda-pêda [peda-peda] *adj* completely, totally
pêjandin [pezhandyn] *v* bake
pêk [pek] *adj* organized
pêkanîn [pekanin] *f* organization
pêkhatin [pek'hatyn] *f* preparation; luck; organization
pêkve [pekvä] *adv* together
pêl [pel] *f* wave; gust of wind; time, period
pêlav [pelav] *f* wave; page; shoes
pênc [pendj] *num* five
pêncşemb [pendjsämb] *f* Thursday
pêra [pera] *adv* together; immediately
pêsîr [pesir] *f* chest, breast
pêş [pesh] *prep* before, against
pêşasêgeh [peshasegäh] *f* obstacle
pêşber [peshbär] *adv* across from; opposite to
pêşda [peshda] *adv* forward
pêşe [peshä] *m* speciality
pêşgîr [peshgir] *f* napkin
pêşî [peshi] *f* front side; wave

pêşîbir [peshibyr] *m* leader
pêşîv [peshiv] *f* perspective, future
pêşkêş [peshkesh] *f* gift, present; reward
pêşmal [peshmal] *f* façade; front side
pêşva [peshva] *adv* forward; in exchange for
pêve [pevä] *adv* hence, from now on
pêvir [pevyr] *f* star
piçek [pychäk] *adv* a little
piçikandin [pychykandyn] *v* turn around
pifîn [pyfin] *f* breath
pijandin [pyzhandyn] *v* bake; fry; cook
pijyayî [pyzhyayi] *adj* baked; fried
pingav [pyngav] *f* swamp
pir [pyr] *adj* many *adv* very
pirafêsor [pyrafesor] *m* professor
pirayî [pyrayi] *m* majority; abundance
pirbûn [pyrbun] *f* expansion
pirç [pyrch] *f* hair
pirçûk [pyrchuk] *m* sadness
pirxaş [pyrkhash] *m* war; fight; battle
pirîn [pyrin] *v* fly *f* brighhtness
pirîsk [pyrisk] *f* flame
pirkirin [pyrkyryn] *f* expansion; reproduction
pirs [pyrs] *f* question
pirsîn [pyrsin] *v* ask
pirsyar [pyrsyar] *f* question

pirtî [pyrti] *m* part, piece; material

pirtir [pyrtyr] *adv* more

pistik [pystyk] *f* pistachio

piş [pysh] *prep* after, behind

pişik [pyshyk] *f* lungs

pişkoj [pyshkozh] *m* button

pişt [pysht] *f* back, spine

piştdawî [pyshtdawi] *adj* last

piştxurtî [pyshhtkhörti] *f* revenge

pişto [pyshto] *f* gun

pite-pit [pytä-pyt] *f* whisper

plan [plan] *f* plan

poç [poch] *f* tail

poêm [poem] *f* poem

pol [pol] *m* coin; shoulder

pola [pola] *m* steel

polon [polon] *m* Pole

polonî [poloni] *adj* Polish

polûs [polus] *f* pole

portmijî [pormyzhi] *adj* upset

portoxal [portoghal] *m* orange; orange color

posatşer [posatshär] *m* ammunition, arms

poşte [poshtä] *f* post office

poştebir [poshtäbyr] *m* mailman

poz [poz] *m* nose

pozbilind [pozbylynd] *adj* proud, haughty

pozbilindî [pozbylyndi] *f* pride, haughtiness
prafêsor [prafesor] *m* professor
pragram [pragram] *f* program
praktîke [praktikä] *m* practice
praktîkî [praktiki] *adj* practical
prodûksî [produksi] *f* production
proje [prozhä] *f* project
pronav [pronav] *f* pronoun
propoganda [propoganda] *f* propoganda
prosês [proses] *f* process
pûç [puch] *adj* empty; aimless
pûxtane [pukhtanä] *adj* ripe
pûpû [pupu] *m* cuckoo
pûrt [purt] *f* hair
pût [put] *f* cork

R

ra [ra] *m* root
pabûn [rabun] *v* ascend, go up
raçandin [rachandyn] *v* stretch
rad [rad] *m* generosity
radîo [radio] *f* radio
radîostansî [radiostansi] *f* radio station
rafet [rafät] *f* compassion
rahet [rahät] *adj* calm, quiet; easy; comfortable

rehetî [rahäti] *f* rest, repose; calm; easiness
rahiştin [rahyshtyn] *v* lift; take
rahejandin [rahäzhandyn] *v* shake
raketin [rakätyn] *v* lie; sleep
rakirin [rakyryn] *v* wake; raise
raqetandin [raqätandyn] *v* drive away, expel
raman [raman] *f* novel
rarû [raru] *adv* face to face
raser [rasär] *adv* opposite to
raserkirin [rasärkyryn] *f* direction
rast [rast] *adj* straight, smooth
rastbêj [rastbezh] *adj* truthful
rastdilî [rastdyli] *f* sincerity
rastek [rastäk] *f* rule
raste-rast [rastä-rast] *adv* straight
rastgoşe [rastgoshä] *f* rectangle
rasthatî [rast'hati] *f* meeting
rastnivîsar [rastnyvisar] *f* spelling
ratib [ratyb] *adj* hard *f* order
raw [ra'w] *f* hunt; game
rawçî [ra'wchi] *m* hunter
raweşandin [rawäshandyn] *v* wave
rawkar [ra'wkar] *m* hunter
ray [ra'y] *m* opinion *f* spirit
razanxane [razankhanä] *f* bedroom; dormitory
razî [razi] *adj* agreeable, content

razîbûn [razibun] *f* concordance, agreement; satisfaction

razînebûn [razinäbun] *f* disagreement

reb [räb] *m* Lord, ruler

reben [räbän] *adj* miserable, unhappy

reca [rädja] *f* request

red [räd] *v* disappear; end

redbûn [rädbun] *f* disappearance; end; death

refîq [räfiq] *f* comrade; companion

rehim [rähym] *f* mercy, kindness, compassion

rehmanî [rähmani] *adj* merciful, kind, compassionate

reh û ol [räh u ol] *f* root, basis

rex [räkh] *m* side

rexber [räkhbär] *f* clothes

reis [räîs] *m* head, boss

req [räq] *adj* stale *m* lobster

reqas [räqas] *f* dance

reqasçî [räqaschi] *m* dancer

reqem [räqäm] *f* number

reqî [räqi] *f* hardness

remil [rämyl] *f* fortelling; magic

remz [rämz] *f* secret, mystery

ren [rän] *m* hip

reng [räng] *m* color

rengdar [rängdar] *adj* colored; colorful

rengîn [rängin] *adj* big, huge
repandin [räpandyn] *v* beat, hit
resm [räsm] *f* look, appearance
resmî [räsmi] *adj* official
resûl [räsul] *m* prophet
reş [räsh] *adj* black
reşandin [räshandyn] *v* sprinkle
reşbelek [räshbäläk] *f* letter; handwriting
reşgirîn [räshgyrin] *f* mourning
reşmar [räshmar] *f* cobra
reş-tûzî [räsh-tuzi] *adj* black
rev [räv] *f* run
revîn [rävin] *v* run
revîvan [rävivan] *m* hunter
rewa [räwa] *f* gift; reward
rewac [räwadj] *f* demand (market)
rewal [räwal] *m* walk; young man
rewan [räwan] *m* soul; ardor
rewîn [räwin] *f* flame
rewindayî [räwyndayi] *m* bum, vagrant
rewnek [räwnäk] *f* brightness
rewş [räwsh] *f* brilliance, brightness, dazzle
reyat [räyat] *f* population, people
reza [räza] *f* agreement, approval
rezîlî [räzili] *f* shame, disgrace
rezm [räzm] *f* battle

rîşî [rishi] *m* beard
rê [reh] *f* road, way, path
rêbir [rebyr] *m* bandit, highwayman
rêç [rech] *f* trace, footprint
rêjîm [rezhim] *f* regime
rênîş [renish] *f* guide
rêtin [retyn] *v* pour
rêvin [revyn] *adj* dirty
rêvmatîzm [revmatizm] *f* rheumatism
rêvolvêr [revolver] *f* revolver
rêwî [rewi] *m* traveller, wanderer
rêwîngî [rewingi] *f* travel
rêzan [rezan] *m* tourist; one who knows the way
rêzik [rezik] *f* row
rih [ryh] *m* spirit, soul
rijandin [ryzhandyn] *v* pour
rikrikîn [rykrykin] *v* knock
rimj [rymzh] *f* thunder, thunderstorm
rind [rynd] *adj* good, beautiful
rindayî [ryndayi] *f* beauty
risxet [ryskhät] *f* permission
rist [ryst] *f* thread, chain
riswa [ryswa] *m* dishonor, disgrace
ritibe [rytybä] *f* rank, position
rivîn [ryvin] *f* flame
rizgarî [ryzgari] *f* fate, fortune

rizî [ryzi] *adj* dilapidated, old
ro [ro] *f* sun
roava [roava] *f* sunset
rohilat [rohylat] *f* sunrise
roj [rozh] *f* sun; day
rojname [rozhnamä] *f* newspaper; journal; diary
rojniş [rozhnish] *f* calendar
rojnivîs [rozhnyvis] *f* diary
roke [rokä] *adv* once
rom [rom] *m* Turk
ronayî [ronayi] *f* light; brightness; liquid
rondar [rondar] *adj* light
ronî [roni] *f* light; liquid
rotob [rotob] *adj* grey
ruh [röh] *m* soul, spirit
ruhnik [röhnyk] *f* light
rux [rökh] *m* face
rutib [rötyb] *f* rank, position
rû [ru] *m* face, visage; side; page
rûbar [rubar] *m* river
rûçik [ruchik] *m* face
rûkar [rukar] *m* surface
rûmet [rumät] *f* honor, glory; authority
rûn [run] *m* butter
rûnerm [runärm] *adj* quiet, humble
rûniştin [runyshtyn] *v* sit

rûperde [rupärdä] *f* mask
rûreşî [rurāshi] *f* shame; confusion
rûs [rus] *m* Russian
rûsî [rusi] *adj* Russian
rûspîtî [ruspiti] *f* honor
rût [rut] *adj* naked
rûtirş [rutyrsh] *adj* sad, morose
rûvî [ruvi] *m* fox

S

sabiq [sabyq] *adj* previous, former
sabûn [sabun] *f* soap
sac [sadj] *f* baking pan
sade [sadä] *adj* easy; clear
sadiq [sadyq] *adj* faithful, true
safîtî [safiti] *f* clarity
sahîb [sahib] *m* owner
sahil [sahyl] *m* shore, bank
saẍ [sakh] *adj* healthy
sakar [sakar] *f* basket
saq [saq] *m* shank; vine
saldat [saldat] *m* soldier
salî [sali] *adj* annual
salif [salyf] *adj* last
salix [salykh] *m* information; story

salname [salnamä] *f* calendar; chronicle
salûs [salus] *adj* false
sar [sar] *adj* cold
sarayî [sarayi] *f* cold
savar [savar] *m* groats
saw [sa'w] *f* terror, horror
seba [säba] *prep* for
sebah [säbah] *f* morning
sebeb [säbäb] *f* cause
sebir [säbyr] *f* patience, endurance
sebûr [säbur] *adj* patient
secde [sädjdä] *f* chair
seda [säda] *m* voice
sefer [säfär] *f* trip
sefîh [säfih] *adj* silly
sefîl [säfil] *adj* simple
sefîre [säfirä] *m* ambassador
seh [säh] *v* listen
seher [sähär] *m* morning
sehet [sähät] *f* hour; health
sehhar [säh'har] *adj* charming
sehîn [sähin] *f* part; dish
sehl [sähl] *adj, adv.* easy
sehm [sähm] *f* fear
sehn [sähn] *m* plaza
sekin [säkyn] *f* country

selah [sälah] *f* honesty
selam [sälam] *f* greeting
selat [sälat] *f* salad
sema [säma] *f* sky
semt [sämt] *m* county
sendûq [sänduq] *f* cashbox
sepe [säpä] *adj* secret
ser [sär] *prep* on
serac [säradj] *f* lamp
serbanî [särbani] *m* roof
serberjêr [särbärzher] *f* downstairs
serbest [särbäst] *adj* independent
serbilind [särbylynd] *adj* proud
serborî [särbori] *f* biography
sercil [särdjyl] *f* clothes
serçav [särchav] *m* face
serçeq [särchäq] *f* brain
serdan [därdan] *f* visit
serdeb [särdäb] *f* basement
serderge [särdärgä] *m* balcony
serdilk [särdylk] *f* dream
sere [särä] *adj* old
serecem [särädjäm] *f* content
serecî [särädji] *m* motherland
serederî [särädäri] *f* understanding
serek [säräk] *m* boss

serekdewlet [säräkdäwlät] *m* head of the government

serenav [säränav] *m* proper noun

sergerdan [särgärdan] *adj* poor

sergiran [särgyran] *adj* silly, idiotic

sergirtin [särgyrtyn] *v* close

serguzeşt [särgözäsht] *f* biography

serhêl [särhel] *f* height

serî [säri] *m* head; *adj* swift

serêş [säresh] *f* headache

serêşanî [säreshanee] *f* worry

sermaye [särmayä] *m* bank, capital

sermest [särmäst] *adj* drunk

sermeşq [särmäshq] *m* example

sernav [särnav] *m* title

sernerm [särnärm] *adj* quiet

serpola [särpola] *adj* strong

serrastî [särrasti] *f* truth

serrû [särru] *m* surface

sersera [särsära] *n* greetings

serşîr [särshir] *m* cream

serşok [särshok] *f* bathroom

ser û bin [sär u byn] *m* basis

serwext [särwäkht] *adj* clever

serwer [särwär] *m* head

serwêt [särwet] *f* universe

sewalî [säwali] *f* question
sewda [säwda] *m* intellect
sewde [säwdä] *m* commerce
sews [säws] *adj* mad, crazy
seyda [säyda] *m* teacher
seyran [säyran] *f* walk
seyvan [säyvan] *f* umbrella
seyyare [säyyarä] *f* planet
sîgar [sigar] *f* cigar
sîm [sim] *m* silver; string
sîng [sing] *m* breast
sînor [sinor] *m* border
sîpkan [sipkan] (name of a Kurdish tribe in
    Armenia and Turkey) Sipkan
sîpkî [sipki] *f* garlic
sîyaset [siyasät] *f* politics
sêlav [selav] *f* storm
sêlqelî [selqäli] *f* stew
sêntir [sentyr] *f* center
sêntyabir [sentyabyr] *f* september
sêrîda [serida] *adv* again
sêşemî [seshämi] *f* Tuesday
sêv [sev] *f* apple
sêzde [sezdä] *num.* thirteen
sibat [sybat] *f* February
sibe [sybä] *f* morning

sifet [syfät] *m* picture; quality
sihik [syhyk] *f* vinegar
sihr [syhr] *f* line
sike [sykä] *f* coin
sikenc [sykändj] *f* cough
silq [sylq] *f* beet
sincebî [syndjäbi] (name fo a Kurdish tribe in
   Iran) Sendzhebi
sinet [synät] *m* Sunni
sinetî [synäti] *f* Sunni Islam
sinf [synf] *m* kind
sinhet [synhät] *f* art; speciality; industry
sinîd [synid] *m* identification card
sipîçal [sypichal] *f* sheet
sipipor [sypipor] *adj* grey
siping [sypyng] *f* spinach
sirê [syreh] *f* line
sirişk [syryshk] *f* tear
sist [syst] *adj* weak
sofî [sofi] *m* sufi
sofîtî [sofiti] *f* sufism
sohbet [sohbät] *f* conversation
soqaq [soqaq] *f* street
sol [sol] *f* shoes
sone [sonä] *f* duck
sor [sor] *adj* red

sorahî [sorahi] *f* bottle
soz [soz] *m* promise
spar [spar] *f* errand
spas [spas] *f* gratitude
sport [sport] *f* sport
stî [sti] *f* lady, Mrs.
stukur [stökör] *f* neck
stûr [stoor] *adj* thick
surman [sörman] *m* muslim
sûc [sydj] *m* fault
sûk [suk] *f* market
sûr [sur] *m* feast
şa [sha] *adj* gay, happy
şadab [shadab] *adj* humid
şade [shadä] *m* witness
şadrewan [shadräwan] *f* swimming pool
şax [shakh] *f* branch
şaxsar [shakhsar] *m* garden
şal [shal] *m* trousers *f* scarf
şalik [shalyk] *f* apron
şalvar [shalvar] *m* trousers
şandi [shandy] *m* deputy
şandyar [shandyar] *m* sender
şane [shanä] *f* comb
şans [shans] *f* chance; luck, success
şanzde [shanzdä] *num.* sixteen

şaper [shapär] *m* cap, hat
şaşî [shashi] *f* mistake
şaşmayî [shashmayi] *adj* surprised
şatir [shatyr] *m* doorman; police officer
şayîr [shayir] *m* poet
şayîş [shayish] *f* care
şebeş [shäbäsh] *m* watermelon
şeîd [shä'id] *adj* strong, severe
şedname [shädnamä] *f* I.D.
şefqe [shäfqä] *f* cap
şefqet [shäfqät] *f* caress, kindness
şehamet [shähamät] *f* perfidy
şeher [shähär] *m* city
şeheristan [shähärystan] *f* culture
şehervan [shähärvan] *m* city dweller
şehervanî [shähärvani] *f* citizenship
şehreza [shähräza] *adj* knowledgeable
şekir [shäkyr] *m* sugar
şekirleme [shäkyrlämä] *m* sweets, candies
şekirok [shäkyrok] *m* appeal
şembî [shämbi] *f* Saturday
şems [shäms] *m* sun
şemsikî [shämsyki] *the name of a Kurdish tribe in southern Armenia* Shamsiki
şene [shänä] *f* comb
şeng [shäng] *adj* refined, elegant

şengeşox [shängäshokh] *adj* beautiful

şerab [shärab] *f* wine

şeref [shäräf] *f* honor

şerh [shärh] *m* explanation

şerîet [shärnät] *m* Shariat (compilation of Muslim religious laws)

şerîf [shärif] *adj* famous, noble

şrîr [shärir] *adj* angry

şerq [shärq] *f* east

şerqî [shärqi] *adj* eastern

şerqîn [shärqin] *f* noise

şerqnasî [shärqnasi] *f* oriental studies

şerm [shärm] *f* shame

şerpeze [shärpäzä] *adj* interrupted

şert [shärt] *m* agreement

şeş [shäsh] *num.* six

şet [shät] *m* river

şev [shäv] *f* night

şevîn [shävin] *adj* nightly

şevorî [shävori] *f* insomnia

şevroj [shävrozh] *f* 24 hours (day)

şewat [shäwat] *f* fuel

şewişandin [shäwyshandyn] *v* shake

şeytan [shäytan] *m* devil

şeyvan [shäyvan] *m* cry

şîlan [shilan] *f* rose hips
şîlav [shilav] *f* liquid, juice
şîn [shin] *adj* green *f* grief
şîr [shir] *m* milk; juice
şîranî [shirani] *f* sweetness; sweets
şîret [shirät] *f* suggestion
sîrêçk [shirechk] *f* plant
şîrêz [shirez] *f* juice
şîkir [shikyr] *f* gratitude
şên [shen] *f* flourishing; comfortable
şênî [sheni] *f* building
şêr [sher] *f* poem
şêrdil [sherdyl] *adj* bold
şibhe [shybhä] *f* suspicion, doubts
şibt [shybt] *f* hall
şixul [shykhöl] *m* business, work
şixulîn [shykhölin] *v* burn, shine
şixulkar [shykhölkar] *m* worker
şikandin [shykandyn] *v* break
şikestî [shykästi] *n. math* fraction
şikev [shykäv] *f* pelvis
şikil [shykyl] *m* image; copy
şikilçî [shykylchi] *m* artist
şil [shyl] *adj* wet

şilik [shylyk] *f* summit *m* pancake

şilope [shylopä] *f* puddle

şima [shyma] *f* candle

şimalî [shymali] *adj* nothern

şimitîn [shymytin] *v* skate

şirîk [shyrik] *m* member

şirîkayî [shyrikayi] *f* membership

şirik [shyryk] *f* tap

şitaet [shyta'ät] *f* nonsense

şiv [shyv] *f* stick

şivet [shyvät] *adv* like

şkav [shkav] *f* closet

şofêr [shofer] *m* driver

şofêrtî [shoferti] *f* profession

şor [shor] *f* word

şor [shor] *adj* salted; bitter

şorb [shorb] *m* liquid

şorbe [shorbä] *f* soup

ştexilî [shtäkhyli] *m* word, conversation

şuret [shörät] *f* greediness

şûl [shul] *f* light

şûnva [shunva] *adv* backwards

şûpî [shupi] *f* humidity

şûşe [shushä] *f* glass; bottle

T

ta [ta] *m* thread, hair; layer, story (of building); sheet; unit; *f* fever; plea; *adj* even; rich; *prep* from...to; *conj* until; *part* even

tab [tab] *f* patience

tabe [tabä] *f* animal

tabet [tabät] *f* self-control

tabe' [tabä] *adj* subordinate

tabî [tabi] *f* submission; publication; *adj* natural

tabileyî [tabyläyi] *adv* of course

tablîsa [tablisa] *f* table

tablo [tablo] *f* painting

tabût [tabut] *f* back; anus

tacir [tadjyr] *m* merchant

tade [tadä] *f* violence

tagir [tagyr] *m* supporter

tajan [tazhan] *f* kidnapping

taq [taq] *m* floor; layer

taqet [taqät] *f* power

tal [ta'l] *adj* sour

talan [talan] *m* robbery

tale [talä] *m* happiness

talektor [taläktor] *adj* unhappy

talî [ta'li] *f* acid

talîf [ta'lif] *f* composition

talîfker [ta'lifkär] *m* compiler
tam [ta'm] *m* taste
tan [ta'n] *m* rebuke
tang [tang] *f* side
tarîx [tarikh] *f* history
tarîxçî [tarikhchi] *m* historian
tarîxî [tarikhi] *adj* historical
tarîstan [ta'ristan] *f* darkness
tas [tas] *f* cup
tat [ta't] *m* cliff
tav [ta'v] *f* sun
tawêr [tawer] *m* stone
tazî [tazi] *adj* naked
tebax [täbakh] *f* plate
tebatî [täbati] *f* peace
tebayî [täbayi] *f* solitude
tebdîl [täbdil] *f* change
tebeqe [täbäqä] *m* layer
tebeşîr [täbäshir] *f* chalk
tebî [täbi] *f* health care
tebîb [täbib] *m* doctor
tebîe't [täbiä't] *f* nature
tecrîb [tädjrib] *f* try
tecrîd [tädjrid] *f* section
tedbîr [tädbir] *f* opinion
tedlîl [tädlil] *f* proof

teglîfat [täglifat] *f* invitation
tehekum [tähäköm] *m* command
tehmûl [tähmul] *f* patience
texalif [täkhalyf] *f* animosity, enmity
texdîr [täkhdyr] *f* estimation
texlît [täkhlit] *m* sort, kind
texmîn [täkhmin] *f* surmise
text [täkht] *m* throne
texdeyûr [täkhdäyur] *m* movement
tek [täk] *f* unit
tekane [täkanä] *adj* one, unique, alone
teker [täkär] *f* death, destruction
tekil [täkyl] *f* mix
tektî [täkti] *f* seclusion
teqez [täqäz] *adv* maybe, possibly
teqle [täqlä] *f* joke
teqleçî [täqlächi] *m* buffoon, joker
teqlîd [täqlid] *f* imitation
teqrîr [täqrir] *f* review
telaq [tälaq] *f* honor, reputation *m* meeting, date
telaqreşî [tälaqräshi] *f* insolence
telandin [tälandyn] *v* hide
telayî [tä'layi] *f* bitterness
telebk [täläbk] *adv* a little
tele-tel [tälä-täl] *adv* secretly
tele't [tälä't] *f* appearance, image

telp [tälp] *m* cloud; fog
tem [täm] *f* desire, intention
temam [tämam] *adj* whole, full
temamî [tämami] *f* wholeness
temaşe [tämashä] *f* performance
temayî [tä'mayi] *f* taste
temedar [tämädar] *m* director, adviser
temene [tämänä] *f* bow; plea
temîn [tämin] *f* advice, guidance
temiz [tämyz] *adj* clean, neat
temizî [tämyz] *f* cleanness, neatness
temsel [tämsäl] *f* imitation
tenahî [tänahi] *adv* just
tenbih [tänbih] *f* advice
tenezul [tänäzöl] *f* humiliation
tengav [tängav] *f* tightness, crowdiness
tengdestî [tängdästi] *f* debility
tengdilî [tängdyli] *f* harshness
tengezarî [tängäzari] *f* grief, suffering
tenê [täneh] *adj* unique, one
tenik [tänyk] *adj* slender, thin
tenqîd [tänqid] *f* criticism
tentene [täntänä] *f* solemnity
tep [täp] *f* madness
tepe [täpä] *f* hill
tepisandi [täpysandyn] *v* press

tepliq [täplyk] *f* drum
ter [tär] *adj* wet, humid; young, adolescent
terayî [tärayi] *f* humidity, wetness
terazû [tärazu] *f* scale
terb [tärb] *m* education
terbîyetdar [täreyätdar] *adj* educated, mannered
terbîyetdarî [tärbiyätdari] *f* education, discipline
tercime [tärdjymä] *f* translation
tercimeçî [tärdjymächi] *m* translator
tercûbe [tärdjubä] *f* temptation
tereb [täräb] *f* joy
terecan [tärädjan] *adj* fresh, new
terx [tärkh] *f* swindle, lie
terxan [tärkhan] *m* part, portion; *adj* free
terx̂îb [tärkhib] *f* nervousness, irritation
terîf [tärif] *f* explanation
terêj [tärezh] *f* lightening
terikî [täryki] *adj* big, huge
terkeser [tärkäsär] *f* wandering
terqe-terq [tärqä-tärq] *f* knock
terqin [tärqyn] *f* explosion; shot
terlan [tärlan] *adj* superb
tertîb [tärtib] *f* rule, order, plan
terz [tärz] *m* form, shape, image; method
tesediq [ttäcädyq] *f* donation
teselî [täsäli] *f* investigation

tesîr [täsir] *f* influence
teslîm [täslim] *m* errand; command
teslîmat [täslimat] *f* obedience
tesrîf [täsrif] *f* change
tesvîl [täsvil] *f* temptation; intrigue
teşkîlat [täshkilat] *f* organization, society
teşkîldar [tashkildar] *f* boss, person in charge
teşqele [täshqälä] *f* trouble, bad luck; *adj* unlucky, troublesome
teşnîtî [täshniti] *f* thirst
teşt [täsht] *f* bath
teşwîş [täshwish] *f* change; mistake; fake
tev [täv] *pron* all, whole *adv* together
teva [täva] *m* animal
tevdan [tävdan] *v* mix; embarrass
tevhev [tävhäv] *adv* together
tevhevbûn [tävhävbun] *f* connection, unity; mix; regret
tevitîn [tävytin] *v* tolerate
tevkar [tävkar] *m* member; colleague
tevkarî [tävkari] *f* membership; participation
tevneçî [tävnächi] *m* tailor
tevsîl [tävsil] *f* temptation
tevsîr [tävsir] *f* description; commentaries
tevz [tävz] *f* trembling; shiver
tewaf [täwaf] *f* death

tewekelî [täwäkäli] *f* light-mindedness
tewekîl [täwäkil] *f* trust
teweqe [täwäqä] *f* request
tewfîq [täwfiq] *f* fulfilment
tewhîd [täwhid] *f* unity
tewijm [täwyzhm] *m* conviction
tewr [täwr] *m* image; *adj.* same
tewrî [täwri] *adv* very
tewsîye [täwsiya] *f* advice; preaching
teyax [täyakh] *adj* strong
teybîr [täybir] *f* loss
teyrok [täyrok] *f* thunder
teze [täzä] *adj* new, fresh
tezede [täzädä] *adv* again, once more
tezedekirin [täzädäkyryn] *f* restoration, rebirth
tezekirin [täzäkyryn] *f* renewal
tezelom [täzälom] *f* complaint
tezîyî [täzi'yi] *f* loss; death
tezwîr [täzwir] *f* lie; fake; deceit
te'bexane [tä'bäkhanä] *f* menagerie
te'cîl [tädjil] *f* hurry
te'eqol [tä'äqol] *f* comprehension, understanding
te'esob [tä'äsob] *f* zeal
te'ew [tä'äw] *f* fury
te'l [tä'l] *m* destiny, fate
te'lîm [tä'lim] *f* teaching; education

te'lîmdar [tä'limdar] *m* instructor

te'mîn [tä'min] *f* protection

te'zîm [tä'zim] *f* bow, obeisance

tîatr [tiatr] *f* theater

tîbûn [tibun] *f* thirst, longing

tîk [tik] *adj* tall; vertical; straight

tîqe-tîq [tiqä-tiq] *f* laughter

tîqîn [tiqin] *f* laughter; whistle

tîmar [timar] *f* care; caress

tîndar [tindar] *adj* strong, robust; bright

tîpî [tipi] *f* thunder; storm; wave

tîr [tir] *f* beam *adj* dense, thick

tîrêj [tirezh] *f* beam

tîrik [tiryk] *f* arrow

tîrme [tirmä] *f* July

tîş-tîş [tish-tish] *m* row

tîtal [tital] *adj* smooth

tîtalî [tetali] *f* smoothness

tîlî [tili] *f* thirst

tê [teh] *adj* real, genuine

têda [teda] *adv* inside

têdan [tedan] *v* destroy; consume

têderxistin [tedärkhystyn] *v* guess

têxnîke [tehnikä] *f* technique

têjber [tezhbär] *f* carpet

têl [tel] *f* thread, rope, string

têlefon [teläfon] *f* telephone
têlgiraf [telgyraf] *f* telegraph
têlgiram [telgyram] *f* telegram
têorî [teori] *f* theory
têr [ter] *adj* sated
têrbez [terbäz] *adj* fat, corpulent
têretijî [terätyzhi] *adj* full; affluent
têrî [teri] *f* abundance
têtî [teti] *f* verity, reality
tibark [tybark] *f* holyness; *adj* holy
tifal [tyfal] *f* child, baby; *adj* lonely
tifalî [tyfali] *f* childhood
tifing [tyfyng] *f* weapon
tifû [tyfu] *f* spit
tihf [tyhf] *f* pride
tixûb [tykhub] *m* boarder
tijî [tyzhi] *adj* stuffed, full
tijîtî [tyzheti] *f* profusion
tilî [tyli] *f* finger
tiling [tylyng] *adj* cursed
tima [tyma] *adj* greedy
timayî [tymayi] *f* greed, avarice
tinaz [tynaz] *m* affectation
tinazker [tynazkär] *m* joker
tiral [tyral] *m* lazy person
tiralî [tyrali] *f* laziness

tirane [tyranä] *m* irony, joke
tiraneyî [tyranäyi] *f* amusement, irony
tirat [tyrat] *f* wrestling
tirb [tyrb] *f* grave, tomb
tirbistan [tyrbystan] *f* cemetery
tirho [tyrho] *f* kidnapping, abduction
tirxes [tyrkhäs] *adj* free
tirên [tyren] *f* train, tram
tirinc [tyryndj] *m* orange
tiringî [tyrynghi] *f* dance, dancing
tirk [tyrk] *m* Turk
tirs [tyrs] *f* fear, dread
tirsandî [tyrsandi] *adj* frightened, scared
tirsek [tyrsäk] *m* coward
tirsonektî [tyrsonäkti] *f* cowardice, shyness
tirtirk [tyrtyrk] *f* butterfly
tisî [tysi] *adj* dry
tişt [tysht] *m* thing, subject
tiştanok [tyshtanok] *adj* materialistic
titûn [tytun] *f* tobacco
tivdarek [tyvdaräk] *m* preparation
tivir [tyvyr] *f* radish
tobe [tobä] *f* regret; oath
tofan [tofan] *f* storm
toxavk [tohavk] *f* sour cream
toxim [tokhym] *m* seed

toq [toq] *m* ring
tol [tol] *f* revenge
ton [ton] *f* ton
tonêl [tonel] *f* tunnel
top [top] *f* weapon
toprax [toprakh] *f* ground; county; motherland
tor [tor] *m* neckless; fence
toraq [toraq] *f* cottage cheese
torat [torat] *f* Old Testament
toravêj [toravezh] *m* fisherman
tore [torä] *m* gender; roots *adj* meritorious
torin [toryn] *m* nephew
tov [tov] *m* seed
toz [toz] *f* dust
trûmbêl [trumbel] *f* automobile
tu [tö] *pron* you
tucar [tödjar] *m* merchant
tucarî [tödjari] *adv* never
tucarî [tödjari] *f* trade, commerce
tum [töm] *adv* always, constantly
tunebûn [tönäbun] *f* absence
tureyî [töräyi] *f* fury
turuş [törösh] *m* bravery, risk
tuşû [töshu] *m* preparation
tutar [tötar] *adj* weak
tutqal [tötqal] *f* glue

tûde [tudä] *f* party
tûj [tuzh] *adj* sharp
tûjî [tuzhi] *f* wit
tûjkirin [tuzhkyryn] *f* sharpening
tûk [tuk] *f* feather
tûn [tun] *m* cave
tûş [tush] *f* valley, plain
tûtî [tuti] *m* parrot
tûzî [tuzi] *m* piece

U

ucre [ödjrä] *f* box
ud [öd] *f* defense, security
ulaq [ölaq] *m* donkey
ulm [ölm] *m* knowledge, science
ulmdar [ölmdar] *m* scientist; knowledgeable person
unda [önda] *adj* lost, disappeared
undabûn [öndabun] *f* loss, disappearance
usr [ösr] *m* difficulty
usûl [ösul] *f* habit
usyan [ösyan] *f* rebellion, insurrection
usyançî [ösyanchi] *m* rebel, insurgent
uzir [özyr] *f* pardon
uzv [özv] *m* member

Û

û [u] *conj* and; but; also
ûceret [udjärät] *f* trade
ûcre [udjrä] *f* rent; hire
ûcredar [udjrädar] *adj* rented; hired *m* hired
   worker
ûlo [ulo] *adv* this way
ûmûd [umud] *f* hope
ûmûr [umur] *m* affair
ûnîvêrsîtê [universiteh] *f* university
ûre [urä] *pl* seeds
ûrisî [urysi] *m* Russian language
ûrt [urt] *f* generation; gender
ûslûb [uslub] *f* method, way
ûstûvank [ustuvank] *n* neckless; collar
ûtêl [utel] *f* hotel

V

va [va] *pron* here
vagon [vagon] *f* carriage
vagzal [vagzal] *f* railroad station
vaqêe'n [vaqe'än] *adv* indeed
vala [vala] *adj* vacant, empty
vandera [vandära] *pron* here

varik [varyk] *f* chicken
vebal [väbal] *prep* to
vebeste [väbästä] *v* tied, binded
veciniqîn [vädjynyqin] *v* frighten
vedawşandin [vädawshandyn] *v* hit
vedizîn [vädyzin] *v* conceal
veger [vägär] *f* return
vegerandin [vägärandyn] *v* return, give back
veguhêrandin [vägöherandyn] *v* change, exchange; *f* exchange
vexwerin [växwäryn] *v* drink; *f* booze
vekirî [väkyri] *adj* opened, unlocked
vekirin [väkyryn] *v* open
vekuştin [väköshtyn] *v* kill; *f* murder
veqetandek [väqätandäk] *m* article
vemalandin [vämalandyn] *v* clean; *n* cleaning
vemirandin [vämyrandyn] *v* kill; *n* murder
vereşandin [väräshandyn] *v* vomit, nauseate
vereşîn [väräshin] *n* nausea attack
verêbûn [värebun] *n* sending; board, management
verêker [värekär] *n* sender; supervisor
verêkirin [värekyryn] *n* sending, package
verêstin [värestyn] *v* fly
verêtin [väretyn] *v* spill
veşartî [väsharti] *adj* hidden, secret

veşartin [väartyn] *v* hide;   *n* funeral
vetirsandin [vätyrsandyn] *v* intimidate, scare
vetirsîn [vätyrsin] *v*   frighten
veweşîn [väwäshin] *v* fall
ve'de [vä'dä] *f* promise, oath *adv* back and forth
vîjik [vizhyk] *f* diarrhea
vîn [vin] *f* desire; love; soul; ghost
vêcar [vedjar] *adv* this time
vêderê [vedäreh] *adv* here
vêga [vega] *adv* this time
vêxistin [vehystyn] *v* ignite, inflame
vêlosîpêd [velosiped] *f* bicycle
vêrgûl [vergul] *f* comma
vine-vin [vynä-vyn] *v* weep, cry
vir [vyr] *adv* here; this way *f* lie
virçikî [vyrchyki] *adj* weak; sticky
virda [vyrda] *adv* this way
virdatir [vyrdatyr] *adv* closer
virek [vyräk] *m* cheater
vireki [vyräki] *f* lie, cheating
virik [vyryk] *f* soup
virişikî [vyryshyki] *adj* crazy
virnî [vyrni] *m* baby
vistan [vystan] *f* case, accident
vitamîn [vytamin] *f* vitamin

W

wa [wa] *adv* this way, in this manner
wacib [wadjyb] *m* duty
wad [wa'd] *f* promise
wade [wa'dä] *m* time, period; term; deadline
wadetî [wa'däti] *adj* temporary
wafiq [wafyq] *adj* informed
wahî [wahi] *f* candidness
wax [wakh] *interj* Oh! Ah! (unfortunately)
wale [walä] *adj* surprised
walî [wali] *m* ruler, mayor
wanî [wani] *adj* similar
wapor [wapor] *f* ship
war [war] *m* place
warge [wargä] *m* place, shelter
warîn [warin] *f* scream
waris [warys] *m* heir
warkor [warkor] *adj* homeless
warocax [warodjakh] *f* dwelling
wa-wa [wa-wa] *interj* really?
wawîk [wawik] *m* curse; anathema
way [wa'y] *interject.* Oops! Alas!; *f* sorrow
wefat [wäfat] *f* death, demise
wefid [wäfyd] *m* unity
wahc [wähdj] *f* face, countenance; image

wehdetî [wähdäti] *adj* temporary
wehe [wähä] *adv* this way
wehîd [wähid] *adj* lonely
wehîdî [wähidi] *f* loneleness; unity
wehş [wähsh] *adj* wild; *m* wild animal; rude
  fellow
wehşî [wähshi] *f* wildness, savagery
wext [wäkht] *f* time period
wextî [wäkhti] *adj* temporary; *adv* temporarily
weê [wä'e] *interjec.* Oh! Ah!
wejunbext [wäzhönbäkht] *adj* miserable
wekaf [wäkaf] *f* contribution
wekan [wäkan] *m* country
weke [wäkä] *adj* equal; corresponding; *adv* at the
  same distance; approximately
wekehevkirin [wäkähävkyryn] *f* similarity
wekî [wäki] *conj* if
wekîl [wäkil] *m* representative; council; lawyer
wekîltî [wäkilti] *f* representation
wekilandin [wäkylandyn] *v* speak, talk
weko [wäko] *conj* like, as
weqe [wäqä] *m* treaty
welat [wälat] *m* motherland
welatî [wälati] *m* fellow countryman
welatjorî [wälatzhori] *m* resindent of the Northern part of a country

wele [wälä] *interj* swear to God
welîlixan [wälilykhan] *f* county
welê [wäleh] *adv* like this *conj* however
welidandin [wälydandyn] *v* give birth
welidîn [wälydin] *v* be born
wellahî [wällahi] *interj* I swear
welle [wällä] *interj* Isn't it? *conj* or
wer [wär] *adv* so, like this
weranîn [wîranin] *v* undress
werdan [wärdan] *v* wash
wergerandin [wärgärandyn] *v* give back; translate; *f* return; translation
wergerandok [wärgärandok] *m* translator
wergerîn [wärgärin] *v* return
wergirtin [wärgyrtyn] *v* dress
werimî [wärymi] *adj* turgid
werimîn [wärymin] *v* bloat
weris [wärys] *m* rope
werq [wärq] *m* sheet (of paper)
werqas [wärqas] *adv* so much
werm [wärm] *f* tumescence, inflammation
wert [wärt] *f* descendence, descendent
werwend [wärwänd] *m* heir
werz [wärz] *f* cultivated earth
wesandin [wäsandyn] *v* instruct; bequeath; *n* instruction; bequeathing

wesefet [wäsäfät] *f* quality, matter
wesf [wäsf] *m* description *v* describe
wesîqe [wäsiqä] *f* reference
wesîle [wäsilä] *f* way, method
wesîyet [wäciyät] *f* advice
west [wäst] *f* suffering; labor; care
westayi [wästayi] *adj* tired
westîn [wästin] *v* tire
weş [wäsh] *f* trembling
weşandin [wäshandyn] *v* shake
weten [wätän] *m* motherland
wetenhiz [wätänhyz] *m* patriot
wetenhizî [wätänhyzi] *f* patriotism
wetîn [wätin] *v* love; *n* love
weto [wäto] *adv* this way
wey [wäy] *interj* Oh!
weyla [wäyla] *interj* Oh
wey-wey [wäy-wäy] *interj* Oh! Alas!
wezaret [wäzarät] *f* ministry
wezîfe [wäzifä] *f* position; service
wezîfedar [wäzifädar] *adj* obligated
wezîfetî [wäzifäti] *f* obligation
wezîretxan [wäzirätkhan] *f* ministry
wezin [wäzyn] f meter, rhythm
we'detî [wä'däti] *adj* temporary
we'z [wä'z] *f* preaching *m* preacher

wêda [weda] *adv* there (in that direction)
wêdatir [wedatyr] *adv* further
wêderê [wedäreh] *adv* there
wêran [waran] *adj* destroyed; *f* ruins
wêranker [werankär] *m* violator
wêrgû [wergu] *f* tax
wêrîn [werin] *v* dare; *n* daring
wiha [wyha] *adv.* this way
wijdan [wyzhdan] *f* conscience
winda [wynda] *adj* lost
windabûn [wyndabun] *f* loss, doom
windakirin [wyndakyryn] *f* loss
wirwirok [wyrwyrok] *f* jabber; *m* talker
wişaq [wyshaq] *m* someone in love, lover
wuşoq [wöshoq] *m* young person

Y

ya [ya] *pron* which, that *interj* Hey! well!
yaban [yaban] *adj* wild
yabanî [yabani] *f* wildness
yax [yakh] *f* collar; skirt
yaqût [yaqut] *m* ruby
yan [yan] *conj* or *m* side
yanzdeh [yanzdäh] *num.* eleven
yanzdehûm [yanzdähum] *num.* eleventh

yar [yar] *m* friend, lover
yarebî [yaräbi] *interjec.* My God!
yarî [yari] *f* friendship, love
yartî [yarti] *f* friendship
yasan [yasan] *f* sadness
yasemîn [yasämin] *f* jasmine
yasîn [yasin] *f* religious book; prayer
yasiyan [yasiyan] *m* interpreter of religious laws
yaşa [yasha] *interjec.* Good job!
yataẍ [yatakh] *f* bed
yazlixan [yaslykhan] *f* balcony
yek [yäk] *num.* one
yekanî [yäkani] *n* unity; *f* singular; *num.* first
yekbang [yäkbang] *gram.* monosyllabic
yekbangî [yäkbangi] *f* agreement
yekî [yäki] *pron* somebody
yekpûtî [yäkputi] *adj* hard
yekrojî [yäkrozhi] *adj* daily
yekrû [yäkru] *adj* same
yeman [yäman] *adj* brave

Z

zabit [zabyt] *m* officer
zad [zad] *f* food

zadepêj [zadäpezh] *m* cook
zagûn [zagun] *f* law
zaha [zaha] *m* expense; *adj* dry
zaẍ [zagh] *f* line
zalim [zalym] *adj* dangerous,; angry; *m* smart aleck
zalimî [zalymi] *f* cruelty
zanak [zanak] *m* sage
zane [zanä] *adj* knowledgeable
zanebûn [zanäbun] *f* knowledge
zang [zang] *f* gorge
zanîngeh [zaningäh] *f* university
zanînî [zanini] *f* knowledge
zar [zar] *m* cry; word; language
zarav [zarav] *m* speech; dialect; gall
zarîn [zarin] *v* cry, weep
zarok [zarok] *f* child
zarutî [zaröti] *f* childhood; *adj* childish
zatî [zati] *f* gist; *adv.* individually
zava [zava] *m* son-in-law
zavod [zavod] *f* plant, factory
zayend [zayänd] *f* gender
zayî [zayi] *adj* born *f* expenditure
zayîn [zayin] *v* give birth; *n* birth, childbirth
zazan [zazan] *m* (name of Kurdish tribe) Zazan
zeca [zädja] *m* glass; crystal

zede [zädä] *f* illness
zef [zäf] *adv* very
zefer [zäfär] *f* victory
zefl [zäfl] *f* chest, breast
zehf [zähf] *adj* many
zehftir [zähftyr] *adv* very
zehmet [zähmät] *m* labor; care
zehmetkêş [zähmätkesh] *m* hard worker; martyr
zexm [zäkhm] *f* power, firmness; *adj* firm
zexmî [zäkhmi] *f* power
zeîf [zä'if] *adj* weak
zelam [zälam] *m* man; youth
zelîl [zälil] *adj* poor, miserable
zeliqandin [zälyqandyn] *v* glue; *f* adherence
zeliqokî [zälyqoki] *adj* sticky
zelûl [zälul] *adj* needy; humble
zelûlî [zäluli] *f* poverty
zeman [zäman] *m* century
zembûr [zämbur] *f* Psalter
zenar [zänar] *f* dervish's hair-shirt
zend [zänd] *f* hand; sleeve
zende [zändä] *f* astonishment
zeng [zäng] *f* bell
zengîn [zänghin] *adj* rich; huge
zengînî [zänghini] *f* riches
zer [zär] *adj* yellow; sandy; pale

zerae't [zäraä't] *f* agriculture
zeraetçî [zäraätchi] *m* farmer
zerarker [zärarkär] *m* delirious person
zerb [zärb] *f* kick, hit
zerbedest [zärbädäst] *adj* strong
zerdele [zärdäl] *f* apricot
zerdeştî [zärdäshti] *f rel.* Zoroastrianism
zere [zärä] *f* atom
zerf [zärf] *pl* dishes; *f* wrap; bag
zerî [zäri] *f* blonde; beautiful woman, beloved
zerîf [zärif] *adj* elegant, charming
zerîn [zärin] *adj* orange
zerik [zäryk] *f* yolk
zerzilî [zärzyli] *adj* torn, broken
zeveş [zäväsh] *m* watermelon
zewac [zäwadj] *f* marriage
zewal [zäwal] *f* damage
zewicî [zäwydji] *adj* married
zewq [zäwq] *f* pleasant taste; joy
zeyî [zäyi] *f* relative
zeytûn [zäytun] *f* plum
zeytûni [zäytuni] *adj* dark green
ze'f [zä'f] *adj* many
zîb [zib] *adj* beatiful, embellished
zîlî [zili] *m* (name of Kurdish tribe) Zili
zîv [ziv] *m* silver

zivker [zivkär] *m* jeweler
zîya [ziya] *adj* dry
zîyan [ziyan] *f* harm, damage
zîyandar [ziyandar] *adj* harmful
zîyaretvan [ziyarätvan] *m* pilgrim
zîyaretvanî [ziyarätvani] *f* pilgrimage
zîz [ziz] *adj* sonorous
zêc [zedj] *f* wife *pl* children
zêde [zedä] *adv* more
zên [zen] *f* resource; cleverness
zênd [zend] *m* (name of Kurdish tribe
　　living in the North-West of Iran) Zend
zêndar [zendar] *adj* bright, gifted
zêndî [zendi] *adj* lively
zêr [zer] *m* gold
zêrav [zerav] *adj* shining
zêrfiroş [zerfyrosh] *m* jewelry seller
zêrîn [zerin] *v* suffer; cry; *f* suffering; cry
zêrker [zerkär] *m* goldsmith
ziaker [zyakär] *m* squanderer
zibr [zybr] *adj* rude
zik [zyk] *m* stomach
zikak [zykak] *f* street
zikêş [zykesh] *f* stomach ache
zikir [zykyr] *f* mentioning
zikreş [zykräsh] *adj* harmful

ziqet [ziqät] *f* sensitivity, understanding
zillet [zyllät] *f* humiliation; mistake; *v* make a mistake
ziman [zyman] *m* language
zimanlîz [zymanliz] *m* verbose person, someone clever in conversation
zimanzan [zymanzan] *m* linguist
zimanzanînî [zymanzanini] *f* linguistics
zinar [zynar] *m* stone
zinê [zyneh] *m* adulterer
zinêkarî [zynekari] *f* adultery
zirar [zyrar] *f* harm
zirarkarî [zyrarkari] *adj* harmful
zirav [zyrav] *adj* slender, straight; gentle *m* gall bladder
zirgurtî [zyrgörti] *f* audacity; disobedience
zirxweh [zyrkhwäh] *f* step-sister
zirîc [zyridj] *f* cement
zirne [zyrnä] *f* oboe
zirneçî [zyrnächi] *m* musician
zirnix [zyrnykh] *f* arsenic
zirt [zyrt] *f* swank
zivar [zyvar] *adj* poor
zivir [zyvyr] *f* return
zivirandin [zyvyrandyn] *v* roll around; *f* return
zivistan [zyvystan] *f* winter

zivistanî [zyvystani] *adj* winter

zivtî [zyvti] *f* guard

ziwa [zywa] *adj* dry

zo [zo] *m* lace

zol [zol] *m* couple

zoltan [zoltan] *f* zoltan (money)

zorbe [zorbä] *adj* strong

zoro [zoro] *m* Zoro (name)

zorzan [zorzan] *adj* smart, bright

zorzanî [zorzani] *f* acuteness

zozan [zozan] *f* Zozan (name)

zucac [zödjadj] *adj* glass, made of glass

zuhum [zöhöm] *m pl.* fats

zurbe [zörbä] *m* Zurba (name)

zuret [zörät] *f* descendence, seed

zû [zu] *adj* quick

zûda [zuda] *adv* long ago

zûrîn [zurin] *v* cry, scream

ENGLISH-KURDISH
DICTIONARY

A

abandon [ubendun] *v* hiştin, hêlandin
abandoned [ubendund] *adj* me'zûl
abduction [ubdukşun] *n* tirho
aborigene [eburicinî] *n* binecî
above [ubuv] *adv* fêz, jorê
absence [ebsins] *n* tunebûn
absent-minded [ebsint-mayndid] *adj* bela-belayî
absurd [ubsurd] *adj* bêmanî
absurdity [ubsurditî] *n* bêmanîbûn
abundance [ebunduns] *n* boşahî, peleseng, pirayî, têrî
acceptance [uksêptuns] *n* îcabet
accident [eksidint] *n* bela, xûsran, vistan
account [ukawnt] *n* hesab, hejmar, jimar
achieve [uçîv] *v* gîhandin, gihîştin
acid [esid] *n* talî
acquaintance [ukwêyntuns] *n* nasî, nasbûn
acrobat [ekrowbet] *n* oyînbaz
across [ekros] *adv* pêşber
act [ekt] *n* ehd, kir *v* kirin
action [ekşun] *n* fel
acuteness [ekyûtnis] *n* zorzanî
address [adris] *n* adrês
adherence [edhurêns] *n* zeliqandin

adolescent [edolêsint] *adj* ter

adulterer [adulturur] *n* zinê

adultery [adulturî] *n* zinêkarî

advance [advens] *n* beha

adventure [advênçur] *n* belaxet, bûyer

adverb [edvurb] *n* fêlnîş, hoker

adversary [edvurserî] *n* e'dû

advertisement [edvurtayzmint] *n* îlan

advice [advays] *n* mesveret, pend, temîn, tenbih, tewsîye, wesîyet

adviser [edvayzur] *n* temedar

affair [afêr] *n* ûmûr

affectation [efêktêyşun] *n* tinaz

affirmation [efurmêyşun] *n* belênî, belêkirin

affluent [eflûint] *adj* têretijî

Afghan (native of Afghanistan) [efgen] *n* efgan

after [eftur] *adv* dû, hindî, paşê *adj* dûra *prep* pey, piş

afterwards [efturwurds] *adv* paşê

again [agêyn] *adv* careke, din, cardin, dîsa *adj* nûva

against [agêynst] *adv* qabil *prep* pêş

age [êyc] *n* e'sir, qurn

agreeable [agrîubl] *adj* razî

agreement [agrîmênt] *n* hevnêrîn, hevbawerî, belênî, ehd, qayîlî

agriculture [egrikulçur] *n* zerae't

Ah! [a] *interj* weê

aim [eym] *n* nîşan, armanc, miraz, berneme, bestem, amac, cihdaxwaz

air [êr] *n* hewir, hewa

airplane [êrplêyn] *n* firinde

airport [êrport] *n* eyredrom, ferange, firindegah

alarmed [alarmd] *adj* bêtewat

Alas! [ales] *interj* way, wey-wey

alien [êylîên] *adj* bêgan

alike [ulayk] *adj* wekhev, yek, hêwan, hevta

alive [ulayv] *adj* çist, zindî, candar, jîndar

Alkan [alkan] *n* alkan

all right [ol rayt] *adj* bila

all [ol] *pron* tev

Allah [Ala] *n* Elah, Îlahî

almonds [elmunds] *n* hincas

alone [alown] *adj* tekane

alphabet [elfabêt] *n* alifba, elfabe

already [olrêdî] *adv* hemîn

also [olsow] *adv* êcgar, *conj* û

altitude [eltitûd] *n* firêz

always [olwêys] *adv* hergav, hercar, herdem, herçax, tum

amazement [amêyzmint] *n* e'cêb, ḧeyret

amazing [amêyzing] *adj* e'zîm, e'cêbokî, gosirmat, ḧeyran

ambulance [embyûluns] *n* ambûlatorîya

American [umêrikin] *n* emirkan, *adj* emirkanî

ammunition [emyûnişun] *n* posatşer

amulet [emyûlit] *n* himelî

amusement [amyûzmênt] *n* tiraneyî

analysis [unelisis] *n* analîz

anathema [anesêma] *n* wawîk

ancient [êynşênt] *adj* antîk, qedîm

and [end] *conj* û

angel [êyncul] *n* milyaket

anger [engur] *n* hêrs, qehr, kerb, bisûtî, fersend, hêrs, qehr, qehirandin

angry [engrî] *adj* bisû, dilgîr, dilgirtî, e'ngir, hêç, şrîr

animal [enumul] *n* canewar, teva, tabe

animals [enimuls] *n* dehbe

animosity [enimasitî] *n* fitne, texalif

annihilate [enayilêyt] *v* qulibandin

annihilation [anayulêyşun] *n* hêçbûn, mehw

announcement [anewnsmint] *n* alan, îlan

annual [enyûul] *adj* salî

answer [enswur] *n* bersîv, *v* lêvegerandin

ant [ent] *n* mûrî
antique [entîk] *adj* antîk
anus [êynus] *n* tabût
anxiety [engzayitî] *n* helecan
anxious [enkşus] *adj* bêtewat
any [ênî] *adj* herkes
apparent [aperint] *adj* melûm, pe'nî
appeal [apîd] *n* xûnkêşî, şekirok
appealing [apîling] *adj* xûnkêş
appearance [apîruns] *n* dirûv, dirb, şêwe, beşer,
    beng, çirûk, eşk
appetizing [epitayzing] *adj* iştehawer
apple [epul] *n* sêv
appraisal [uprêyzul] *n* pesnevedan, *prep* pey
apprentice [aprêntis] *n* berdestî
approval [uprûvul] *n* halan, qebûlbûn, reza
approximately [upraksimatlî] *adv* weke
apricot [eprikat] *n* zerdele
apricots [eprikats] *n* qeysî
April [êyprul] *n* nîsan
apron [êyprun] *n* şalik
apt [ept] *adj* fehmdar
aptitude [eptitûd] *n* fehm
architect [arlitêkt] *n* çîredest
architecture [arkitêkçur] *n* çîredestî

ardor [ardur] *n* rewan
area [êrîa] *n* alî, malbend
argue [argyû] *v* cîdalkirin, pevçûn
argument [argyûmint] *n* pevçûn, raberizîn, geleşe, cibbe, cîdal, genc
aristocracy [eristakrusî] *n* çelebîtî
arm [arm] *n* dest
armchair [armçêr] *n* kursî
Armenian [armîniun] *adj* filekî, *n* ermenî, file, êrmenî
arms [arms] *n* posatşer
army [armî] *n* cinûd, leşker, qişûn, ordî
aroma [arowma] *n* bîhnayî, bîhn, xweşbîn
around [urewnd] *adv* çarnical
arouse [urewz] *v* hawûtin
arrival [arayvul] *n* amade
arrow [erow] *n* tîrik
arsenal [arsinul] *n* cebirxane
arsenic [arsênik] *n* zirnix
art [art] *n* hiner, sinhet
article [artikl] *n* miqale, veqetandek
artificial [artifişul] *adj* destker
artist [artist] *n* nexşkar, şikilçî
as [ez] *adv* qasî, gava ku, hewakî, *conj* maden, weko
ascend [usênd] *v* hilhatin, hilbûn

ascent [asênt] *n* berjor, firêz, hilkês, jêrejorbûn
as if [ez if] *conj* anêka, gak *adv* e'sêba, guya, giva, mîna
ask [esk] *v* pirsîn
assembly [usêmblî] *n* civat
assignment [usaynmint] *n* e'mel
astonishment [ustanişmênt] *n* zende
astute [estût] *adj* fehmdar
atheist [êysîist] *n* xwedênenas
atmosphere [etmusfîr] *n* hewir
atom [etum] *n* zere
attack [etek] *n* hucûm
attention [atênşun] *n* agah
attentive [atêntiv] *adj* agah
attraction [utrekşn] *n* cezbet
attractive [atrektiv] *adj* xûnkêş
audacity [odesitî] *n* zirgurtî
aunt [ont] *n* xalojn, xweltik
authority [osoritî] *n* rûmet
automobile [otomobîl] *n* otomobîl, trûmbêl
autumn [otumn] *n* xezan, payîz
avarice [evuris] *n* desthişkî, çikûsî, timayî
awaiting [uwêyting] *n* hîvî
awake [ewêyk] *adj* hişyar
awful [oful] *adj* bêter
axis [eksis] *n* mihwer
azure [ejur] *adj* erzeq

B

baby [bêybî] *n* biçûk, çûçik, virnî, tifal
bachelor [beçilur] *n* izb
back [bek] *adv* berepaş, bişûnva, paşda *n* pişt, tabût
backwards [bekwurds] *adv* berepaş, şûnva
bad [bed] *adj* bêter, neçê
bad luck [bed luk] *n* teşqele
bag [beg] *n* zerf
bake [bêyk] *n* beriştin *v* birajtin, pijandin, pêjandin
baked [bêykd] *adj* pijyayî
baker [bêykur] *n* firneçî, firinçî, nanpêj
bakery [bêykurî] *n* firne
baking pan [bêyking pen] *n* sac
balcony [belkunî] *n* banoke, şehnişîn, balqon, eywan, heywan, yaslixan
bald [bold] *adj* keçel
ball [bol] *n* hol
band [bend] *n* berbend
bandit [bendit] *n* celal, rêbir
banish [beniş] *v* qewrandin
bank [benk] *n* sermaye, sahil
banquet [benkit] *n* çeşn
bar [bar] *n* meyxane

barbarian [barberîun] *n* berber
barber [barbur] *n* berber, delak
barber shop [barbur şap] *n* delakxane,
   berberxane
barometer [buramitur] *n* hewapîv
barrel [berul] *n* bermîl
base [bêys] *adj* alçax, fehît, nemerd *n* hîm
basement [bêysmint] *n* serdeb, jêrmal
baseness [bêysnis] *n* alçaxî
basic [bêysik] *adj* bingehîn
basil [bezil] *n* belalizk
basin [bêysin] *n* bêrim
basis [bêysis] *n* bingeh, binî, binaxe, binînî, e'sas,
   medar
basket [beskit] *n* sakar
bath [bes] *n* teşt
bathroom [besrum] *n* çêşme, destav, serşok
battle [bedl] *n* ceng, cîdal, pirxaş, rezm
battlefield [betlfîld] *n* best
bay [bêy] *n* derav, xelic
be [bî] *v* heyîn, hebûn
be angry [bî engrî] *v* e'ngirîn, e'nirîn
be born [bî born] *v* welidîn
be tired [bî tayrd] *v* betilîn
beam [bîm] *n* tîr, tîrêj
beans [bîns] *n* lobî

bear [bêr] *v* welidandin
beard [bîrd] *n* rîşî
beast [bîst] *n* den, canewar, fort, hov, ḧeywan
beasts [bîsts] *n* dehbe
beat [bît] *v* xistin, dan, kutan, lê xistin, lê dan,
beautiful [byûtiful] *adj* bedew, wxeşik, sipehî, zîb, cemal, geş, qeşeng
beautiful woman [byûtiful wuman] *n* zerî
beauty [byûtî] *n* bedewî, dilberî, pakî, cemalî, cemal, delalî
because [bikoz] *conj* çimkî, madam, çûnkî, herçend, lema
bed [bêd] *n* bestek, cî-nivîn, yataẍ
bedroom [bêdrûm] *n* razanxane
beet [bît] *n* çewender, silq
before [bifor] *prep* berî, pêş, li pêş *adv* berê, bera, desertberî
beggar [bêgur] *n* parsek, cevîndok, lavakar, berdîvar, berade, gerdan
beginning [bigining] *n* destpêk, îbtîda
behind [bihaynd] *prep* ber, piş, paş
behind [bihaynd] *n* kûn, qûn
behind [bihaynd] *adv* li dû, li paş
belated [bilêytid] *adj* dereng, egle
bell [bêl] *n* ceres, zeng

beloved [biluvid] *n* berdil, delal, hêja, mehbûb, maşoq

beloved [bîluvid] *adj* evindar, e'zîz, dildayî, dilgirtî, dildar

belt [bêlt] *n* berbend, berteng, kember, navbend

bend [bênd] *v* çivandin

bend [bênd] *n* nobe

benefactor [bênifektur] *n* monim

bent [bênt] *adj* ko, qorî

bequeath [bêqwîs] *v* wesandin

bequeathment [bêqwîsmênt] *n* wesandin

best [bêst] *adj* bijare, ala, çê, fayiq, qenc

bestiality [bîstîelitî] *n* dehbetî

better [bêtur] *adj* bijare

bewildered [buwildurd] *adj* gêj

bewilderment [buwildurmint] *n* gêjbûn

bibliography [biblîagrufî] *n* kitêbnasî

bicycle [baysikul] *n* vêlosîpêd

big [big] *adj* givrik, gumreh, gir, qerd, qirinte, rengîn, terikî

bigger [bigur] *adv* mestir

bill [bil] *n* çêk

billion [bilyun] *n* mîlyard

binded [bayndid] *v* vebeste

biography [bayagrafî] *n* serborî, serguzeşt

bird [burd] *n* çîvanok, murẍ

birth [burs] *n* mewlûd, zayîn
bite [bayt] *v* gestin, gezandin *n* gez, gezîn
bitter [bitur] *adj* delû, şor
bitterness [biturnis] *n* telayî
black [blek] *adj* qer, reş-tûzî, reş
blackcurrant [blekkurunt] *n* qereqot
blessing [blêsing] *n* bereket
blind [blaynd] *adj* kor
blindness [blayndnis] *n* koranî
bloat [blowt] *v* werimîn
blockade [blakêyd] *n* hesar
blonde [bland] *adj* çûr *n* zerî
blood [blud] *n* qan
bloodthirsty [bludsurstî] *adj* xûnxur
bloom [blûm] *v* geşan
blooming [blûming] *adj* geş, gulgeş, nûber
blossoming [blasuming] *adj* nûber
blow up [blow up] *v* hilteqandin
blue [blû] *adj* erzeq, kew
boar [bor] *n* beraz
board [bord] *n* verêbûn
boarder [bordur] *n* tixûb
boat [bowt] *n* gemî, qeyk, lotke, niqboq
body [badî] *n* can
boil [boyl] *n* kel
bold [bowld] *adj* delîr, comerd, ḧir, qoçax, şêrdil

boldly [boldlî] *adv* comerdane
boldness [boldnis] *n* comerdî, e'gîtî, xurtebarî
bomb [bamb] *n* qember, qumber
bone [bown] *n* hestî
book [buk] *n* celd, kitêbok
boot [bût] *n* çekme
border [bordur] *n* çephe, hedan, sînor
borderline [bordurlayn] *n* ḧed, qad
boredom [bordum] *n* mikurî
boring [boring] *adj* herîs
born [born] *adj* zayî
borrow [barow] *v* biqerz
boss [bos] *n* gilavî, reis, serek, teşkîldar
bottle [batl] *n* bitulge, sorahî, şûşe
bottom [batum] *n* binî, jêr
bottomless [batumlês] *adj* bêbinî
boulevard [bûlvar] *n* bûlvar
boundary [bawndurî] *n* çephe, hedan, ḧed, qad
bouquet [bûqê] *n* qeseb
bow [baw] *n* temene, te'zîm
box [baks] *n* qab, ucre
boy [boy] *n* kur
brain [brêyn] *n* mejû, serçeq
bran [bren] *n* kapek
branch [brenç] *n* çikil, çilpî, çirpî, liq, şax
brand [brend] *n* daẍ *v* daẍkirin

brave [brêyv] *adj* bêtirs, mêrxas, dilêr, cesûr, delû, dilawer

bravely [brêyvlî] *adv* comerdane

bravery [brêyvurî] *n* turuş

bread [brêd] *n* nan

breadth [brêds] *n* pehnayî

break [brêyk] *v* jekirin, sikenandin, qetandin, qurçimandin, şikandin *n* navbir

breast [brêst] *n* berûk, bistan, guhan, pêsîr, sîng

breath [brês] *n* fûre-fûr, nefes, pifîn

bride [brayd] *n* bûk, xwestik

bright [brayt] *adj* meşfûf, tîndar, zêndar, zorzan

brightness [braytnês] *n* pirîn, rewnek, rewş, pertew, pertab, ronayî

brilliance [brilyuns] *n* ferwarî, rewş

brilliant [brilyunt] *adj* geş, ferwar

bring [bring] *v* anîn, gihîştandin

broad [brod] *adj* ber, pehn

broken [browkin] *adj* dêris, hûrxaş, zerzilî

brook [bruk] *n* co

brothel [brasul] *n* bozxane

brother [brazur] *n* bira

brother-in-law [brazur-in-lo] *n* birajin

brow [brew] *n* birû

brown [brawn] *adj* esmer

bud [bud] *n* bişkoj, gupik

budget [badcêt] *n* bûcê
buffoon [bufûn] *n* teqleçî
building [bilding] *n* xan, xanî, imaret, şênî
bull [bul] *n* gamêş, ga
bullet [bulit] *n* berîk, gulle, qember
bum [bum] *n* berade, dedirî, gerdan, rewindayî
bundle [bundl] *n* boxçe
burn [burn] *v* şixulîn
bury [burî] *v* çalkirin
bush [buş] *n* berih
business [biznus] *n* kar, kirîn, xizmet, kir, îş, şixul
but [but] *conj* belam, feqet, hemîn, û
butter [butur] *n* rûn
butterfly [buturflay] *n* fepûle, minnî, perwane, tirtirk
button [butun] *n* bendik, pişkoj
buyer [bayur] *n* bikirçî, xerîdar, mişterî

C

cabbage [kêbic] *n* kelem
café [kefê] *n* qawexane
cage [kêyc] *n* qefes
calamity [kulemitî] *n* ifaet
calendar [kelêdar] *n* rojniş

calm [kom] *adj* bêba, bêpêl, sehal, firêqet,
   bêẍazende *n* berdengî, hêsabûn, ḧewînî *v*
   ḧewîn
calmness [komnis] *n* firêqetî
calumny [kalumnî] *n* fesadî, qîr
camel [kemul] *n* deve
candidate [kendidit] *n* namzed
candidness [kendidnês] *n* wahî
candle [kendl] *n* find, şekirleme, mûm, şima
candy [kendî] *n* kanfêt
cap [kep] *n* şefqe, şaper
capable [kêypabl] *adj* bîranî
capital (money) [kepital] *n* sermaye
capital (city) [kepitul] *n* paytext
captain [keptin] *n* qeptan
captive [keptiv] *n* hêsîr
captivity [keptivitî] *n* hêsîrî
caravan [kereven] *n* boşe
cards [kards] *n* kart
care [kêr] *n* ḧeyr, xerêq, meraq, tîmar, şayîş,
   zehmet, west
carefree [kêrfrî] *adj* bêtalaş
careful [kêrful] *adj* miqat, mudbir
careless [kêrlês] *adj* bêhemel, bêtalaş
carelessly [kêrlêslî] *adv* ẍafil
carelessness [kêrlêsnês] *n* bêtalaşî, bêhemelî

caress [kurês] *n* tîmar, şefqet
carpet [karpêt] *n* têjber
carriage [keric] *n* vagon
carry [kerî] *v* anîn, birên
case [kêys] *n* vistan
cashbox [keşbaks] *n* sendûq
castle [kestl] *n* qesirbend
cat [ket] *n* kitik
Catholic [kesolik] *n* qatolîk
cattle [ketl] *n* kavran
cause [koz] *n* daîye, sebeb
caution [koşun] *n* baldarî, ewlekarî, tedbîr,
   hajxwehebûn, guhbelî
cautious [koşus] *adj* guhbel, hajxwe, guhmişk,
   mudbir, miqat
cautiously [koşuslî] *adv* hêdî
cave [kêyv] *n* meqam, tûn
caviar [kevyar] *n* xerz
celebrated [sêlêbrêytid] *adj* denngîr
cement [sêmênt] *n* zirîc
cemetery [sêmitêrî] *n* gorxane, qebiristan,
   tirbistan
center [sêntur] *n* xebatgeh, kûranî, nîverast,
   navend, orte, sêntir
central [sêntral] *adj* nîvroyî
century [sênçurî] *n* qurn, zeman

certainly [surtunlî] *adv* elbet, helbet, hilbet
chain [çêyn] *n* cenber, qenter, qeter, rist
chair [çêr] *n* kursî, secde
chairman [çêrmin] *n* gerînendkar
chalk [çok] *n* tebeşîr
champion [çempîun] *n* qehreman
chance [çens] *n* şans
change [çêync] *v* guhêrandin, guhêrin *n*
    guhertin, xurde, tebdîl, tesrîf
chapter [çeptur] *n* fesil
character [karuktur] *n* fitret
charity [çeritî] *n* bimbarek
charm [çarm] *n* delalî
charming [çarming] *adj* delal, sehhar, zerîf
chaste [çêyst] *adj* dêmdur, e'fîf, ḧelal
chastity [çestitî] *n* fedî, ḧelalî
cheap [çîp] *adj* bêvece, bihakêm, bêqîmet, erzan
cheaply [çîplî] *adv* bêqîmet
cheater [çîtur] *n* virek
cheating [çîting] *n* tezwîr, vireki, terx
checkers [çêkurs] *n* çik
cheek [çîk] *n* gep, ḧinarik, gupik
cheese [çîz] *n* penêr
chef [şêf] *n* xurekpêj
cherry [çêrî] *n* belalûk, fişqe, gêlaz, qeresî
chess [çês] *n* kişik

chest [çêst] *n* pêsîr, zefl
chew [çû] *v* cûtin, cûn
chew gum [çû gum] *v* cûm cûtin
chewing gum [çûwing gum] *n* benişt
chicken [çikin] *n* mirîşk, varik
chief [çîf] *n* e'mirdar, gilavî
child [çayld] *n* benî, çûçik, dergûş, ferzend, law, tifal, zarok
childbirth [çayldburs] *n* zayîn
childhood [çayldhud] *n* biçûktî, çûktî, tifalî, zarutî
childish [çayldiş] *adj* zarutî
children [çuldrun] *n* zêc
chin [çin] *n* binçene, çene, çeng
china [çayna] *n* çînî *adj* Chinese
choice [çoys] *n* bijar, întîxab
choke [çowk] *v* xeniqin
choose [çûz] *v* bijartin, e'cibandin
Christian [krisçun] *n* xaçparêz
Christianity [krisçenitî] *n* xaçparêzî
chronic calendar [kronik kelindur] *n* salname
chrystal [kristul] *n* belor *adj* belor
church [çurç] *n* cam, dêr
cigar [sigar] *n* sîgar
cigarette [sigarêt] *n* bizûz

circle [surkl] *n* xelak, çembar, hal, hawir, çarme, daîre, helqe, hol, mafir

circumference [surkumfruns] *n* daîre

citadel [saytadêl] *n* qesirbend

citizenship [sitizinşip] *n* şehervanî

city [sitî] *n* şeher

city dweller [sitî dwêlur] *n* şehervan

clamor [klemur] *n* ẍaze

clan [klen] *n* berek

clarity [kleritî] *n* ferihî, safîtî

class [kles] *n* derskom, ders

classroom [klesrûm] *n* dersxane, hucir

clay [klêy] *n* çamûr, ḧerî

clean [klîn] *adj* nab, pak, temiz *v* vemalandin

cleaning [klîning] *n* vemalandin

cleanness [klînnis] *n* temizî

clear [klîr] *adj* beyan, ferih, kivş, sade

clever [klêvur] *adj* serwext

cleverness [klêvurnês] *n* zên

cliff [klif] *n* lat, tat

climate [klaymut] *n* kilîma

cloak [klowk] *n* beniş

close [klows] *adj* nêzîk *v* sergirtin

close (lock) [dadan] *v* dadan

closely [klowslî] *adv* nêzîkva

closer [klowzur] *adv* virdatir

closet [klazêt] *n* şkav
clothes [klowz] *n* cil, kinc, libas, malbûs, rexber, sercil
cloud [klawd] *n* e'wr, hecac, hewir, telp
cloudy [klawdî] *adj* e'wrane
club [klub] *n* kilûb
coast [cowst] *n* berav
coat [kowt] *n* bêşmêrt, palto
cobra [kabra] *n* reşmar
coffin [kofin] *n* gor, gorxane, mehef
cognac [kanyek] *n* kanyak
coin [koyn] *n* sike
cold [kold] *n* hersim, sarayî, parsim *adj* sar
collar [kalur] *n* ûstûvank, yax
colleague [kalîg] *n* havalkar, hemraz, tevkar
collect [kulêkt] *v* civandin
collection [kulêkşun] *n* îctime
colony [kalunî] *n* kolonî, mostemere
color [kulur] *n* boyax, den, hawak, reng
colored [kulurd] *adj* rengdar
colorful [kulurful] *adj* rengdar
comb [kowmb] *n* şene, şane
come [kum] *v* gihîştin
comedy [kamidî] *n* komêdî, lêpok
comfort [kumfurtubl] *n* şên
comfortable [kumfortubl] *adj* rahet

comma [kama] *n* vêrgûl
command [kumend] *n* ferman
commander [kumendur] *n* e'mirdar
commentaries [kamênterîs] *n* tevsîr
commerce [kamurs] *n* sewde, tucarî
commiseration [kumizurêyşun] *n* hevderdî
committee [kumitî] *n* komîtê
common folks [camon fowks] *n* am
companion [kumpenyun] *n* eshab, hevkar, mişterek, refîq
company [kumpunî] *n* bir, fîrme
comparison [kamperisun] *n* angortî, danberhevî, berhvdanî, qiyas, eman, dilhişyarî
compassionate [kumpeşinit] *adj* dilovan, mihrîban, rehmanî, dilhişyar
competition [kampitişun] *n* lec
compiler [kumpaylur] *n* talîfker
complaint [kumplêynt] *n* e'rze, gure-gur, tezelom
completely [kamplîtlî] *adv* qet, lap, pêda-pêda
completion [kumplîşn] *n* cîanîn
complex [kamplêks] *adj* çetin
compliant [kumplayunt] *adj* mûtî
composed [kumpowzd] *adj* e'qilremîde
composition [kampuzişun] *n* talîf
comprehension [kamprihênşun] *n* te'eqol
compulsion [kumpulşun] *n* qisare

comrade [kamrêyd] *n* hemraz, heval, hingor, refîq

conceal [kunsîl] *v* vedizîn

concentrate [kansuntrêyt] *v* civandin

concert [kansurt] *n* konsêrt

concordance [kunkorduns] *n* razîbûn

condition [kundişun] *n* ḧewal

confederation [konfêdurêyşun] *n* êlat

conference [kanfruns] *n* konfêrênsî

confident [kanfidint] *adj* emîn

confiding [kunfayding] *adj* bista

confinement [kunfaynmint] *n* ḧebs

confirmation [kanfurmêyşun] *n* belêkirin, belênî

conflict [kanflikt] *n* e'davet

confused [kunfyûzd] *adj* perîşan

confusion [kunfyûjun] *n* rûreşî

congratulation [kungredyûlêyşun] *n* bimbarek

congress [kangris] *n* encimen, hevkom, hemcivat, kongirê

conjunction [kuncunkşun] *n* gihanek, pevgirêk

connect [kunêkt] *v* hevgihandin

connection [kunêkşun] *n* berbend, eleqet, girêdanî, mihwer, pevgirêk, tevhevbûn

conscience [konşêns] *n* island, ada, wijdan

consciousness [kanşusnês] *n* olan

consequently [kansikwêntlî] *adv* îda

consider [kunsidur] *v* begem
conspicuous [kunspikyûwus] *adj* berbiçav, e'yan, xweyan
constancy [kanstunsî] *n* dayîmî
constant [kanstunt] *adj* beqa, dayîm
constantly [kanstuntlî] *adv* herçax, tum
constitution [kanstitûşun] *n* konstîtûsî
consul [kansul] *n* qonsûl
consulate [kansulut] *n* konsûltî
consume [kastyûm] *v* têdan
contemplate [kantimplêyt] *v* fikirîn
contemplation [kantêmplêyşun] *n* fikir
content [kantênt] *n* naverok, têr, besitî, serecem
　　adj memnûn, mohenna, razî
continent [kantinênt] *n* bej
continuation [kuntinyûêyşun] *n* dehol
continuity [kantinûitî] *n* dayîmî
continuous [kuntinyûus] *adj* dayîm
contract [kantrekt] *n* belêkirin, qayîme, name
contradiction [kantradikşun] *n* qabilbêjî
contribution [kantribyûşun] *n* wekaf
conversation [konvursêyşun] *n* cir, galegal, axaftin, behs, gilî, xeberdan
conviction [kunvikşun] *n* înandin, qane, tewijm
convince [kunvins] *v* înandin
cook [kuk] *n* çêştker, xurekpêj, pijandin, zadepêj

cool [kûl] *adj* germosarî, hênik
coolness [kûlnis] *n* hênikayî
copper [kapur] *n* mîs, paxir
copy [kapî] *v* bernivîsarkirin *n* nesxe, şikil
copyist [kapîist] *n* bernivîs
corageous [kuricus] *adj* cimcimî
cork [kork] *n* pût
corn [korn] *n* garis
corner [kornur] *n* goşe, qulç
corpse [korps] *n* berate, cinyaz, cendek
corpulent [korpyûlint] *adj* gewde, têrbez
correct [kurêkt] *adj* dûz
correspondence [karuspandêns] *n* muxabere
corresponding [karuspanding] *adj* weke
corridor [koridor] *n* dalan
cost [kost] *n* xerc, hêjayî
costly [kostlî] *adj* giranbiha
cottage cheese [katuc çîz] *n* toraq
couch [kawç] *n* dîwan
cough [kof] *n* kuxik, sikenc
council [kewnsil] *n* mesveret, wekîl
councilor [kewnsilur] *n* berdevk
count [kewnt] *v* jimartin
countenance [kewntinuns] *n* wahc
counterfeit [kewnturfit] *adj* deẍel
countless [kewntlês] *adj* bêjimar

country [kuntrî] *n* gund, hêl, iqlîm, sekin, wekan

countryman [kuntrîmên] *n* axeban, hemwelat, welatî

county [kewntî] *n* semt, toprax, welîlixan

couple [kupl] *n* zol

couplet [kuplêt] *n* beyt

courage [kuruc] *n* metirsî, bêgefî, culhet, cesaret, dilawerî, mêranî

courageous [kurucus] *adj* egîd, mêr, mêrxas, cesûr, dilawer

course [kors] *n* kûrs

court [kort] *n* dadge, mehkeme

cousin [kuzin] *n* xaloza

cousin (female) [kuzin] *n* dûxtmam

cow [kaw] *n* çêlek, mange

coward [kawurd] *n* bizdonek, nemêr, tirsek

cowardice [kawurdays] *n* nemêrî, tirsonektî

cowherd [kawhurd] *n* gaajo

crab [kreb] *n* xerçeng

crack [krek] *n* qeliştek

cradle [krêydl] *n* bêşîk, colan, helecan

craft [kreft] *n* hiner

craftsman [kreftsmen] *n* hostakar, mihendiz

crazy [krêyzî] *adj* bêaqil, dîn, mecnûn, sews, virişikî

cream [krîm] *n* serşîr

creased [krîsd] *adj* bodelan
create [krîêyt] *v* e'firandin
creation [krîêyşun] *n* aferin, e'firandkarî, îcat
creator [krîêytur] *n* e'firandkar, xwedan
crescent [krêsint] *n* hîv, meh
crime [kraym] *n* cinêh, guneh
criminal [kriminul] *n* fasiq, gunehkar, ĥerambaz
crisis [kraysis] *n* boran, kirîzîs
criticism [kritisizm] *n* tenqîd
crooked [krukid] *adj* xar, qîloqaç, ko, mohenna
crowd [krewd] *n* bir, elalet
crowdedness [krewdînis] *n* tengav
crown [krewn] *n* efser
cruel [krûwul] *adj* alçax, desthişk, nemerd
cruelty [krûwultî] *n* alçaxî, desthişkî, dehbetî,
    zalimî
crumble [krumbl] *v* hilşîn
cry [kray] *n* çirîn, çarîn, fixan, hinarî, qûjînî,
    şeyvan *v* girîn, qîrîn, zarîn, zûrîn
crying [kraying] *n* girî
crystal [kristal] *n* zeca
cub [kub] *n* çêje
cuckoo [kûkû] *n* pûpû
cucumber [kyûkumbur] *n* xiyar
culprit [kulprit] *n* gunehkar
culture [kulçur] *n* irfan, kûltûr, şeheristan

cunning [kuning] *n* al, berfende, dek, fêldarî,
    fen, hîle, mek *adj* degenek, fêldar
cup [kup] *n* fîncan, efser, kas, qedeh
cupboard [kuburd] *n* îşkav, dolav, xizana
cure [kyûr] *v* kewandin
curiosity [kyurîasitî] *n* merekat
curious [kyurîus] *n* hewesker
curse [kurs] *n* çîr, kirin, nifir, cehnem, dijûn
cursed [kursd] *adj* tiling
curtain [kurtin] *n* perde
curve [kurv] *n* çivane
curved [kurvd] *adj* ko
custom [kustum] *n* e'det
customary [kustumerî] *adj* e'detî
customer [kustomur] *n* bikirçî, mişterî
cut [kat] *v* behandin
cut off [kut of] *v* hilqetandin, jêbirîn

D

daily [dêylî] *adj* yekrojî
damage [demic] *v* därisandin *n* mazeret, niqis,
    zîyan, zewal
damaged [demicd] *adj* dêris
dame [dêym] *n* xanim
dampness [dempnis] *n* xunav, nemayî

dance [dens] *n* reqas, tiringî

dancer [densur] *n* reqasçî

danger [dêyncur] *n* ifaet, mazeret

dangerous [dêyncurus] *adj* xeder, zalim

daring [dêring] *n* wêrîn *v* wêrîn

dark [dark] *adj* bêronahî, qer

dark green [dark grîn] *adj* zeytûni

darkness [darknis] *n* dûman, xubar, moşk, tarîstan

date [dêyt] *n* ejmar, hejmar, telaq

daughter [dotur] *n* qîz, keç

dawn [don] *n* berbang, ferec, hingor, rewş

day [dêy] *n* şevroj, roj

dazzle [dezl] *n* pertew

dead [dêd] *adj* candayî, givirdar, mirî

deadline [dêdlayn] *n* wade

deaf [dêf] *adj* bêguh, ker, kero

dear [dîr] *adj* e'zîz

death [dês] *n* mirin, felak, fote, helaket, hêçbûn

debility [dêbilitî] *n* tengdestî

debt [dêt] *n* deyn, borc, qeneyî,

deceit [disît] *n* mizaxilî, xapandin, al, alçaxî, fen

deceitful [disît] *adj* fenok, fendar, merazaxil, xapînok, alçax

December [dusêmbur] *n* çirîya paşin

decency [dîsinsî] *n* cindîtî

decision [disijun] *n* qirar

decoration [dêkurêyşun] *n* xemil

deed [dîd] *n* fel

deep [dîp] *adj* bêbinî, kûr

deer [dîr] *n* gakûvî, nask

defeat [difît] *n* hezêmet, meïlubîyet

defender [difêndur] *n* paşmer

defense [difêns] *n* paristin, berbestî, muhafiz, mihafize, midafe

definite [dêfinit] *adj* ferih, kivş

definition [dêfinişun] *n* kivşkirin

degree [digrî] *n* pay

delay [dilêy] *n* derengî

demand [dimend] *n* daxwez

demand (market) [dimend] *n* rewac

demise [dêmays] *n* wefat

demon [dîmun] *n* dêw, kabûs

dense [dêns] *adj* tîr

depart [dipart] *n* ferqût

department [dipartmint] *n* organ

departure [diparçur] *n* firqet

dependence [dipêndins] *n* pî

depict [dipikt] *v* nitrandin

depiction [dipikşun] *n* e'kis

depressed [diprêst] *adj* berxweketî

depression [diprêşun] *n* kerb

depth [dêps] *n* kûranî

deputy [dêpyûtî] *n* cîhgirtî, şandi

dervish [durviş] *n* dewrês

descend [disênd] *v* berjêr, dahatin, daçûn

descendence [disênduns] *n* zuret, wert

descendent [disêndunt] *n* wert

descent [disênt] *n* e'sil, îrq, mewlûd, nijad, nizmbûn

describe [diskrayb] *v* nitrandin, wesf

description [diskripşun] *n* tevsîr

desert [dêzurt] *n* berîstan, çol

desire [dizayr] *n* berîya, menc, miraz, tem, vîn

despair [dispêr] *n* bêûmûdî, miqur

desperate [dêspurat] *adj* bêûmûd

despite [dispayt] *conj* herçend

despondent [dispandint] *adj* gerdenkestî

destiny [dêstinî] *n* axiret, aqûbet, peşk, te'l

destroy [distroy] *v* hilsandin, hilwesandin, hedimandin, ẍaret

destroyed [distroyd] *adj* xirab, wêran

destruction [distrukşun] *n* heravî, ẍaret, mehw, qir, teker

detail [dîtêyl] *n* hûrgilî

detailed [dîtêyld] *adj* kit-kit

devil [dêvul] *n* dêw, îblîs, şeytan

dew [dû] *n* xunav

dialect [dayulêkt] *n* lehze, lesan, zarav
diamond [daymund] *n* almas
diarrhea [dayurîa] *n* vîjik
diary [dayurî] *n* rojname, rojnivîs
dictionary [dikşunerî] *n* ferheng, xebernivîs, loẍet
difference [difruns] *n* cudabûn, cudayî, ferq, firqî
different [difrunt] *adj* cihê, cuda
difficult [difikult] *adj* dijwar, tade, zor, çetin, dijwar, giran, mişkil
difficulty [difikultî] *n* dijwarî, usr, zorbun, tode, aloz, giranî
dig [dig] *v* çikandin, qelişandin, kolan, kolandin
dilapidated [dilepidêytid] *adj* rizî
dinner [dinur] *n* firavîn
diploma [diplowma] *n* dîplom
direct [durêkt] *v* gerandîn
direction [durêkşun] *n* alî, ber, hêl, hindav, beravan, henda
director [dirêktur] *n* dirêktor, gerînendkar, temedar,
dirt [durt] *n* çamûr, ḧerî, gû, qirêj, qilêr
dirty [durtî] *adj* gemarî, qilêrî, qirêjî, ḧeram, pîs
disagreement [disagrîmint] *n* qabilbêjî, razînebûn

disappear [disapîr] *v* wenda, wendabûn, mina, qulibîn

disappearance [disupîruns] *n* neman, kokhatin, minabûn, redbûn, wendabûn

disappeared [disupîrd] *adj* unda

disaster [dizestur] *n* bobelat

discern [dissurn] *v* qeşîrandin, qişirandin

discipline [disiplin] *n* eteb, întîzam, terbîyctdarî

disconnect [diskunêkt] *v* jêveqetandin

discussion [diskuşun] *n* behs, genc

disease [dizîz] *n* bîmarî

diseased [dizîzd] *adj* bîmar, canêş

disgrace [disgrêys] *n* e'deb, riswa, rezîlî

disgraceful [disgrêysful] *adj* bêhurmet

disgusting [disgusting] *adj* qermiçî, qebe

dish [diş] *n* sehîn

dishes [dişes] *n* zerf

dishonor [disonur] *n* bextreş, e'yb, fezihet, riswa

dishware [dişnêym] *n* derdan

disobedience [disobîdîins] *n* zirgurtî

disobedient [disobîdîint] *adj* bêîtae't

disorder [disordur] *n* bêîntîzamî, lewandî

disordered [disordurd] *adj* bêteher

dispersed [dispurst] *adj* bela-belayî, jihevbela

dispute [dispyût] *n* fitin

disrespect [disrispêkt] *n* bêxatirî

dissolve [disolv] *v* bişavtin

distance [distuns] *n* dûrî, dûranî, mesafe

distant [distunt] *adj* dûr

distinct [distinkt] *adj* cuda

distinction [distinkşn] *n* cudayî, cudabûn, firqî, ferq

distortion [distorşun] *n* qelp

distributor [distribyûtur] *n* belavker

distrustful [distrust] *adj* nebawar

disturbed [disturbd] *adj* bêtewat

ditch [diç] *n* çal

divide [divayd] *v* jihevcudakirin

division [divijun] *n* parbûn

do [dû] *v* kirin

do not [dû nat] *adv* ne

doctor [daktur] *n* tixtor, doktor, bijîşk

dog [dog] *n* seg, fendo, kelb, kûçik

doll [dol] *n* bûk

donation [downêyşun] *n* tesediq

donkey [dunkî] *n* ulaq

doom [dûm] *n* windabûn

door [dor] *n* derge, derî

doorman [dormen] *n* bekçî, dergevan, hacib, şatir

dormitory [dormitorî] *n* razanxane

dot [dat] *n* nuqte

double [dubl] *n* cêwî
doubts [dewts] *n* şibhe
dough [dow] *n* hevîr
downcast [dewnkest] *adj* gerdenkestî
downstairs [dewnstêrs] *n* serberjêr
draw [dro] *v* neqişandin
drawing [drowing] *n* neqiş
dream [drîm] *n* xew, xulî, nivistin, pesin, serdilk
dress [drês] *n* kinc, libas *v* wergirtin
drink [drink] *v* xwerin, vexwerin
drip [drip] *v* gulgulîn
drive away [drayv awêy] *v* berîdan, raqetandin
driver [drayvur] *n* şofêr
drop [drap] *n* çir, niqitk, nuqte *v* niqitandin
drought [drewt] *n* bêbaranî, firk
drown [drewn] *v* xeriqîn, xeniqin
drum [drum] *n* dewl, dawul, dehol, tepliq
drunk [drunk] *adj* cemmaş, mest, mexmûr, sermest
dry [dray] *adj* bêav, ḧişk, tisî, zaha, ziwa, zîya
dryness [draynis] *n* ḧişkayî
duck [dak] *n* hevo, kevjal, sone, ordek
dull [dul] *adj* herîs
dusk [dusk] *n* e'sir, hingor, meẍrîb
dust [dust] *n* xubar, toz
Dutchman [duçmen] *n* holandî

duty [dûtî] *n* bêş, qeneyî, xizmet, wacib
dwelling [dwêling] *n* qonax, warocax

E

each time [îç taym] *adv* hercar
ear [îr] *n* guh
earlier [urliur] *adv* berê
earning [urning] *n* dexl
earnings [urnings] *n* ked, kar
ears [îrs] *n* guh
earth [urs] *n* belelerz, ax, bej, e'raz, e'rd
earthquake [urskwêyk] *n* e'rdlerzîn
ease [îz] *n* hêsabûn
easily [îzilî] *adv* bêzehmet
easiness [îzînês] *n* rehetî
east [îst] *n* şerq
eastern [îsturn] *adj* şerqî
easy [îzî] *adj* hêsa, hêsan, pêkan, bêvece,
    bêzehmet, gengaz
eat [ît] *v* xwerin
eau de Cologne [o du kulown] *n* gulavgirî
ecstasy [êkstusî] *n* cezbe, xulî
edition [êdîşun] *n* neşir
editor [êdîtur] *n* neşirkar
educated [êcukêytid] *adj* terbîyetdar

education [ecukêyşun] *n* te'lîm, terbîyetdarî, terb
effort [êfurt] *n* cefa, xirêt
egg [êg] *n* hêk
egoism [îgowism] *n* anantî, e'ne'ne, mayî
egoist [îgoist] *n* xwehebîn
egotistical [îgotistikul] *adj* anan, xwehebîn
Egyptian [îcipşun] *n* misirî *adj* misirî
eight [êyt] *num* heyşt
eighteen [êytîn] *num* hîjdeh
eighty [êytî] *num* heyştê
elect [êlêkt] *v* bijartin
election [ilêkşun] *n* întîxab
elections [êlêkşuns] *n* bijar
elector [êlêktur] *n* bijarkar
elegance [êliguns] *n* cindîtî
elegant [êligunt] *adj* şeng, zerîf
element [êlimênt] *n* osaf
elephant [elifant] *n* fîl
eleven [ulêvên] *num* yanzdeh
eleventh [ulêvêns] *num* yanzdehûm
embarassment [imberusmunt] *n* aloz
embarrass [imberus] *v* tevdan
embassador [umbesador] *n* sefîre
embellished [imbêlişd] *adj* zîb
embrace [êmbrêys] *n* axuş, hemêz
emigrant [êmigrant] *n* mihacir

emigration [êmigrêyşun] *n* hîcret, mihaceret
emotion [imowşun] *n* his
emperor [êmpurur] *n* qeyser, kayser
empire [êmpayr] *n* orket
employee [êmployî] *n* qulixçî
empty [êmtî] *adj* culf, cewt, xalî, vala, pûç
enamoured [inemurd] *adj* bengî, eşqî, dildayî
encircle [insurkl] *v* çarmekirin
encircling [insurkling] *adv* çarnical
encouragement [inkurucmint] *n* halan
end [ênd] *n* kutasî, kuj, serî, axirî, encam *v* kuta, red
ending [ênding] *n* kutasî
endless [êndlês] *adj* bêaxir, bêserbêbînî
endurance [indûrans] *n* sebir
enemy [ênimî] *n* berber, dijmin, e'dû, neyar
English [ingliş] *adj* înglîzî
enjoyment [incoymint] *n* lihvan
enmity [ênmitî] *n* texalif
enough [enuf] *adv* besanî
entrance [êntrens] *n* derî
envious [ênvîus] *adj* e'rnûs, dixesî, hosûd
envy [ênvî] *n* dexs, çavbelî, dexesî, çavreşî
  v çavberdan, xwezandin, berçîn, dixesîn
epidemic [êpidêmik] *n* belqîtk
epoch [êpak] *n* dem, e'sir, hana, qurn

equal [îqwul] *adj* wekhev, hevber, wek, beraber, angorî, hemta

equal [îqwul] *n* hingor

equality [îqwalitî] *n* wekhevî, hevberî, beraberbûn, angortî

era [êra] *n* dem, hengam

eraser [irêysur] *n* lastîk

errand [êrund] *n* spar, teslîm

especially [ispêşulî] *adv* îlahî

essence [êsuns] *n* abad, mezmûn, meal, qinyat, nihêt

essential [isênşul] *adj* bikêr, xusûs

esteem [êstîm] *n* xatirgirtin

estimation [êstimêyşun] *n* texdîr

eternal [iturnul] *adj* abad, dayîm, e'bdî, e'zelî

eternity [iturnitî] *n* abad, dayîmî, ezelî, ezel

European [yûropîun] *adj* firengî

European [yûropîun] *n* fireng

evaluation [êvelyûêyşun] *n* bihabirîn

even [îvin] *adj* ta *conj* ta

evening [îvning] *n* êvar

event [ivênt] *n* bûyer, macira

everlasting [êvurlesting] *adj* e'zelî, e'bdî

every [êvrî] *adj* herkes

everybody [êvrîbadî] *pron* gî, gişan

everyday [êvrîdêy] *adj* herroj

everything [êvrîsing] *pron* gî, gişt
everywhere [êvrîwêr] *adv* herder, hercîya
evil [îvul] *n* dûje, dijûn, dejûnî, qidîk, neçêyî
    adj mifsid
exactly [igzektlî] *adv* hemîn, xût
example [igzempl] *n* delîl, ebret, sermeşq
except [iksêpt] *adv* be'zî, qerez, masowa, cîale,
    ẍerez
exercise [êksursayz] *n* meşq
exchange [iksçêync] *v* veguhêrandin,
    veguhêrandin
excite [iksayt] *v* hawûtin
excuse [ikskyûs] *n* behane
executioner [êgzêkyûşunur] *n* qesas
executive [ugzêkyûtiv] *n* cabdar
exhaltation [êgzultêyşn] *n* cezbe
exile [êgzayl] *n* ẍurbet, nefî
exist [igzist] *v* hebûn, heyîn
existence [igzistins] *n* heyînî, mewcûd
exit [êgzit] *n* derî, cîderk
expanse [iskpens] *n* berînî, firehî
expansion [ikspenşun] *n* firebûn, fireyî, pirkirin,
    pirbûn
expectation [êkspiktêyşun] *n* çavnêrîn, hîvî
expel [êkspêl] *v* raqetandin
expenditure [êkspêndiçur] *n* zayî

expense [ikspêns] *n* xerc, mesref, zaha
expensive [ikspênsiv] *adj* nerx
experience [ikspîrîins] *n* cêrb
experienced [ikspîrîinsd] *adj* gerîyayî, ehl
experiment [ikspêrimênt] *v* cêribandin
explanation [êksplunêyşun] *n* terîf, şerh
explode [iksplowd] *v* hilteqandin
exploiter [iksploytur] *n* xûnxur
explosion [iksplowjun] *n* terqin
expression [iksprêsun] *n* axawik, loxet
exquisite [êkskwizit] *adj* ferwar
extinguish [ikstingwiş] *v* damirandin
extoll [êkstol] *v* payîdan
eyes [ays] *n* çeşm, çeşmek, çav
eyeglasses [ayglesis] *n* e'ynik
eyebrow [aybraw] *n* qaş
eyelash [ayleş] *n* bijang
eyelid [aylid] *n* bijang
eyes [ay] *n* çeşm, çeşmek

F

facade [fasad] *n* bermal, pêşmal
face [feys] *n* mirûz, wech, ber, çirûk, çehr, serçav
factory [fekturî] *n* fabrîke, karxane, zavod
fade [fêyd] *v* çilmisîn

fair [fêr] *adj* biînsaf *n* çarsû
fairly [fêrlî] *adv* biînsafî
faith [fêys] *n* bawerî, yekînî, aminî, dîn, guman, îtbar
faithful [fêysful] *adj* bawermend, bilexî, sadiq
fake [fêyk] *adj* destker *n* qelp, tezwîr, teşwîş
fall [fol] *v* daketin, hilşîn, veweşîn
false [fols] *adj* salûs
falsehood [folshud] *n* berfende, çavbestin, derew, qelp
falsely [folslî] *adv* çat-pat
falsification [folsifikêyşun] *n* qelpkirin
fame [fêym] *n* navbang, navdarî
familiar [fumilyur] *adj* nas
familiarity [fumilyeritî] *n* nasbûn
family [femilî] *n* e'sil, famîl, e'yal, îlet, mal, malbat
famous [fêymus] *adj* binavûdeng, navdayî, berbiçav, abrûdar, navdar, namwer
fanatic [fenetik] *adj* biînad
fantastic [fentestik] *adj* bêdevan
fantasy [fentisî] *n* fantazî, mêxûlî
far away [far uwêy] *adv* dûredûr
far-sighted [farsaytid] *adj* dûrbîna
far-sightedness [farsaytidnis] *n* dûrbînayî
farewell [fêrwêl] *n* hicran

farm [farm] *n* fêrme

farmer cheese [farmur çîz] *n* cacî

farmer [farmur] *n* zeraetçî

fashion [feşun] *n* mod

fast [fest] *adj* çeleng, deman, çist, cilakî, birûskîn, lez

fat [fet] *adj* bezgîr, givir, xurt, kok, têrbez

fatal [fêytul] *adj* xeder

fate [fêyt] *n* axiret, çarenûs, aqûbet, felek, qeder, oxir

father [fazur] *n* aba

fats [fets] *n* zuhum

fault [folt] *n* guneh, xeta, qar, sûc

favor [fêyvur] *n* xwestek

fear [fîr] *n* etlahî, xewf, sehm, tirs

fearless [fîrlês] *adj* bêhavil

feast [fîst] *n* bezm, çeşn, sûr

feather [fêzur] *n* tûk

February [fêbrûerî] *n* sibat

federation [fêdurêyşn] *n* fêdêrasî

feeling [fîling] *n* his, hewas, hesas

feet [fît] *n* bizût

female [fîmêyl] *n* mê

fence [fêns] *n* çeper, caẍ, çît, hesar, tor

fertile [furtul] *n* berxweş

festival [fêstivul] *n* mihrecan

festivity [fêstivitî] *n* e'yd
feud [fyûd] *n* fitne, e'davet
feudal [fyûdul] beg
fever [fîvur] *n* ta
few [fyû] *adv* çîçîk
fiancée [fîansê] *n* xwestik
field [fîld] *n* zevî, mêrg, erd, qad, dewl, çayr, çol
fierceness [fîrsnis] *n* gurî
fifteen [fiftîn] *num* panzde
fight [fayt] *n* ceng, şer, lej, cîdal
fight [fayt] *v* serkirin, têkoşîn, cîdalkirin,
    hevxistin, pevçûn
figure [figyûr] *n* qilafet
fill [dagyrtyn] *v* dagirtin
filled [fild] *adj* lebaleb
film [film] *n* fîlm
filth [fils] *n* gemar, gû
final [faynul] *adj* dawîn, paşîn
finally [faynêlî] *adv* dawiya, talîyê, axirîye,
    dawîyê, paşwextî
finger [fingur] *n* tilî
finish [finiş] *v* gîhandin, kuta
Finnish [finiş] *adj* fînî
fire [fayr] *n* agir, nar
fire-place [fayrplêys] *n* buxari
firm [furm] *n* fîrme *adj* zexm

firmness [furmnis] *n* zexm
first [furst] *adj* pêşîn, yekem, yekemîn, birincî, ewle
fish [fiş] *n* aẍu, masî
fisherman [fişurmen] *n* masîvan, toravêj
five [fayv] *num* pênc
flame [flêym] *n* alav, rivîn, pirîsk, rewîn
flat [flet] *adj* hilû
flatterer [fleturing] *n* çilçiçik
flattering [fleturing] *adj* çilçiçik
flawless [flolês] *adj* bêkêmasî
fleet [flît] *n* nêrevan
flight [flayt] *n* fir, firkirin
flood [flad] *n* lêmişt
floor [flor] *n* ewlî, taq
flourishing [flurişing] *n* şên
flow [flow] *v* çûyîn
flower [flawur] *n* çîçek, kulîlk, gul, gulking
flowerbed [flawurbêd] *n* çîmange, gulistan
flower vase [flawur vêys] *n* guldan
flowering [flawuring] *adj* geş, gulgeş *n* guldan
flu [flû] *n* buxari, hersim, grîp
flute [flût] *n* bilûr
fly [flay] *v* firîn, pirîn, perîn, verêstin *n* mêş
foe [fow] *n* berber
fog [fag] *n* dûman, telp

folklore [folklor] *n* folklor
follower [faluwur] *n* paşmer
folly [falî] *n* bêaqilî, dînanî, dînîtî
food [fûd] *n* debar, emek, xwarin, xwerin, êm, xwer, zad
fool [fûl] *n* efsene
foolish [fûliş] *adj* ehmeq
foot [fut] *n* qedem
football [futbol] *n* fûtbol, fotbal
football player [futbol plêyur] *n* fûtbolçî
footprint [futprint] *n* e'ser, parone, rêç
for [for] *prep* bêî ku, bo, seba
force [fors] *n* cebrî, cebir, hêz, qewat, mecal
forehead [forhêd] *n* cebhet, e'nî, ne'tik, navçav
foreign [forin] *adj* ecnebî
forest [forêst] *n* bêş, cengel
foreword [forwurd] *n* dîbace
forgetful [forgîtful] *adj* bîrereş
forgive [furgiv] *v* e'fu
forgiveness [furgivnês] *n* e'fu, eman, e'nayet
forgotten [forgatin] *adj* bîrkirî
form [form] *n* lewm, terz
former [formur] *adj* sabiq
formula [formyûla] *n* formûl
foretelling [fortêling] *n* remil

fortitude [fortitûd] *n* delîrî, cesaret, curet, fêrisî, dilawerî

fortress [fortris] *n* qesirbend

fortunate [forçunut] *adj* felekbaz

fortune [forçun] *n* felek, qeder, êẍbal, rizgarî, oẍir

forward [forwurd] *adv* berpêş, pêşva, pêşda

foundation [fawndêyşun] *n* hîm, mebna, medar

founder [fawndur] *n* danî

fountain [fewntin] *n* qulteyn

four [for] *num* çar

fourth [fors] *num* çaranî

fox [faks] *n* rûvî

fraction [frekşun] *n math* şikestî

frail [frêyl] *adj* naz, nask

frailty [frêyltî] *n* nazî

fraudulent [frodyûlint] *adj* deẍel

free (of charge) [frî] *adj* belaş

free [frî] *adj* azad, serbest, badilhewa, bêvece, bêheq, gerdenazadî

freedom [frîdum] *n* azadî, firehî, fireyî, firêqetî, felat, haşîtî

freeze [frîz] *v* qerimîn, qefilîn

French [frênç] *adj* feransizî, firengî

Frenchman [frênçmun] *n* feransiz, fireng

frenzy [frênzî] *n* harî

fresh [frêş] *adj* hênik, nestêl, terecan, teze
freshness [frêşnis] *n* hênikayî
Friday [fraydêy] *n* cuma, înî
fried [frayd] *adj* pijyayî
friend [frênd] *n* eshab, heval, hemkar, yar
friendship [frêndşip] *n* hevaltî, olfet, yarî, yartî
frighten [fraytun] *v* vetirsîn, veciniqîn
frightened [fraytund] *adj* tirsandî
from [frum] *prep* ji
from where [frum wêr] *adv* kuva
front side [frunt sayd] *n* pêşî
frost [frost] *n* cemed
fruit [frût] *n* mêwe, fêkî ber, çerez
fruitful [frûtful] *n* berxweş
fry [fray] *v* biraştin, pijandin, pijîn, birajtin,
    qijilandin
fuel [fyûwul] *n* şewat
fulfilment [fulfilmênt] *n* tewfîq, cîanîn
full [ful] *adj* lebaleb, tijî, temam, têretijî
function [funkşun] *n* fûnksî
funeral [fyûnirul] *n* veşartin
funny [funî] *adj* commaş, gosirmat, oyîn
fur [fur] *n* mû
furious [fyurîus] *adj* har
furnace [furnis] *n* ocax
fury [fyurî] *n* harî, te'ew, tureyî

further [furzur] *adv* wêdatir
futile [fyûtil] *adj* boş, hawa, herze
future [fyûçur] *n* paşdawî, paşwextî, pêşîv

G

gain [gêyn] *n* kar
gambling [gembling] *n* qumar
game [gêym] *n* lîzk, lîstîk, raw
garage [guraj] *n* garaj
garbage [garbac] *n* gemar
garden [gardun] *n* bostan, parîz, şaxsar
gardener [gardunur] *n* bostançî
garlic [garlik] *n* sîpkî
gas [gez] *n* gaz
gasoline [gezolîn] *n* bênzîn
gate [gêyt] *n* derî, hasarî, hesar
gates [gêyts] *n* derge
gather [gezur] *v* civandin, gihîştandin
gathering [gezuring] *n* civat
gay [gêy] *adj* şa
gaze [gêyz] *n* nezer, mêzek
gender [cêndur] *n* tore, ûrt, zayend
general [cênurul] *n* ceneral, gênêral, jeneral
generation [cênurêyşun] *n* nesl, nijad, ûrt

generosity [cênurositî] *n* ciwanbextî, çavfirehtî, camêrî, comerdî

generous [cênurus] *adj* ciwanbext, comerd, çavfireh, destvehirî, çavtêr, camêr

generously [cênuruslî] *adv* comerdane

gentle [cêntl] *adj* helîm, nask, naz, zirav

gentleness [cêntlnis] *n* nazî

genuine [cênwin] *adj* tê

geography [cîagrufî] *n* cexrafî, gêografî

geometry [cîamitrî] *n* gêometrî

Georgian [corcun] *n* gurc

Georgian [corcun] *adj* gurcikî

German [curmin] *n* gêrmanî, jêrmen *adj* jêrmenî

ghost [gowst] *n* qeratû, vîn

giant [cayunt] *n* fêris

gift [gift] *n* dîhar, dabas, pêşkêş, rewa

gifted [giftid] *adj* ehl, zêndar

Gipsy [cipsî] *n* çengene

girl [gurl] *n* birkîyam, keç, qîzik

gist [cist] *n* zatî

glance [glens] *n* mêzek, nezer

glass [gles] *n* îskan, piyan, piyale, cam, îstekan

glasses [glesis] *n* berçavk, çavberk

gloomy [glûmî] *adj* dilgiran

glory [glorî] *n* celal, navbang, muta, rûmet

glue [glû] *n* çirîş, tutqal *v* zeliqandin

go [gow] *v* çûyîn, meşîn, perîn
goat [gowt] *n* bizin
goblet [gablut] *n* cam, fîncan, kas
God [gad] *n* Elah, Xwedê, Îlahî, Êzdan, Xuda
gold [gold] *n* zêr
goldsmith [goldsmis] *n* zêrker
good [gud] *adj* baş, çê, çak, rind, çê, qenc *n* kerem, qencî
goodness [gudnis] *n* fezilet, xweykeremî, qencî
goods [guds] *n* emte'e, kala
gorge [gorc] *n* zang
gorgeous [gorcus] *adj* dilbar
Gospel [gaspul] *n* Încîl
gossip [gasip] *n* geveztî
government [guvurmint] *n* hikumet
governor [guvurnur] *n* gilavî
gown [gewn] *n* beniş
grab [greb] *v* girtin
gradually [grecûalî] *adv* bere-bere
grain [grêyn] *n* lib
grammar [gremur] *n* giramar
granite [grenit] *n* nihêt
grass [gres] *n* çayr, gîha
gratis [gretis] *adj* bêheq
gratitude [gretitûd] *n* şîkir, spas

grave [grêyv] *n* mezel, tirb, çalxane, gorxane, giran

greed [grîd] *n* têrnebûn, cavnebarî, gurî, timayî

greediness [grîdînis] *n* çikûsî, şuret

greedy [grîdî] *adj* çavxur, çavbirçî

Greek [grîk] *adj* hurumî

Greek [grîk] *n* hurum

green [grîn] *adj* hêşîn, şîn

greeting [grîting] *n* selam

greetings [grîtings] *n* sersera

grey [grêy] *adj* belek, bor, gewr, sipipor, rotob

grey-haired [grêyhêrd] *adj* belekpor

grief [grîf] *n* azar, jan, derd, xem, gurdil, ẍusse

groats [growts] *n* savar

ground [grewnd] *n* toprax

group [grûp] *n* kom, çêkirin, civîn, berek, destek, firqe

grow up [grow up] *v* gihîştandin

growth [grows] *n* bejn, firebûn

grudge [gruc] *n* kêmî

guard [gard] *n* pasvan, parezgêr, nobedar, bekçî *v* xwedî, pawtandin

guess [gês] *v* têderxistin

guidance [gayduns] *n* temîn

guide [gayd] *n* berdevk, rênîş

guilt [gilt] *n* guneh, xeta, ifad

guilty [giltî] *adj* xweyguneh
gulf [gulf] *n* derav
gum [gum] *n* cûm
gun [gun] *n* depançe, pişto
Gypsy [cipsî] *n* qeraçî, mirtib

H

habit [hêbit] *n* e'det, ins, usûl
habitation [hebitêyşun] *n* ajinî
hair [hêr] *n* mû, pûrt, pirç, ta
half [hef] *n* nîvek
hall [hol] *n* dalan, şibt
halvah [halva] *n* hewle, mirtoxe
hand [hend] *n* nêzîk, derdest, çepil, çikil, çeng,
    çepik
handbag [hendbeg] *n* çelte
handcuffs [hendkufs] *n* destbend
handful [hendful] *n* çeng
handkerchief [henkurçif] *n* destmal
handle [hendl] *n* destî
handrail [hendrêyl] *n* destî
handsome [hendsum] *adj* qeşeng, letîf
handwriting [hendrayting] *n* reşbelek
happiness [hepînis] *n* şadî, dileşqî, dilgeşî,
    bextewarî

happy [hepî] *adj* şad, dilşad, bextewar, dileşq, dilgeş, bextiyar

harbor [harbur] *n* bender, gemîstan, xelic

hard [hard] *adj* berk, çetin, deşwar, dijwar, ḧişk

hardness [hadrnis] *n* berkî, berkbûn, reqî

harm [harm] *n* zîyan, zirar

harmful [harmful] *adj* zikreş, zirarkarî, zîyandar

harmonious [harmownyus] *adj* xweşbang

harmony [harmunî] *n* xweşbangî

harshness [harşnis] *n* tengdilî

hat [het] *n* kum

hatred [hêytrid] *n* boẍz, e'davet, hased, irin

haughtily [hotilî] *adv* kubar-kubar, qude-qude

haughtiness [hotinês] *n* anantî, qudetî, pozbilindî

haughty [hotî] *adj* anan, kaw, qude, pozbilind

haven [hêyvin] *n* bender

havoc [hevak] *n* hêwirze, hurmîn

head [hêd] *n* ser, serok, sereta, serî, qehf, kelle, kele

headache [hêdêyk] *n* sereş

health [hêls] *n* çakî, sehet

health care [hêls kêr] *n* tebî

healthy [hêlsî] *adj* cansaẍ, xweşhal, saẍ

hear [hîr] *v* bihîstin

heart [hart] *n* dil, qelb,

heat [hît] *n* germî, qijavî, kel, xumam

heath [hîs] *n* cansaxî

heaven [hêvun] *n* cenet, cennet, eflak, felek, e'sman, hawêr

heaviness [hêvînis] *n* giranî

heavy [hêvî] *adj* giran

heel [hîl] *n* pe'nî, pehnî

height [hayt] *n* bejn, afraz, bilindayî, firêz, hêl, qilafet, serhêl

heir [êr] *n* waris, werwend

hell [hêl] *n* cehnem, dûje

help [hêlp] *n* destgirî, çare, hewil, komek, îlac

helper [hêlpur] *n* berdestî

helpless [hêlplês] *adj* bêpergal, bêhal, bêçar, aciz, çarneçar

helplessness [hêlplêsnês] *n* bêçarî, çarneçarî

hence [hêns] *adv* pêve

here [hîr] *adv* vir, vira, der, hira, îreda, livêderê, lora

heredity [hurêditî] *n* îlet

heritage [hêrituc] *n* bermayî, mîrat

hermit [hurmit] *n* koçek

hero [hîrow] *n* afet, fêris, mêrxas

heroic [hirowik] *adj* pîroz

herself [hurself] *pron* xwe

Hey! [hêy] *interj* ya

hidden [hidun] *adj* xewle, neeşkela, veşartî
hide [hayd] *v* hilandin, qulibîn, telandin,
    veşartin
high [hay] *adj* bilind, hilneyî
highly [haylî] *adv* hilneyî
highest [hayist] *adj* bilintir, fayiq, hêlekan
highway [haywêy] *n* cade
highwayman [haywêymen] *n* rêbir
hill [hil] *n* beyar, hawêr, tepe
himself [himself] *pron* xwe
hip [hip] *n* ren
hire [hayr] *n* îcare, ûcre
hired [hayrd] *adj* ûcredar
hissing [hising] *n* fîkîn, fîkandin, fişe-fiş, fîşîn,
    fize-fiz
historian [historiun] *n* tarîxçî
historical [historikul] *adj* tarîxî
history [histurî] *n* tarîx
hit [hit] *v* lêketin, hingaftin, kutan, xistin, lêdan,
    lêxistin *n* zerb
hobby [habî] *n* mijûl
hole [howl] *n* kol, qulqulk
holiday [halidêy] *n* cejin, e'yd
holy [howlî] *adj* tibark
holiness [howlînês] *n* tibark

homeless [howmlês] *adj* bêwar, berdîwar, dêran, warkor

homelessness [howmlêsnês] *n* bêwarî

honest [onist] *adj* ebrûhelal, xudanbext, xwedînamûs

honesty [onistî] *n* selah

honey [hunî] *n* hingiv

honor [onur] *n* serbilindî, bext, ada, îkram, namûs, rûmet, şeref

hook [huk] *n* êramûk

hop [hap] *v* lotin

hope [howp] *n* hêvî, aminî, guman, mikûn, menzûr, ûmûd

hopeless [howplês] *adj* bêhêvî, neçar, bêûmûd, bêçare, derhal

hopelessness [howplêsnês] *n* bêûmûdî, bêgavî

horizon [hurayzun] *n* horîzon, lûce

horn [horn] *n* qoç

horrible [harubul] *adj* bêteher, beter

horror [haror] *n* saw

horse [hors] *n* abdar, bor, hesp

hospital [haspitul] *n* bîmarxane, boşpîtal, xesterane, nexweşge

hospitality [haspitêlitî] *n* îkram

hostage [hastuc] *n* berdêlvan

hot [hat] *adj* germ, har, qijavî

hotel [howtêl] *n* mêvanxane, otêl, ûtêl
hour [awur] *n* sehet
house [haws] *n* xanî, xan, mal
how [haw] *adv* ça, çitewr, çer
how? [haw] *interj* ha?
however [hawêvur] *conj* welê
huge [hyûc] *adj* gir, girs, gewde, derhal, bêrabit, pir
human being [hyûmen bîing] *n* însan, meriv
humanity [hyûmanitî] *n* mirovahî, mirovatî, beşer, bişaret, însan
humble [humbl] *adj* rûnerm, zelûl
humid [hyûmid] *adj* şadab, ter
humidity [hyûmiditî] *n* rewa, şilî, nemayî, şûpî, terayî
humiliation [hyûmilîêyşun] *n* şerm, rûreşî, tenezul, zillet
hunchback [hunçbek] *n* qûzo
hunchbacked [hunçbekd] *adj* qûz
Hungarian [hungerîun] hûncarî, macarî
Hungarian [hungerîun] *n* macar
hunger [hungur] *n* xelayî, nêz
hunt [hunt] *n* raw
hunter [huntur] *n* rawçî, rawkar, revîvan
hurricane [hurikêyn] *n* firtone, fizildûman
hurry [hurî] *v* bilezbûn, te'cîl

husband [husbend] *n* mêr
hymn [himn] *n* beyt, gîmin

I

I [ay] *pron* min
I.D. [ay dî] *n* şedname
ice [ays] *n* bûz, cemed
idea [aydîa] *n* îdêya
ideal [aydîul] *adj* îdêalî *n* îdêal
idealist [aydîulist] *n* îdêalîst
identification card [aydêntifikêyşun kard] *n* sinîd
idiocy [idîusî] *n* axmaxî
idiom [idîum] *n* îstîlah
idiot [idîut] *n* axmax
idiotic [idîatik] *adj* sergiran
idle [aydl] *adj* bêxizmet, bêemel
idleness [aydlnês] *n* bêemelî
idol [aydul] *n* bot
if [if] *conj* heger, herke, mafir, wekî
ignite [ignayt] *v* vêxistin
ignorance [ignuruns] *n* bêfe'mî, cuhl
ignorant [ignurunt] *adj* bêxeber
ill [il] *adj* nexweş, nexas, xerab, xesle, xweyês, kulek

illiteracy [illiturasî] *n* bêxwenditî, cuhl
illiterate [illiturat] *adj* bêxwendî
illness [ilnis] *n* derd, êşayî, kul, êş, zede, jan
illusion [ilûzun] *n* xulî
image [imuc] *n* gewher, nimûş, terz, tele't, wahc, şikil, wahc, tewr
imagination [imecinêyşun] *n* mêxûlî
Imam [imam] *n* îmam
imitation [imitêyşun] *n* temsel, teqlîd
immediately [imîdîetlî] *adv* aniha, tavilê, dest-dest, destxweda
immense [imêns] *adj* bêrabit, pir, mezin
impatience [impêyşêns] *n* bêsebirî, netevitî
impatient [impêyşênt] *adj* bêtab, bêsebir, netevitî
impolite [impolayt] *adj* bêmerîfet, bêterbyet
importance [importuns] *n* ferzî
important [importunt] *adj* ferzan, xwediehmîyet, qedirgiran
impossible [impasibl] *adj* bêpergal
impotent [impotênt] *adj* bêtab, bîmar
improvement [imprûvmint] *n* dûzbûn, dûzkirin
imprudence [imprûdêns] *n* bêfesalî
impudence [impyûdêns] *n* bêe'debî
in [in] *adv* daxil *prep* li nav
in back of [in bek uv] *adv* para
in love [in luv] *adj* evindar, dilhebandî, wişaq

incense [insêns] *n* bîhnayî
incident [insidint] *n* hadîse
inclination [inklinêyşun] *n* meyl
income [inkum] *n* îrad
incompetent [inkampitunt] *adj* fehmkor
inconvenient [inkunvînîint] *adj* bêfesal
incorrect [inkurêkt] *adj* ewt
incurable [inkyurubl] *adj* xeder
indeed [indîd] *adv* vaqêe'n
independence [indupênduns] *n* serbixwebûn,
    serxwebûn, xwexwetî, nebindestî
independent [indipêndint] *adj* azad, serbixwe,
    biserxwe, nebindest
Indian [indîun] *adj* hindî *n* hind
indifference [indifruns] *n* bêhewasî
indifferent [indifrunt] *adj* bêteẍayûr, bêhewas
indispensable [inispênsibl] *adj* bijîşk
individually [induvicûulî] *adv* zatî
indubitable [indûbitabl] *adj* bêşik
industry [industrî] *n* îndûstrî, sinhet
inept [inêpt] *adj* fehmkor
ineptness [inêptnus] *n* fehmkorî
inexpensive [inêkspênsiv] *adj* bêqîmet
inexpensively [inêkspênsivlî] *adv* bêqîmet
inexperienced [inêkspîrîênsd] *adj* xeşîm, xizan
infant [infant] *n* biçûk, çûçik
infect [infêkt] *v* belqitandin
infection [infêkşun] *n* belqîtk

infinite [infinit] *adj* bêserbêbînî
inflame [inflêym] *v* vêxistin
inflammation [inflamêyşun] *n* werm
influence [inflûêns] *n* nifûs, tesîr
information [infurmêyşun] *n* danezan, haj, salix
informed [informd] *adj* wafiq
inheritance [inhêritins] *n* mirês, mîrat
inn [in] *n* meyxane
innocence [inusêns] *n* bêgunehî, cahilî
innocent [inusênt] *adj* bêgune, bêtexsîr, dêmdur,
  me'sûm
insane [insêyn] *adj* bêaqil, dîn
insanity [insenitî] *n* bêaqilî, dînanî, dînîtî,
  gêjbûn
insect [insêkt] *n* bihok
inside [insayd] *n* hundur *adj* daxil *adv* nav, têda
inside-out [insayd-ewt] *adj* beropaşo *adv* berepaş
insignificant [insignifikunt] *adj* hêç
insolence [insulins] *n* telaqreşî
insomnia [insamnîa] *n* bêxewî, şevorî
instead of [instêd uv] *adv* bêî ku
instruct [instrukt] *v* bersîv, wesandin
instruction [instrukşun] *n* nesîhet, namenasî,
  wesandin
instructor [instruktur] *n* te'lîmdar
instrument [instrumênt] *n* alem, hesincawî

insulted [insultid] *adj* dilgirtî
insurgent [insurcint] *n* usyançî
insurrection [insurêkşun] *n* usyan
intellect [intilêkt] *n* hiş, olan, sewda
intelligence [intêlicuns] *n* fehm
intelligent [intêlicint] *adj* aquilmend, fehmdar
intention [intênşun] *n* bestem, qesd, nîyet, meremet, tem
intentionally [intênşunulî] *adv* qestana
interest [inturêst] *n* hewas
intermission [inturmişun] *n* navbir
international [inturneşunul] *adj* ortemiletî
interpret [inturprit] *v* axivandin
interpreter of religious laws [inturpritur uv rêlicus los] *n* yasiyan
interrupted [inturuptid] *adj* şerpeze
intimate [intimit] *adj* nêzîk
intimidate [intimidêyt] *v* vetirsandin
into [intû] *adv* daxil
intoxicated [intaksikêytid] *adj* cemmaş
intrigue [intrîg] *n* tesvîl
invent [invênt] *v* e'firandin, dahênan
invention [invênşun] *n* e'firandkarî, îcat
inventor [invêntur] *n* e'firandkar, îcatkar
investigation [invêstigêyşun] *n* teselî
invitation [invitêyşun] *n* e'zîmet, teglîfat

iron [ayrun] *n* ḧesin
irony [ayrunî] *n* tiraneyî, tirane
irritation [iritêyşun] *n* bisûtî, terẍîb
Islam [islam] *n* Îslamiyet
island [aylund] *n* cizîr
isn't it? [isn't it] *part* axir, welle
itself [itself] *pron* xwe

J

jabber [cebur] *n* wirwirok
jacket [cekut] *n* cakêt, jakêt
jam [cem] *n* mûrabe
January [cenyûerî] *n* kanûn
Japanese [cepenîz] *n* japon
Japanese [cepenîz] *adj* japonî
jasmine [cesmin] *n* yasemîn
jaw [co] *n* hestîçene
jealous [celus] *adj* dixesî, hosûd
jealousy [celusî] *n* çavreşî
jester [cêstur] *n* oyînbaz
Jew [cû] *n* cihûd
jewel [cûwul] *n* micewher, zêrker, xişir, coher,
    gewher, cewahir
jeweler [cûwulur] *n* zivker, zêrfiroş
jewelry [cûwulrî] *n* micewherat

job [cab] *n* e'mel, qulix
joke [cowk] *n* ḧenek, lêpok, teqle, tirane
joker [cowkur] *n* letîf, teqleçî, tinazker
journal [curnul] *n* kovar, rojname
joy [coy] *n* dileşqî, tereb, zewq
joyous [coyus] *adj* eşqlû, dileşq
judge [dadvan] *n* dadvan, qazî
juice [cûs] *n* ezva, şîlav, şîr, şîrêz
July [culay] *n* îyûl, tîrme
jump [cump] *n* cotikî, çilape, lot, quloz *v* lotin
June [cûn] *n* ḧeziran, îyûn
just [cust] *adj* biînsaf *adv* tenahî
justice [custis] *n* biînsafî, îsaf

K

key [kîy] *n* anaxdar, açar, kilît, mifte
kick [kik] *n* zerb
kidnapping [kidneping] *n* tirho, tajan
Kika (name of Kurdish tribe) [kîka] *n* kîka
kill [kil] *v* fetisandin, kuştin, nejîyandin,
    vekuştin
kind [kaynd] *n* cûre, sinf, texlît
kind [kaynd] *adj* rehmanî
kindness [kayndnis] *n* nermî, çakî, xûnermî,
    devnermî, ehsan

king [king] *n* kayser, qeyser, melîk, padşah
kingdom [kingdum] *n* padşahî
kiss [kis] *v* paçkirin
kiss [kis] *n* paç
kitchen [kiçin] *n* kûxnî, xurekxane
kitchenware [kiçinwêr] *n* aman
knee [nî] *n* çok, nûjen
knife [nayf] *n* kêr
knock [nak] *v* rikrikîn *n* terqe-terq
know [now] *v* nasîn, zanîn
knowledge [nalêc] *n* e'rifî, zanîn, hay, ferheng,
    haydarî, zanînî
knowledgeable [nalêcubl] *adj* e'rif, gerîyayî,
    şehreza, zane, beled, ahil
Koran [kuran] *n* quran
Korean [kurîun] *n* korê
Kurd [kurd] *n* kurd
Kurdish [kurdiş] *adj* kurdî
Kurmandji [kurmancî] *adj* kurmancî

L

labor [lêybur] *n* cefa, zehmet, west
laboratory [laburutorî] *n* laboratorî
lace [lêys] *n* zo
lack [lek] *n* kêmasî, qar

ladder [ledur] *n* derince, nerdewan
lady [lêydî] *n* stî
lake [lêyk] *n* gol
lamb [lemb] *n* berx, hemel
lame [lêym] *adj* kulek
lamp [lemp] *n* çira, serac
land [lend] *n* e'raz
language [lengwuc] *n* lesan, zar, ziman
lantern [lenturn] *n* fener
large [larc] *adj* gumreh
lark [lark] *n* dûmeqesk
last [lest] *adj* axir, dawîn, piştdawî, paşîn, salif
late [lêyt] *adj* dereng, egle
lateness [lêytnis] *n* derengî
later [lêytur] *adv* hindî
laugh [lef] *n* devkenî, ken
laughing [lefing] *adj* xendan
laughter [leftur] *n* pîrq, pîrqînî, piqpiq, narîn,
    tîqîn, tîqe-tîq
laundry [londrî] *n* kineşo, kelişo
law [lo] *n* heq, qanûn, zagûn
lawfulness [lofulnês] *n* qanûntî
lawn [lon] *n* bihnûnî
lawyer [loyur] *n* wekîl
layer [lêyur] *n* çîn, tebeqe, ta, taq
laziness [lêyzînês] *n* bêemelî, tiralî

lazy [lêyzî] *adj* bêemel
lead [lîd] *v* birên, gerandîn
leader [lîdur] *n* qaid, pêşîbir
leaf [lîf] *n* belçîm, belg, berû, lîst, pel
leak [lîk] *v* herikîn, niqitandin
learn [lurn] *v* hîn
learning [lurning] *n* hînbûn, ilm
lease [lîs] *n* daman
leave [lîv] *v* hiştin, hêlandin
lecher [lêçur] *n* fecar
lechery [lêçurî] *n* qabî
left [lêft] *adj* çep
leftovers [lêftowvurs] *n* dûmayî
leg [leg] *n* qedem, laq, ling, pê
legend [lêcind] *n* efsane, hadîs, mejvema
legs [lêgz] *n* qudûm
lemon [lêmun] *n* lîmon
lemonade [lêmunêyd] *n* lîmoned
lend [lênd] *v* biqerz
lesson [lêsun] *n* ders, ebret
letter [lêtur] *n* tîp, herf, reşbelek, kaxet, name,
    mektûb, nivîsar
liar [layur] *n* derewçî, morewir
liberal [liburul] *n* lîbêral
liberation [liburêyşun] *n* felat
liberty [liburtî] *n* haşîtî

library [laybrurî] *n* kitêbxane

lie [lay] *n* berfende, debar, derew, çavbestin, vir, tezwîr *v* razan, raketin

life [layf] *n* e'mir, ebûrî

lift [lift] *v* heldan, hîldan, hilkirin, berizandin, hilandin

light [layt] *adj* binûr, hêsahec, kej, meşfûf, rondar *n* negirîng, qels, îşq, tenik, ronî, ruhnik

light-mindness [layt-mayndêdnês] *n* tewekelî

lightning [laytning] *n* terêj, berq, birûsk

like [layk] *adv* begem, hewakî, şivet *conj* weko

likely [layklî] *adv* îhtîmal

likeness [layknês] *n* mişabih

line [layn] *n* rê, çixîz, xaz, xet, sirê

linen [laynin] *n* cî-nivîn

lingerie [lincurî] *n* binîş

linguist [lingwist] *n* zimanzan

linguistics [lingwistiks] *n* zimanzanînî

liquid [liqwid] *n* meya, ronayî, ronî, şîlav, şorb

listen [lisun] *v* bihîstin, seh

liter [litur] *n* lîtir

literature [lituruçur] *n* lîtêratûr

little [litl] *adj* biçûk, çûçik, çûk, hûr *adv* hindik, kêm

little-by-little [litl-bay-litl] *adv* bere-bere

live [liv] *v* jîyîn
livelihood [layvlîhud] *n* ebûrî, ebûr
lively [layvlî] *adj* zêndî
living [living] *adj* ajinî, candar, e'mirdar
loaf (of bread) [lowf ov brêd] *n* derem
loan [lown] *n* borc
lobster [labstur] *n* xerçeng, req
lock [lak] *n* anaxdar, qifil, kilît, quflik
lodge [lac] *n* qonax
logic [lacik] *n* mentîq
loneliness [lownlînês] *n* wehîdî
lonely [lownlî] *adj* bêheval, dêran, tifal, wehîd
long ago [long egow] *adv* zûda
longing [longing] *n* hesret, xwest, tîbûn
look [luk] *v* nihêrtin, fekirin, nêrîn, fekrandin,
      nihêrandin *n* nêrîn, resm
lord [lord] *n* beg, xudan, Xuda
Lord [lord] *n* Xuda, Xwedê, reb
loss [los] *n* xisar, wundakirin, jidestçûn, xûsran,
      niqis, windakirin, windabûn
lost [lost] *adj* unda, winda
loud [lawd] *adj* qewî
love [luv] *n* evîn, evîndarî, bengîtî, dildarî,
      hezkirin, wetîn *v* evindar, dilgirtî, ḧubandin,
      wetîn
lover [luvur] *n* berdilk, mohib, yar

lower [lowur] *v* dahiştin, dahilanîn
luck [luk] *n* pêkhatin, şans
lucky [lukî] *adj* oẍirxêr
lullaby [lulubay] *n* lûrî
lunch [lunç] *n* firavîn
lungs [lungs] *n* pişik

M

machine [maşîn] *n* alem
machine-gun [maşîngun] *n* xweberajo
mad [med] *adj* har, sews
madam [medum] *n* xanim, madam
madness [mednês] *n* bêhişî, tep
magazine [meguzîn] *n* kovar
magic [mecik] *n* ce'dûgerî, remil
magician [mucişn] *n* ce'dû
magnet [megnit] *n* meqletûz
magnificence [megnifisuns] *n* fort, fortan
magnificent [megnifisuns] *adj* bêhevta, dilbar
magnitude [megnitûd] *n* celal, hişmet
maiden [mêydin] *n* keç
mailman [mêylmen] *n* poştebir
majesty [mecistî] *n* hezret
majority [mecoritî] *n* pirayî
male [mêyl] *n* nêr

malice [melis] *n* boxz, e'rnokî, kîn

man [men] *n* adem, mêr, zelam

management [menecmênt] *n* verêbûn

maneuvers [manûvrs] *n* manawira

manifesto [menifêsto] *n* manîfest

manliness [menlînis] *n* mêranî

mannered [menurd] *adj* terbîyetdar

many [mênî] *adv* pir, ze'f, zehf

map [mep] *n* xarite, kart

marauding [muroding] *n* berîde

marble [marbl] *n* nihêt, mermer

march [març] *n* marş

March [març] *n* adar, mart

market [markit] *n* alvêr, bazar, alişveriş, çarsû

marriage [meric] *n* mar, nikeh, jinxwestin, zewac

married [merîd] *adj* xweykulfet, jindar, zewicî

martyr [martur] *n* zehmetkêş

mask [mesk] *n* rûperde

master [mastur] *n* axa, hostakar, xwedan, xudan, xweyî, mihendiz, mazûban

match [meç] *n* ezva

matches [meçês] *n* pîçke

material [matîrîul] *n* e'ciza, madde, bûjen, berk, matêryal, made, *adj* xusûs

materialistic [matîrîulistik] *adj* tiştanok

maternal [maturnal] *adj* adî

matter [metur] *n* wesefet
maturity [muçûritî] *n* kemal
May [mêy] *n* gulan
maybe [mêybî] *adv* dibe, dibit, heye, belkî, teqez
mayor [mêyur] *n* walî
me [mî] *pron* min
meadow [mêdow] *n* çayr, çîmenzarîn, mêrg
mean [mîn] *adj* fehît, nemerd, neçê
meaning [mîning] *n* qinyat, mana, meal
means [mîns] *n* esibil, gêl, îlac
measure [mêjur] *v* çapkirin, pîvan *n* çap, kêşan
meat [mît] *n* goşt
meatballs [mîtbols] *n* kifte
medal [mêdul] *n* mêdal
medicine [mêdisin] *n* derman, dû û derman
mediocre [mîdîowkr] *adj* bêhunur
meeting [mîting] *n* civat, hevdîn, lîqa, rasthatî, telaq, jwan
melancholy [mêlankolî] *n* bêkêfî
melody [mêludî] *n* melodî, aheng, hewa, nexme, meqam, newa
member [mêmbur] *n* şirîk, tevkar, uzv
membership [mêmburşip] *n* şirîkayî, tevkarî
memory [mêmurî] *n* bîr
menagerie [minecurî] *n* te'bexane
mentioning [mênşuning] *n* zikir

mentor [mêntur] *n* berdevk

merchant [murçunt] *n* bezaz, tacir, tucar

merciful [mursiful] *adj* kerîm, rehmanî

merciless [mursîlês] *adj* bêtexsîr

mercy [mursî] *n* rehm, dilovanî, lêborîn, bereket, merhemet

meritorious [mêritorîus] *adj* tore

merry [mêrî] *adj* berxweş, commaş, kêfxweş, xweşdîl

message [mêsuc] *n* muxabere, peyẍam

messenger [mêsuncur] *n* qasid

meter [mîtur] *n* mêtir, wezin

method [mêsud] *n* gêl, mêtod, terz, ûslûb, wesîle

midday [middêy] *n* nîvro

middle [midl] *n* çat, navçe, nîvek, navbeyn, navend, nîverast

midnight [midnayt] *n* nîvşev

might [mayt] *n* celal, hêz, gumrehî, mecal

mightiest [maytîist] *adj* hêlekan

mighty [maytî] *adj* boke

migration [maygrêyşun] *n* hîcret, mihaceret

mile [mayl] *n* mîl

milk [milk] *n* şîr

milkmaid [milkmêyd] *n* bêrîvan

milliard [milyurd] *n* mîlyard

million [milyun] *n* mîlyon

millionaire [milyunêr] *n* mîlyondar

mind [maynd] *n* hiş

minister [minustur] *n* mînîstir

ministry [minustrî] *n* wezaret, wezîretxan

minute [minut] *n* deqe, qiç

miracle [mirakul] *n* e'cêbî, mûcize

mirage [miraj] *n* leylan

mirth [murs] *n* commaşi

miserable [mizurabul] *adj* bextreş, reben, wejunbext, zelîl

miserly [mayzyrlî] *adj* çavbirçî

misfortune [misforçûn] *n* bedbext, bedhal, bervale, bêçarî, medet, misîbet

mist [mist] *n* mij

mistake [mistêyk] *n* çewtî, xeletî, şaşî, çewt, cibbe, qelet, teşwîş

mix [miks] *v* hevxistin, tevdan *n* tevhevbûn, tekil

mode [mowd] *n* mod

model [madul] *n* modêl

modest [madist] *adj* e'fîf

modesty [madistî] *n* hişmet

Moldavian [moldevîun] *adj* moldavî *n* moldav

mom [mam] *n* in

moment [mumint] *n* bis, bist, lehze, pêlek, deqe, gav, qas

momentarily [mumintlî] *adv* carekêra

mommy [mamî] *n* in
monarch [manurk] *n* ḧukumdar, qral, key, manarx
monarchy [monurkî] *n* orket
money [munî] *n* pere, dirav
monk [munk] *n* êris, keşîş
monkey [munkî] *n* qird, meymûn
monopoly [munapulî] *n* monopolî
monosyllabic [manosilebik] *adj* yekbang
monster [manstur] *n* dêw
month [muns] *n* meh
monument [manyûmint] *n* heykel
mood [mûd] *n* beşer, beng, kêf
moon [mûn] *n* hîv, meh
moral [morul] *n* ebret
more [mor] *adv* zêdetir, hîn, hêj, tir, bêtir, îda, mezintir, pirtir
morning [morning] *n* seher, sebah, sibe
morning bell [morning bêl] *n* berbang
morose [morows] *adj* bêkêf, dilgiran, rûtirş
mosque [masq] *n* meçit
most [mowst] *adj* ala
mother [muzur] *n* da, mak, dad
motherland [muzurlend] *n* serecî, toprax, welat, weten
motive [mowtiv] *n* meqam

motor [mowtur] *n* mator
motorcycle [mowtursaykl] *n* motosîkil
mountain [mewntun] *n* afraz, çîya
mountain range [mewntin rêync] *n* beyar
mournful [mornful] *adj* melûl
mourning [morning] *n* hevşîn, reşgirîn
mouse [mews] *n* mişk
mouth [maws] *n* dev, gep
move [mûv] *v* bezav, herikîn, lepitandin
movement [mûvmint] *n* hereket, lebat, liv,
      tevger, teẍdeyûr
mover [mûvur] *n* palançî
Mrs. [misus] *n* xanim
much [muç] *adv* bêjimar, boş, gelek
multiplication [multuplukêyşun] *n* carbûn
murder [murder] *n* qetil, vekuştin
murderer [murdurur] *n* xûnkar
museum [myûzîum] *n* entikxane, mûzê
mushroom [muşrum] *n* karî
music [myûzik] *n* mûzîk
musician [myûzişun] *n* zirneçî
Muslim [muslim] *adj* misilmanî, surman
Muslim [muslim] *n* misilman
mute [myût] *adj* bêziman, lal
mutually [myûçûulî] *adv* hevra, hev
My God! [may gad] *interj* yarebî

mysterious [mistîrîus] *adj* x̄eyb, neeşkela
mystery [misturî] *n* neeşkelayî, pene, remz

N

nail [nêyl] *n* bizmar, mix
naïve [naîv] *adj* xeşîm, xizan, nestêl
naked [nêykid] *adj* berehne, rût, tazî
name [nêym] *n* nav, inwan, îsm
nameless [nêymlês] *adj* bênav
napkin [nepkin] *n* pêşgîr
narration [nerrêyşun] *n* behs, gilîgotin
narrative [nerrativ] *n* neqil
narrator [nerrêytur] *n* gilîbêj
narrow [neruw] *adj* cemik
nasty [nestî] *adj* mifsid
nationality [neşunelitî] *n* milet, nijad
native land [nêytiv lend] *n* cîmisken
natural [neçurul] *adj* tabî
nature [nêyçur] *n* xwerist, xweza, jêza, xû, fitret, nihad
nausea [nosîa] *n* vereşîn
nauseate [nosîêyt] *v* vereşandin
Nazi [natsî] *n* nazî
near [nîr] *adv* berda, êmanê, liber
nearby [nîrbay] *adv* berda

neatness [nîtnis] *n* temizî

necessary [nêsisêrî] *adj* pêwîst, hewce, pêdivî, bijîşk, gerek, îqin, xwezî

necessity [nisêsitî] *n* pêwîstî, bivênevêyî, divêyî, gerekî, ferzî, hacet, hewce

neck [nêk] *n* gerden, lehane, mil, stukur

necklace [nêklis] *n* ûstûvank, tor

need [nîd] *n* destengî, feqîrî, hewce, hacet, newa

needed [nîdid] *adj* gerek, kêr, lazim

needle [nîdl] *n* niştir

needy [nîdî] *adj* desteng, fiqare, feqîr, e'bdal, zelûl

neighbor [nêybur] *n* cewar, mişirîk

neighborhood [nêyburhud] *n* dayre

nephew [nêfyû] *n* birazê, biraza, xwarzê, torin

nervousness [nurvisnis] *n* terxîb

nest [nêst] *n* hêlîn

never [nêvur] *adv* tucarî

new [nûw] *adj* nû, teze, terecan

news [nûwz] *n* cab, peyẍam, nûwînî

newspaper [nûspêypur] *n* gazêt, kovar, rojname

next [nêkst] *prep* ber

niece [nîs] *n* xwarzî

night [nayt] *n* şev *adj* şevîn

night guard [nayt gard] *n* gezme

nightmare [naytmêr] *n* cehnem, kabûs

nine [nayn] *num* neh
nine hundred [nayn hundrid] *num* nod
nineteen [nayntîn] *num* nozdeh
ninety [nayntî] *num* nehwêd
nipple [nipul] *n* çiçik
no [now] *conj* tu, qet, na, nana
nobility [nowbilutî] *n* çavtêrî, cindîtî, comerdî, çelebîtî, camêrî
noble [nowbl] *adj* zadegan, esilzade, bresil, camêr, ciwanmêr, cindî, maqûl
nobly [nowblî] *adv* comerdane
nobody [nowbudî] *pron* nekes, tukes, kesek *adv* nakes
noise [noyz] *n* çirîn, hurmîn, deng, dengzar, teqreq, guje-guj, hêwirze
non-Muslim [nan-muslim] *n* gawir
nonsense [nansins] *n* şitaet
noon [nûn] *n* nîvro
normal [normul] *adj* normal
northern [norzurn] *adj* şimalî
Norwegian [norwîcun] *adj* nerwêcî *n* nerwêc
nose [nowz] *n* bîhnî, bêvil, difin, kep, meşam, poz
nostril [nastrul] *n* firing, finc
nostrils [nastruls] *n* bêvil, firing
not [nat] *adv* ne *conj* nî, na

note [nowt] *n* note, sirinc, muz
nothing [nusing] *n* hêç, neyîn, netiştek, tiştek,
    nehin *prep* netutişt
novel [navul] *n* raman
November [nowvêmbur] *n* çirîya evel
now [naw] *adv* hala, hêja, hina, aniha, niha, naka
number [numbur] *n* erqem, ejmar, nomêr, jimar,
    hejmar, jima
numeral [nûmurul] *n* jimar

O

oak [owk] *n* çilû, palûd
oar [or] *n* bêr
oath [ows] *n* ad, qeseb, tobe, ve'de
obedience [ubîdîins] *n* gor, îmam, teslîmat
obedient [ubîdîint] *adj* mûtî
object [abcêkt] *n* eşîya, e'ciza, objêkt
objection [abcêkşun] *n* îtîraz
objective [abcêktiv] *adj* objêktîv
objectivity [abcêktivitî] *n* objêktîvî
obligated [abligêytid] *n* wezîfedar
obligation [abligêyşun] *n* wezîfetî
oboe [owbow] *n* zirne
obstacle [abstukul] *n* aloz, pêşasêgeh
obstinacy [abstinusî] *n* gerdenkêşî, e'nadî

obstinate [abstinut] *adj* gerdenkêş, ḧir
obvious [abvîus] *adj* beyan, melûm, pe'nî
occasion [ukêyjun] *n* daîye, car, fersend
occasionally [ukêyjunulî] *adv* dem-demî, carna, caran, geh-geh
occupation [akyûpêyşun] *n* qulix, dagirtin
ocean [owşun] *n* okîan
October [aktowbur] *n* aktyabir, çirî
odd [ad] *adj* bêdevan
of course [of kors] *adv* elbet, hilbet, helbet, tabileyî
offense [afêns] *n* buxtan
officer [ofisur] *n* efser, ofîsêr, zabit
official [afişul] *adj* resmî
often [oftin] *adv* bêtir
oh! [ow] *interj* hay, weê, wax, wey, weyla, wey-wey
oil [oyl] *n* bizir
okay [owkêy] *part* bira *adv* bera
old [owld] *adj* kevn, kal, mecin, demborî, ixtîyar, pîr, antîk
old age [owld êyc] *n* extîyarî
old lady [old lêydî] *n* e'cûze, pîrek
old man [old men] *adj* kal
old woman [old wumen] *n* jinepîr
Old Testament [old têstumênt] *n* torat

older [oldur] *adv* mestir

on [an] *prep* li, ser

on purpose [on purpus] *adv* enqest, e'mden

once [wuns] *adv* roke

once more [wuns mor] *adv* tezede

one [wun] *adj* tekane, tenê, *num* yek

onion [onyun] *n* pîvaz

only [ownlî] *adv* elle, hêja, mehza

Oops! [ûps] *interj* way

open [owpin] *adj* menfehet, meftûh, vekirin

open [owpin] *v* jihevvekirin

opened [owpind] *adj* vekirî

opera [apura] *n* opêra

operation [apurêyşun] *n* opêrasîon

opinion [upinyun] *n* tedbîr, ray, nêt

opportunist [apurtûnist] *n* oportûnîst

opposite [apusit] *n* hevrûbûn

opposite to [apusit tu] *adv* pêşber, raser

opposition [apuzişun] *n* opozîsî

oppositionist [apuzişunist] *n* opozîsîonêr

oppression [uprêşun] *n* e'zeb

or [or] *conj* ango, yan

orange [orunc] *n* portoẍal, tirinc, zerîn

orator [orator] *n* otarbêj

orbit [orbit] *n* govek

orchestra [orkistra] *n* mûzîk

order [ordur] *n* rêz, pergal, sazûman, serûberî,
    destûr, ferman, eteb
ordinary [ordinurî] *adj* çentîn
organization [orgunizêyşun] *n*
    organ, pêkhatin, organîzasî, teşkîlat,
    rêxistin, komel, sazûman
organized [orgenayzd] *adj* pêk
oriental studies [orîêntul studîs] *n* şerqnasî
original [uricinul] *n* metne
ornament [ornumênt] *n* xemil
other [uzur] *adj* adîne, êdin
outcome [ewtkam] *n* axirî, kutasî
outdoors [ewtdor] *adv* derva
outside [ewtsayd] *adv* derva
outstanding [ewtstending] *adj* ala
owner [ownur] *n* xweyî, sahîb
ox [aks] *n* ga

P

package [pekic] *n* verêkirin
packet [pekit] *n* boxçe
pact [pekt] *n* qayîme, name
page [pêyc] *n* pêlav, rû
pail [pêyl] *n* dewl, qenter

pain [pêyn] *n* elem, keder, êş, kul, jan, xem, êşandin
paint [pêynt] *v* neqişandin
painter [pêyntur] *n* nexşkar
painting [pêynting] *n* tablo, neqiş
pair [pêr] *n* cot
pale [pêyl] *adj* qîçolek, zer
paleness [pêylnis] *n* qîçolekî
palm (of hand) [pom] *n* navlep
pancake [penkêyk] *n* bîşî, şilik
paper [pêypur] *n* kaxet
parade [purêyd] *n* parad
Paradise [peridays] *n* cenet, cennet
paragraph [perugref] *n* made, paragraf
paralysis [puralusus] *n* belqîtk, felc
paralyze [parulayz] *v* belqitandin
pardon [pardun] *n* e'fu, uzir *v* e'fu, bexşîn
park [park] *n* parîz
parliament [parlimênt] *n* parlamênt
parrot [perut] *n* tûtî
part [part] *n* behr, pirtî, parî, terxan, beş, bir, pişk
participant [partisipint] *n* hevkar
participation [partisipêyşun] *n* hevkarî, tevkarî
parting [parting] *n* dûrî, firqet, ferqût, hicran

partner [partnur] *n* havalkar, beşdar, hevkar, şirîk

party (political) [partî] *n* firqe

party [partî] *n* tûde

passport [pespurt] *n* paşport

pass [pes] *v* daborîn

passage [pesic] m bihur

passenger [pesincur] *n* pasajîr

passion [peşun] *n* bengîtî, eşq, îşq, menc

passport [pesport] *n* pasport

past [pest] *adj* bihurî

pastime [pestaym] *n* mijûl

path [pes] *n* esibil, rê

patience [pêyşuns] *n* mohlet, sebir, tab, tehmûl

patient [pêyşunt] *adj* sebûr

patriot [pêytrîat] *n* patrîot, wetenhiz

patriotism [pêytrîutizm] *n* wetenhizî

patron [pêytrun] *n* patron, hemayetger, xweyî, xudan, xwedan

patronage [pêytrunic] *n* destgirî, perest, hemayet, xwedîtî, xudantî

patronize [pêytrunayz] *v* pawtandin

pauper [popur] *n* dewrês, kasib, xwezok, e'vdal, pepûk, kûtxur

pavillon [puvilyun] *n* ḧucir

payment [pêymint] *n* eda, heqdest, îcret

peace [pîs] *n* haşîtî, hêsabûn, tebatî, aşitî, lihehatin, bêdengî

peaceful [pîsful] *adj* amin, bêẍazende, hêsa, milahîm

pear [pêr] *n* karçin

pearl [purl] *n* almas, gewher, guher

peasant [pêsunt] *n* gundî

pedagogue [pêdagag] *n* pêdagog

pelvis [pêlvis] *n* şikev

pencil [pênsul] *n* xame, qelemzirêç, qelem, pênûszirêç

people [pîpl] *n* beşer, alet, xelq, mexlûqet, gel, ehl, mirov

pepper [pêpur] *n* filfil, bîber

perfection [purfêkşun] *n* fezilet

perfidy [purfidî] *n* şehamet

performance [purformins] *n* temaşe

period [pîrîud] *n* hengam, hana, hingam, muẍdar, midet, pêl, wade

period of time [pîrîud ov taym] *n* derav, esna

permanent [purmanunt] *adj* medam

permission [purmişn] *n* cewaz, îbahat, îzin, risxet

Persian [purjun] *n* fars *adj* farsî

person [pursun] *n* e'bd, merov, merî, kes, şexs

personality [pursunelitî] *n* nifûs
perspective [purspêktiv] *n* pêşîv
petal [petul] *n* belçik, pel
pharmacy [farmusî] *n* dermanxane
philologist [filalucist] *n* fîloloj
philology [filalucî] *n* fîlolojî
philosopher [filasufur] *n* fîlosof
philosophy [filasufî] *n* felsefî, fîlosofî
phonetics [funêtiks] *n* fonêtîk
photo [fowtow] *n* e'kis
photograph [fowtugref] *n* foto
photographer [futagrufur] *n* fotograf *n* fotografî
phrase [frêyz] *n* firaz, îstîlah
physical [fizikul] *adj* fîzîkî
physics [fiziks] *n* fîzîke
pick up [pik up] *v* hilgirtin, hildan, hilandin
picture [pikçur] *n* neqiş, sifet, wêne, risim
piece [pîs] *n* kerî, qut, loq, parî, parçe, pirtî, tûzî
pig [pig] *n* beraz
pigeon [picun] *n* kew
pilaf [pilef] *n* birinc
pilgrim [pilgrim] *n* zîyaretvan
pilot [paylut] *n* firindevan
pince-nez [pens-nê] *n* berçavk
pinch [pinç] *v* quncirandin
pistachio [pistaçîow] *n* pistik

pit [pit] *n* çal
pity [pitî] *n* eman, cscf
place [plêys] *n* dews, cî, cîgeh, dewl, der, warge
    v danîn
plain [pleyn] *n* best, tûş *adj* kor
plan [plen] *n* plan, tertîb
planet [plenêt] *n* seyyare
plant [plent] *n* sîrêçk, zavod
plate [plêyt] *n* tebax
play [pley] *n* pîyês, lîsk, leyîsk, lîstin
plaza [plaza] *n* meydan, dewl, ger, sehn
plea [plî] *n* ta, temene
pleased [plîzd] *adj* memnûn
pleasingly [plîzinglî] *adv* xweş-xweş
pleasure [plêjur] *n* hilawet, lezet, qenaet, mijûl
plight [playt] *n* bendewarî
plum [plum] *n* alû, zeytûn
plump [plump] *adj* xurt
pocket [pakit] *n* cêb
poem [powum] *n* poêm, şêr
poet [powit] *n* şayîr
poetry [powitrî] *n* e'şar
point [poynt] *n* nuqte
poison [poyzun] *n* jehr
poisonous [poyzunus] *adj* jehrdar

pole [powl] *n* qutb, polûs
Pole (native of Poland) [powl] *n* lêh, polon
police officer [pulîs afisur] *n* şatir
Polish [powliş] *adj* polonî
polished [palişd] *adj* mat
politeness [polaytnês] *n* adab, e'deb, perdaq
politics [palitiks] *n* sîyaset
pollute [pulût] *v* ḧerimandin
pollution [pulûşun] *n* qilêrkirin
pomp [pamp] *n* fort, fortan
pond [pand] *n* gol
poor [pûr] *adj* bêçar, bêhêz, belengaz, bêpergal,
     ixtîyar, lawaz, perîşan, reben, xizan
popular [papyûlar] *adj* belû
population [paplyûlêyşun] *n* xelq, reyat
port [port] *n* bender, îskela
portion [porşun] *n* terxan
position [puzişun] *n* ritibe, rutib, wezîfe
possession [puzêşun] *n* xwedêdan
possibility [pasibilitî] *n* imkan, mimkûn
possible [pasibl] *conj* belkî
possibly [pasublî] *adv* teqez
post office [powst ofis] *n* poşte
potato [potêytow] *n* kartol
pour [por] *v* rijandin, rêtin

poverty [pavurtî] *n* belengazî, hêsîrî, destengî, feqîrî, mehrûmî, perîsanî, xisanî, zelûlî

power [pawur] *n* birh, hikumet, karin, taqet, xurtî, qudret, zexmî

powerful [pawurful] *adj* hur

practical [prektikul] *adj* praktîkî

practice [prektis] *n* praktîke

praise [prêyz] *n* medhet, pesnevedan, pesin, pesinandin, payî *v* payîdan

prayer [prêyur] *n* de'wet, ibadet, yasîn

preacher [prîçur] *n* we'z

preaching [prîçur] *n* tewsîye, we'z

precious [prêşus] *adj* giranbiha, nerx, qedirgiran

precise [prisays] *adj* ferih

precision [prisijun] *n* ferihî

preface [prêfis] *n* dîbace

pregnant [prêgnunt] *adj* hemil

preparation [prêpurêyşun] *n* pêkhatin, tivdarek, tuşû

prescription [purskripşun] *n* dermanivîs

presence [prêzuns] *n* hezret, hazirbûn, mewcûd

present [prêzunt] *n* dîhar, dîyarî, pêşkêş

presently [prêzuntlî] *adv* hina, naka

preserve [prizurv] *n* mûrabe

press [prês] *v* tepisandi

previous [prîvîus] *adj* sabiq

price [prays] *n* biha, fiyat, fîyat, hêjayî, hêja,
    qîmet
priceless [prayslis] *adj* giranbiha
pricing [praysing] *n* bihabirîn
pride [prayd] *n* anantî, e'ne'ne, kawî, qudetî,
    qutetî, pozbilindî, tihf
priest [prîst] *n* êris, papaz
prison [prizun] *n* hebs, girtîgen
prisoner [prisanur] *n* bend, dîl, dîlbend, hêsîr
privilege [privilic] *n* extîyar, extîyarî
probability [prabubilutî] *n* mimkûn
problem [prablum] *n* mesele
process [prasis] *n* prosês
product [pradukt] *n* mehsûl
production [pradukşun] *n* prodûksî
productive [pradaktiv] *adj* adan
profession [prufêşun] *n* îş, şofêrtî, mitexesîs
professor [prufêsur] *n* pirafêsor, prafêsor
profit [prafit] *n* fayîde, hewil, kar
profitable [prafitubl] *adj* fayîdekar, kardar,
    mifade
profusion [profyûjun] *n* tijîtî
program [prowgrem] *n* berneme, pragram
progress [pragris] *n* çelengkirin
project [pracêkt] *n* proje
prominent [praminint] *adj* bilîmet

promise [pramis] *n* wad, ve'de, soz
pronoun [prownawn] *n gram* cînav, pronav
proof [prûf] *n* delîl, tedlîl
proper noun [prapur newn] *n* serenav
property [prapurtî] *n* emte'e
prophet [prafit] *n* enbî, nebî, resûl
propaganda [prapagenda] *n* propoganda, agîtasî
prosperous [praspurus] *adj* oxirxêr
prostitution [prastitûşun] *n* boztî, qabî
protect [prutekt] *v* xwedî
protection [prutêkşun] *n* hemayet, xwedîtî,
    te'mîn
protector [prutêktur] *n* hemayetger
protest [prowtêst] *n* îtîraz
proud [prewd] *adj* anan, kaw, qude, qure,
    pozbilind. serbilind
proudly [prawdlî] *adv* kubar-kubar, qude-qude
province [pravins] *n* hêl, olk
provocation [pravokêyşun] *n* fesadî
prune [prûn] *n* alû
psalter [psoltur] *n* zembûr
pub [pub] *n* meyxane
public [publik] *n* cimaet
publication [publikêyşun] *n* çapkirin, neşir, tabî
publisher [publişur] *n* neşirkar

puddle [pudl] *n* şilope
punishment [punişmint] *n* bobelat, ceza, îza, ifad
pure [pyûr] *adj* ebrûhelal, ḧelal, xarû, nab
purple [purpl] *adj* erẍewanî
purpose [purpus] *n* e'rbab, e'md
purposely [purpus] *adv* e'mden, qestana, qazîk
purse [purs] *n* kîs
put [put] *v* danîn

Q

quack [qwak] *n* belelerz
quality [qwalitî] *n* cûre, çawabûn, fola, xastî,
　　xuya, sifet, osaf, wesefet
quantity [qwantitî] *n* çendî, çendanî
quarrel [qwarul] *n* fitne, fitin, qal *v* pevçûn
question [qwêşçun] *n* mesele, sewalî, pirsyar,
　　pirs
quick [qwayut] *adj* zû, alçax, bêdeng, bêẍazende,
　　kip, rahet, rûnerm, sernerm
quiet [qwayut] *adj* as, bêdeng, bêpejn, hêmin,
　　sehal
quietly [qwayutlî] *adj* hêdî
quietness [qwayêtnis] *n* alçaxî

R

race [rêys] *n* îrq, lec
racket [rekit] *n* girme-girm, gurîn, qalme-qalm
radio [rêydîow] *n* radîo
radio station [rêydîow stêyşun] *n* radîostansî
radish [rediş] *n* tivir
rage [rêyc] *n* fersend, hêrs, xeşm, xezeb, îdam,
    irin, qehir *v* ẍezibîn, qehirîn
railroad station [rêylrowd stêyşun] *n* vagzal
raise [rêyz] *v* hilgirtin, hildan, rakirin
raisin [rêyzin] *n* mehûj, mewuj
ram [rem] *n* beran
rank [renk] *n* pay, ritibe, rutib
rat [ret] *n* beleban, mişko, mişk
raving [rêyving] *n* mêxûlî
ravished [revişd] *adj* dilhebandî, dilgîr
raw [ro] *adj* xavî, xam
ray [rêy] *n* îşq
razor [rêyzur] *n* hûzan
razor blade [rêyzur blêyd] *n* dûzan, gûzan
reach [rîç] *v* gihîştin
read [rîd] *v* xwendîn
reader [rîdur] *n* xwendevan
readiness [rêdînis] *n* hazirbûn
ready [rêdî] *adj* hazir

real [rîul] *adj* tê
reality [rîelitî] *n* heqî, têtî
really? [rîlî] *interj* ha? wa-wa?
reason [rîzun] *n* daîye, mana, mehne
rebel [rêbul] *n* usyançî
rebellion [ribêlyun] *n* usyan
rebirth [riburs] *n* tezedekirin
rebuke [ribyûk] *n* tan
receipt [risît] *n* îbra
recently [rîsintlî] *adv* hêja
receptivity [riseptivitî] *n* behistî
recognize [rêkugnayz] *v* nasîn
rectangle [rêktengl] *n* rastgoşe
red [rêd] *adj* alîsor, erẍewanî, xumrî, kej, sor
red-haired [rêd-hêrd] *adj* kej
reference [rêfuruns] *n* wesîqe
refined [rîfaynd] *adj* şeng
reflection [riflêkşun] *n* e'kis
refuge [rêfyûc] *n* penah
refusal [rifyûzul] *n* înkar
regime [rêjîm] *n* rêjîm
regiment [rêcimênt] *n* bêlûk
region [rîcun] *n* malbend, bêlûk
regret [rigrêt] *n* tevhevbûn, tobe
regular [regyûlar] *adj* adetî
rejection [rîcêkşun] *n* nanayî

relative [rêlativ] *n* aqar, kinêz, zeyî *adj* adî
relatives [rêlutivs] *n* malbat
religion [rulicun] *n* mezheb, ol
religious [rîlicus] *adj* xwedanterîqet
remaining [rimêyning] *adj* mayî
remains [rimêyns] *n* bermayî
remembrance [rîmêmbrans] *n* bîr
remnants [rêmnants] *n* dûmayî
renewal [rinûwul] *n* tezekirin
rent [rênt] *n* kirê, îcare, ûcre
rented [rêntid] *adj* ûcredar
repeat [rêpît] *v* axivandin
repel [ripêl] *v* berîdan
replace [riplêys] *v* guhartin
reporter [ruportur] *n* miqaledar
repose [rîpowz] *n* rehetî
representation [rêprisêntêyşun] *n* wekîl, wekîltî
reproach [riprowç] *v* xurîn *n* melamet, lome
reproduction [rîprowdukşun] *n* pirkirin
reputation [rêpyûtêyşun] *n* telaq, namûs
request [riqwêst] *n* lava, reca, teweqe
resembling [rizêmbling] *adj* hêwan
resistance [rizistuns] *n* bervanî
resource [rîsors] *n* zên
respect [rispêkt] *n* hurmet, xatirgirtin, hişmet, qedir

respectable [rispêktabl] *adj* qedirgiran, maqûl
respected [rispêktid] *adj* e'zîz
respectful [rispêktful] *adj* xatirnas
response [ruspans] *n* cab
responsibility [rispansubilitî] *n* berpirsîyarî, cabdarî
responsible [ruspansubl] *adj* cabdar
rest [rêst] *n* rehetî
restless [rêstlês] *adj* netevitî
restlessness [rêstlêsnês] *n* netevitî
restoration [ristorêyşun] *n* tezedekirin
restraint [ristrêynt] *n* xwebergirî
result [rêzult] *n* bermayî, e'ser, encam, mowacib
return [riturn] *v* paşdahatin, ve, vegerandin, zivirandin, wergerîn *n* veger, zivir, hatin, wergerandin
revenge [rêvênc] *n* piştxurtî, tol
review [rivyû] *n* teqrîr
revolver [rivalvur] *n* rêvolvêr
reward [riword] *n* hucret, mokafat, mikafat, rewa, pêşkêş
rheumatism [rûmatizm] *n* rêvmatîzm
rhythm [rizm] *n* wezin
rib [rib] *n* parxan
rice [rays] *n* birinc
rich [riç] *adj* ẍenî, ta, zengîn

riches [riçis] *n* dewlemendî, dewlet, zengînî
rich person [riç pursun] *n* dewlemend
riddle [ridl] *n* metel
right [rayt] *n* extîyar, extîyarî, heqyat, heq, îzin
right [rayt] *adj* dûz
righteous [rayçus] *adj* abid
ring [ring] *n* xeleq, xatim, negîn, toq
ripe [rayp] *adj* pûxtane
rise [rayz] *v* hilhatin, hilbûn
risk [risk] *n* fêde, fedî, turuş
rival [rayvl] *n* ce'dû
river [rivur] *n* co, coybar, cew, ça, çem, rûbar,
    şet
river bank [rivur benk] *n* berçem
road [rowd] *n* rê
roar [ror] *n* narîn
rob [rab] *v* ẍaret
robber [rabur] *n* celal, êrîşbir
robbery [raburî] *n* destdirêjî, berîde, êrîşkirin,
    ẍaret
robust [rowbust] *adj* tîndar
rock [rak] *n* hucur, taht, qîş, çêl, lat
    v qeliqandin, leqandin
roll up [rol up] *v* dagerîn
roof [rûf] *n* xaneban, serbanî
room [rûm] *n* ḧucir, xan, otax

root [rût] *n* kok, ra, reh û ol

roots [rûts] *n* tore

rope [rowp] *n* ben, têl, weris

rose [rowz] *n* gulking, gul

rose hips [rowz hips] *n* şîlan

round [rewnd] *adj* gulol, gulover, ẍeltan

row [row] *n* qelf, qeter, rêzik, tîş-tîş

rub [rub] *v* perxandin

rubbish [rubiş] *n* qilêr, qirêj

ruby [rûbî] *n* aqût, yaqût

rude [rûd] *adj* bêmerîfet, bêterbyet, qubet, zibr

rudeness [rûdnis] *n* qubetî

rug [rug] *n* xalîçe, merş

ruin [rûin] *adj* xirab

ruined [rûind] *adj* malkavil

ruins [rûins] *n* gamboẍ, kambax, wêran, mexer

rule [rûl] *n* adet, e'det, hikim, hikumet, îdare, qanûn, zagon

ruler [rûlur] *n* e'mirdar, ḧukumdar, melîk, walî, serekdewlet

run [run] *v* bezîn, revîn *n* fêr, rev

Russian [ruşun] *n* rûs *adj* rûsî

rye [ray] *n* açar

S

sacrifice [sekrifays] *n* qurban
sad [sed] *adj* bêkêf, dilgirtî, dilbirîn, dilgêr, hezîn, xemgîn, keserbar, melûl
sadness [sednis] *n* berxweketin, bêkêfî, hizin, kul, dilgiranî, kerb, xem, xemgînî, ẍusse
safe [sêyf] *adj* amin, bêxeber, firêqet
safety [sêyftî] *n* firêqetî, bêxederî, amindarî
sage [sêyc] *n* zanak
sailor [sêylur] *n* gemîçî
salad [selud] *n* selat
sale [sêyl] *n* firotan
salesman [sêylsmin] *n* firoşçî
salt [solt] *v* xwê
salty [soltî] *adj* şor
same [sêym] *adj* tewr, yekrû
sand [send] *n* qûm
sandals [senduls] *n* kişik
sandy [sendî] *adj* zer
sated [soltid] *adj* têr
satisfaction [setisfekşun] *n* razîbûn
Saturday [seturdêy] *n* şembî
savagery [sevicurî] *n* gurî, wehşî
saw [so] *n* mişar
say [sêy] *v* axaftin

scale [skêyl] *n* terazû
scandal [skendul] *n* cencele, gosirmatî
scandalous [skendulus] *adj* gosirmat
scantily [skentilî] *adv* kêm
scar [skar] *n* qereh
scarcity [skersitî] *n* kêmasî
scare [skêr] *v* vetirsandin
scared [skêrd] *adj* tirsandî
scarf [skarf] *n* şal
scarlet [skarlit] *adj* erxewanî
scent [sênt] *n* meşam, bîhnî, bîhn, bîhnayî
school [skûl] *n* dersxane, hînxane, xwendegeh,
    dibistan, xwendînxanî, mekteb, îşkol
science [sayuns] *n* ferheng, elm, ilm, zanistî
scientific [sayuntifik] *adj* ilmî, zanyarî, zanistî
scientist [sayuntist] *n* ulmdar, zanistyar
scissors [sizurs] *n* cawbir, meqes
scold [skold] *v* xurîn
scratch [skreç] *v* quncirandin
scream [skrîm] *n* fize-fiz, hurmîn, qalme-qalm,
    qîrîn, qîrînî, pe ketin, xaze *v* qarîn, qîjandin,
    qûjîn
screen [skrîn] *n* çît
scruples [skrûpls] *n* ebûrî
sculpture [skulpçur] *n* heykel
sea [sî] *n* dengiz

seal [sîl] *n* pêçat

seashore [sîşor] *n* delav

season [sîzun] *n* fesil, mewsim

seclusion [siklûjun] *n* tektî, muferdat

secret [sîkrit] *n* dildizî, nehîn, nehênî, ezîr, xewlet, neeşkelayî *adj* xewle, ẍeyb, mehfî, veşartî

secretary [sêkritêrî] *n* katib

secretive [sîkritiv] *adj* mehfî

secretly [sîkritlî] adv tele-tel

section [sêkşun] *n* fesil, tecrîd

secure [sikyûr] *adj* bêxeber

security [sikyûritî] *n* mihafize, bêxederî, pawanî, ud

see [sî] *adj* behrî

sight [sayt] *n* behr

seed [sîd] *n* tov, toxim, zuret

seek [sîk] *v* lêgerîn

select [sêlêkt] *v* bijartin

self-control [sêlf-kuntrol] *n* tabet

Shemsiki [şemsikî] (the name of a Kurdish tribe in South America) Şemsikî

sender [sêndur] *n* verêker, şandyar

sending [sênding] *n* verêbûn

sense [sêns] *n* nêt

sensible [sênsibl] *adj* bîranî, bîrbir, aquilmend, jîr

sensitive [sênsitiv] *adj* hezmekar

sensitivity [sênsitivitî] *n* hezmekarî, ziqet

sentence [sêntuns] *n* hizir, hevok

separate [sêpurut] *adj* cuda, cihê, cihade

separation [sêpurêyşun] *n* cudabûn, cihêbûn

September [sêptêmbur] *n* îlon, sêntyabir

serious [sîrîus] *adj* cidî, xwediehmîyet

servant [survint] *n* berdest, berdestî, bende, xulam, çawîş, hodax, qerebaşî

service [survis] *n* çeyk, wezîfe

set free [sêt frî] *v* berdan

seven hundred [sêvin hundrid] *num* hevtsed

seventy [sêvintî] *num* heftê

severe [sivîr] *adj* şeîd

shake [şêyk] *v* herikîn, kil, lerizandin, hejandin, lerizîn, qeliqandin, leqandin

shame [şêym] *n* bêabrûyî, ebûr, e'yb, rûreşî, şerm, fedî, eyb, fehêt

shameful [şêymful] *adj* bêhurmet

shameless [şêymlis] *adj* berxweneketî, bêwijdan

shamelessness [şêymlisnis] *n* berxweneketî

shank [şenk] *n* saq

shape [şêyp] *n* terz

Shariat (compilation of Muslim religious laws)
[şerîet] *m* şerîet
sharp [şarp] *adj* çist, nehriz, pîj, tûj
sharpening [şarpining] *n* tûjkirin
sheep [şîp] *n* mî, pez
sheet [şît] *n* ta, sipîçal
sheet (of paper) [şît] *n* werq
shelf [şêlf] *n* îşkav
shelter [şêltur] *n* warge
shepherd [şêpurd] *n* bizinvan
shin [şin] *n* çîp
shine [şayn] *v* şixulîn
shining [şayning] *adj* zêrav
ship [şip] *n* folk, gemî, wapor
shirt [şurt] *n* kiras
shiver [şivur] *n* tevz
shock [şak] *n* gêjbûn
shocked [şakt] *adj* gêj
shoelace [şûlêys] *n* pejî
shoes [şûz] *n* midas, sol
shop [şap] *n* mixaze
shore [şor] *n* sahil
short [şort] *adj* bejnkurt, kin, kurt, kêm, qol
shortcoming [şortkuming] *n* naqos
shortness [şortnis] *n* kurtbûn
shot [şat] *n* gulleagirkirin, terqin

shoulder [şoldur] *n* mil, pol
shrewd [şrûd] *adj* mekranî
shyness [şaynês] *n* tirsonektî
sick [sik] *adj* bêhal, bîmar, e'lîl, xesle, kulek, qola
sickly [siklî] *adj* canêş
sickness [siknis] *n* bîmarî
side [sayd] *n* alî, hind, berpal, rex, rû, tang, yan
siege [sîyc] *n* hesar
sigh [say] *n* efẍan, e'nîn, hêzing, êzing, nefes
sign [sayn] *n* işaret, nîşan
signature [signaçur] *n* îmza
significance [signifikens] *n* ferzî
significant [signifikent] *adj* ferzan
silence [saylêns] *n* bêdenganî, hişbûn
silent [saylênt] *adj* bêdeng
silk [silk] *n* herir
silliness [silînis] *n* gosirmatî
silly [silî] *adj* kêmaqil, kerîgêj, sergiran, sefîh
silver [silvur] *n* niqar, sîm, zîv
similar [simulur] *adj* angorî, fena, hemta, hevreng, ji rengê, mina, wanî
similarity [simileritî] *n* hevrûbûn, angortî, lêçûn, mişabih, şibîn, wekehevkirin
simple [simpl] *adj* bêvece, sefîl
sin [sin] *n* guneh
since [sins] *conj* madam

sincere [sinsîr] *adj* ebrûhelal, xudanbext
sincerity [sinsîritî] *n* rastdilî
sinful [sinful] *adj* xweyguneh
single [singl] *adj* bêjin
sinner [sinur] *n* fasiq, gunehkar
Sipkan [sipkan] (the name of a Kurdish tribe in Armenia and Turkey) Sîpkan
sister [sistur] *n* dûxtmam, xûsk
sit [sit] *v* rûniştin
six [siks] *num* şeş
sixteen [sikstîn] *num* şanzde
size [sayz] *n* meqyas
sizeable [sayzubl] *adj* gir, giran, givrik, gumreh, qerd
skate [skêyt] *v* şimitîn
skin [skin] *n* çerm
skinny [skinî] *adj* bêzuhum, qor, jar
skirt [skurt] *n* yax
sky [skay] *n* erzeq, e'wr, eflak, lûce, e'sman, sema
slander [slandur] *n* buxtan
slave [slêyv] *n* e'vdal, bend, qerebaşî, xulam, kol, qûl
slavery [slêyvurî] *n* bendewarî, hêsîrî, qûltî
sleep [slîp] *n* xew, raketin, nivistin
sleepless [slîplês] *adj* bêxew
sleeve [slîv] *n* zend

slender [slêndur] *adj* tenik, zirav
slim [slim] *adj* çê
slippers [slipurs] *n* kişik
slope [slowp] *n* berpal, berwar, berjêr
slow [slow] *adj* dereng
sly [slay] *adj* degenek, fêldar, fendar
slyness [slaynis] *n* fêldarî
small [smol] *adj* biçûk, cemik, piçûk, çûçik, çûk
smart [smart] *adj* aquilmend, bîrbir, xweyhiş, zorzan
smell [smêl] *n* bîhnî
smile [smayl] *n* devkenî, ken
smiling [smayling] *adj* xendan
smoke [smowk] *n* xubar
smooth [smûs] *adj* hilû, mat, rast, tîtal
smoothness [smûsnês] *n* tîtalî
snake [snêyk] *n* mar
snow [snow] *n* berf
so [sow] *adv* wer
so much [sow muç] *adv* hingî, werqas
soap [sowp] *n* sabûn
sob [sab] *n* fişe-fiş, fîşîn, hinarî *v* girîn
sobbing [sabing] *n* girî
sociable [sowşubl] *adj* kinêz
society [susayutî] *n* cimaet, enbazî, mafir, teşkîlat

sock [sak] *n* gore
soft [soft] *adj* helîm, nerm
soldier [solcur] *n* lesker, nezam, saldat
sole [sowl] *n* binpî, ax, binsol
solemnity [salêmnitî] *n* tentene
solitude [salityûd] *n* tebayî
solution [solûşun] *n* bişav
somber [sambur] *adj* bêronahî
somebody [sumbadî] *pron* yekî
somehow [sumhaw] *adv* cûrekî, qene
someone [sumwun] *pron* qeys
something [sumsing] *n* çîz
sometimes [sumtayms] *adv* caran, geh-geh
son [san] *n* kur, benî
son-in-law [san-in-lo] *n* zava
song [song] *n* kilam, newa, leylan
sonorous [sanurus] *adj* zîz
soot [sut] *n* qîr
sorcery [sorsurî] *n* ce'dûgerî
sorrow [sorow] *n* dilgiranî, hizin, way, hesret
sort [sort] *n* celeb, cur, babet, texlît, am, havil,
    qelb, vîn
sound [sawnd] *n* hewa, deng, derxistin, guje-guj,
    xumîn *v* lê xistin
soup [sûp] *n* şorbe, virik
sour cream [sawr krîm] *n* toxavk

sour [sawr] *adj* tal

source [sors] *n* e'ynik, qunî

South [saws] *n* cenûb, nîvro

sow [sow] *v* çandin

spark [spark] *n* birûsk

sparkle [sparkl] *v* geşan

sparsely [sparslî] *adv* hindik

speak [spîk] *v* axivandin, axaftin, saygotin, wekilandin

speaker [spîkur] *n* oratorxeberdar

spear [spîr] *n* e'rş

special [spêşul] *adj* xusûs

speciality [spêşelitî] *n* sinhet, pêşe

specimen [spêsimin] *n* delîl

specter [spêktur] *n* qeratû

speech [spîç] *n* axaftin, peyv, xeberdan, xeber, gotar, gilî, kêlm

speed [spîd] *n* lezgînî

speedy [spîdî] *adj* çeleng, deman, cilakî

spelling [spêling] *n* rastnivîsar

spend [spênd] *v* bihurandin

sphere [sfîr] *n* hol

spill [spil] *v* verêtin

spinach [spinuç] *n* îspenax

spine [spayn] *n* pişt

spirit [spirit] *n* havil, ruh, rih, ray

spit [spit] *n* tifû

splendid [splêndid] *adj* cemal, dilbar, xûnkêş,
  şahare, bedew, bi rewş keleş

splendor [splêndur] *n* delalî, ferwarî, husin,
  xûnkêşî, dilbarî

split [split] *v* behandin

splitting [spliting] *n* behandin

sponge [spunc] *n* hewir

sport [sport] *n* sport

spot [spat] *n* deq

spouse [spaws] *n* hemser

spring [spring] *n* bihar, e'ynik, qunî

sprinkle [sprinkl] *v* reşandin

sprout [sprawt] *n* gupik

spy [spay] *n* xufye

squanderer [sqwendurur] *n* ziaker

square [skwêr] *n* çarçik

staircase [stêrkêys] *n* derince, nerdewan

stale [stêyl] *adj* req

stamp [stemp] *n* pêçat

star [star] *n* necm, pêvir

station [stêyşun] *n* gehînek, îstasîon

statue [steçyû] *n* heykel

steam [stîm] *n* dû, hulmgulm

steel [stîl] *n* pola

stem [stêm] *n* çirpî, bist

step [stêp] *n* binpî, nerdewan
step-sister [stêpsistur] *n* zirxweh
stepmother [stêpmasur] *n* jinbav
steppe [stêp] *n* best, çol, berî
stew [stûw] *n* sêlqelî
stick [stik] *n* kopal, *n* şiv
sticky [stikî] *adj* virçikî, zeliqokî
still [stil] *adj* bêdeng *adv* hemîn, hê
stillness [stilnês] *n* bêdenganî
sting [sting] *v* gezandin
stocking [staking] *n* gore
stomach [stumuk] *n* hûr, berûk, zik
stomach ache [stumuk-êyk] *n* zikêş
stone [stown] *n* ber, hucur, kevir, kuç, tawêr,
   zinar
stop [stap] *n* cîgeh
store [stor] *n* miẍaze
storm [storm] *n* firtone, fizildûman, sêlav, tofan,
   bazor, beger
story [storî] *n* çîrok, behs, ewlî, e'ne'ne, gilîgotin,
   neqil
story (of building) [storî] *n* ta
stove [stowv] *n* ocax
straight [strêyt] *adj* dûz, rast,
   tîk, zirav *adv* raste-rast

straightening out [strêytning awt] *n* dûzkirin, dûzbûn

strange [strêync] *adj* beter, behît, bêgan, biyanî, nejê, gosirmat, bêdevan

strangeness [strêyncnis] *n* gosirmatî

strangle [strêngl] *adj* fetisandin

stream [strîm] *n* çirik, cew, co, lehî, pelemîşk

street [strît] *n* dermal, kûçe, soqaq, zikak

streetlamp [strîtlemp] *n* fener

strength [strêngs] *n* berkbûn, birh, gac, gûc, hêl, hêz, qayîmî, qidûm

stretch [strêç] *v* raçandin

strict [strikt] *adj* çist

string [string] *n* sîm, têl

striped [straypd] *adj* moxetet

stroll [strol] *adj* gerîn

strong [strong] *adj* berk, betîn, hêzdar, hur, qayîm, xurt, mitîn, mehkem, serpola

stronger [strongur] *adv* bêtir

struggle [strugl] *n* gulaşgirî, gulaş

student [stûdint] *n* xwendevan

studies [studîs] *n* xwêndewarî, pend

study [studî] *n* fêrbûn, hînbûn *v* hîn

stuffed [stufd] *adj* tijî

stupid [stûpid] *adj* bale, bêmejî, bêaqil, fehmkor, ehmeq, kêmheş, kêmaqil

stupidity [stûpiditî] *n* bêaqilî, bêfe'mî, fehmkorî
sturdiness [sturdînês] *n* qayîmî
sturdy [sturdî] *adj* berk, qayîm, qahîm, mehkem, mitîn
subject [subcêkt] *n* tişt
submission [submişun] *n* miteyî, tabî
subordinate [subordinat] *adj* bindest
subordination [subordinêyşun] *adj* tetabe
subway [subwêy] *n* mêtro
success [suksês] *n* destanînî, bext, mizeferîyet, şans
succombing [sukambing] *adj* alçax
such [suç] *adj* ha
sudden [sudin] *adj* bêḧeya, nişkêva
suddenly [sudinlî] *adv* ha-hanga, bêḧeyam, xepe-xep, ẍafil, nagah, nişkêva
suffer [sufur] *v* qacqicîn, zêrîn, kişandin, êşin, ezibîn, rakirin
suffering [sufuring] *n* berxweketin, danavî, îza, keder, êş, êşîn, kul
suffix [sufiks] *n* paşpartik
Sufism [sûfizm] *n* sofîtî
Sufi [sûfî] *n* sofî
sugar [şugur] *n* qend, şekir
suggestion [sugcêşçun] *n* şîret
suit [sût] *n* cil, kastûm

suitcase [sûtkêys] *n* çemedan
sulk [sulk] *v* e'ngirîn
summer [sumur] *n* havîn, qijavî, şilik
sun [sun] *n* ferx, xewer, mihr, ro, tav, şems, roj
Sunni (Islam) [sûnî] *n* sinetî, sinet
sunrise [sunrayz] *n* rohilat
sunset [sunsêt] *n* mexrîb, roava
superb [sûpurb] *adj* terlan
superficial [sûpurfişl] *adj* culf
supervisor [sûpurvayzur] *n* verêker
supporter [suportur] *n* tagir
surface [surfus] *n* serrû, rûkar
surmise [surmayz] *n* texmîn
surname [surnêym] *n* famîl
surprised [surprayzd] *adj* wale, şaşmayî
surround [surawnd] *v* çarmekirin, qurijîn
surroundings [surawndings] *n* govek
suspicion [suspişun] *n* şibhe
swallow [swaluw] *v* daqurtandin, dabeliyandin,
    hişavtin, qurtandin *n* firkirin
swamp [swamp] *n* lîl, merziq, pingav
swank [swenk] *n* zirt
sweat [swêt] *v* xûdan *n* xweydan
sweating [swêting] *n* xweydan
sweet [swît] *n* şîranî
sweets [swîts] *n* hilawet, qend, şekirleme

swift [swift] *adj* lez, serî
swiftness [swiftnus] *n* xerez, leztî
swimming pool [swiming pûl] *n* şadrewan
symbol [simbul] *n* işaret, nîşan

T

table [têybl] *n* mase, tablîsa
tail [têyl] *n* dûv, poç
tailor [têylur] *n* tevneçî, cûmker
take away [têyk awêy] *v* birên
take [têyk] *v* hilandin, girtin
tale [têyl] *n* hadîs
talent [telint] *n* hiner, kemal
talented [telintid] *adj* ehl, xweykemal
talisman [telismun] *n* himelî
talk [tok] *v* saygotin, wekilandin
talker [tokur] *n* wirwirok
tall [tol] *adj* bejnbilind, hilneyî, gir, tîk
tap [tep] *n* bûlbûlk, çirik, şirik
target [targit] *n* amac
taste [têyst] *n* tam, temayî
tasty [têystî] *adj* bite'm
tax [teks] *n* bêş, îrad, wêrgû
tea [tî] *n* çay

teacher [tîçur] *n* dersdar, hînker, melûm, seyda

teaching [tîçing] *n* te'lîm

teapot [tîpat] *n* çaynik

tear [têr] *v* çirandin, gincirandîn, hilqetandin, qelişandin, qelaştin

tear [tîr] *n* hêsir, hêstir, mecar, sirişk

tears [tîrs] *n* hêstir

technique [têknîk] *n* têxnîke

telegram [têligrem] *n* têlgiram

telegraph [têligref] *n* têlgiraf

telephone [têlifown] *n* têlefon

temperament [tempirament] *n* fitret

temple [têmpl] *n* cênîk, gulak, ibadetgeh

temporarily [têmporerilî] *adv* wextî

temporary [têmpurerî] *adj* wextî, wadetî, wehdetî, we'detî

temptation [têmptêyşun] *n* belwa, tesvîl, tercûbe, tevsîl

ten [tên] *num* deh

tendency [têndinsî] *n* meyl

tent [tênt] *n* çadir

term [turm] *n* wade

terrace [têris] *n* eywan, heywan, xaneban

terrible [têribul] *adj* bêter, bitirs

terror [têrur] *n* xewf

text [têkst] *n* metne

Thank God! [senk gad] *excl* erhemdula
Thank Allah! [senk Ala] *excl* erhemdula
that is [zet iz] *conj* ango
that [zet] *conj* çi, ya, ku, çiko
that much [zet muç] *adv* hilqeys
theater [sîurtur] *n* tîatr, pîyês
theft [sêft] *n* destdirêjî
then [zên] *adv* îda
theory [sîurî] *n* têorî
there [zêr] *adv* liwê, livêderê, wêderê
there (in that direction) [zêr] *adv* wêda
thermometer [surmamitur] *n* germpîv
thick [sik] *adj* stûr, tîr
thin [sin] *adj* bêzuhum, kelax, qor, jar, tenik
thing [sing] *n* çîz, eşîya, e'ciza, kel, tişt
things [sings] *n* hûrmûr
think [sink] *v* fikirîn
thinker [sinkur] *n* fikirdar, Ḧişker
thirst [surst] *n* teşnîtî, tîbûn, tîlî
thirteen [surtîn] *num* sêzde
this way [zis wêy] *adv* vir, virda, wehe, ûlo, weto,
  wiha
this time [zis taym] *adv* vêga, vêcar
thorn [sorn] *n* pej
thought [sot] *n* fikir, xeyal, nêt
thousand [sawzund] *num* ḧezar

thread [srêd] *n* dezî, rist, tê, têl, ta, rakirin
threat [srêt] *n* e'rnokî, geſ, gur
threshold [sreşhold] *n* berderek
throat [srowt] *n* boẍaz, gerden, gewrû, xeneq
throne [srown] *n* e'rş, mezheb, text
through [srû] *adv* kura, navra *prep* lay
throw [srow] *v* çerpandin, firqandin
thunder [sundur] *n* gure-gur, gurîn, gumgume, rimj, gimîn, teyrok, tîpî
thunderstorm [sundurstorm] *n* rimj
Thursday [surzdêy] *n* pêncşemb
thus [zus] *adv* ewha, lema
ticket [tikit] *n* bilêt
tie [tay] *n* pevgirêk
tied [tayd] *v* vebeste
tier [tîr] *n* ewlî
tiger [taygur] *n* ejder
time [taym] *n* geh, esna, hengam, muẍdar, wade, wext, kat, nifş
time period [taym pîrîud] *n* wext
tin [tin] *n* qela
tiny [taynî] *adj* hûr
tire [tayr] *v* westîn
tired [tayurd] *adj* xesle, perîşan, westayi
title [taytul] *n* inwan, sernav
to [tu] *prep* vebal

tobacco [tubekow] *n* titûn
together [tugêzur] *adv* hevra, pêkve, pêra, tevhev, tev
toil [toyl] *n* ked
toilet [toylit] *n* çêşme
tolerate [talurêyt] *v* tevitîn
tomato [tumêytow] *n* pamîdor
tomb [tûm] *n* çalxane, tirb
ton [tun] *n* ton
too [tû] *adv* îcgar
too much [tû muç] *adv* gelek
tool [tûl] *n* hesincawî, alem
toothbrush [tûsbruş] *n* firçak
top [tap] *n* hêl, kele, jor
torn [torn] *adj* gincorî, zerzilî
torrent [torint] *n* lehî
torture [torçur] *n* e'zîyet, e'zeb *v* ezibandîn, qacqicandin
totally [towtulî] *adv* gişt, qet, qey, lap, pêda-pêda
tourist [torist] *n* rêzan
trace [trêys] *n* e'ser, parone, rêç
trade [trêyd] *v* gorandin, guhêrandin, guhêrin, *n* ûceret, tucarî, bazirganî, ticaretî
tradition [tradişun] *n* adet
train [trêyn] *n* tirên
traitor [trêytur] *n* mixenet

tramp [tremp] *n* bozebelî, berdîwar

transfer [trensfur] *v* bihurandin

translate [trenslêyt] *v* bihurandin, wergerandin

translation [trenslêyşun] *n* tercime, wergerandin

translator [trenslêytur] *n* dîlbend, tercimeçî,
    wergêr, wergervan, wergerandok

trap [trep] *n* dehfik, dek

trash [treş] *n* gemar

travel [trevul] *n* rêwîngî

traveller [trevulur] *n* misafir, rêwî, rêwîng

tray [trêy] *n* xûnçe

treacherous [trêçurus] *adj* deẍel, fendar

treachery [treçurî] *n* dek, fen

treason [trîzun] *n* xayînî, xiyanet

treasure [trêjur] *n* define, gencîne, xesne

treasury [trêjurî] *n* define

treat [trît] *v* kewandin

treatment [trîtmint] *n* derman, dû û derman

treaty [trîtî] *n* weqe

tree [trî] *n* derext

tremble [trêmbl] *v* lerizîn

trembling [trêmbling] *n* pertab, tevz, weş

trial [trayul] *n* belwa

tribe [trayb] *n* ber, berek, çêlî

trifle [trayfl] *n* hûrayî

trip [trip] *n* sefer

triumph [trayumf] *n* mizeferîyet, pîrozî
triumphant [trayumfunt] *adj* pîroz
trouble [trubl] *n* teşqele
troublesome [trublsum] *adj* teşqele
trousers [trewzurs] *n* şalvar, şal
true [trû] *adj* amin, heqîq, mecît, sadiq
trumpet [trumpit] *n* lûle
trust [trust] *n* îtbar, tewekîl, bawerî, yeqînî *v* pê,
    bawer bûn, bawerî
trustworthiness [trustwurzînês] *n* amindarî
trustworthy [trustwurzî] *adj* amin
truth [trûs] *n* heqî, heq, heqyat, serrastî, mecîtî
truthful [trûsful] *adj* rastbêj
try [tray] *v* cêribandin, xesirîn *n* tecrîb
Tuesday [tûzdêy] *n* sêşemî
tumescence [tumêsins] *n* werm
tunnel [tunul] *n* tonêl
turgid [turcid] *adj* werimî
Turk [turk] *n* tirk, rom
turkey [turkî] *n* cûrcûr
turn [turn] *v* çivandin, fitilandin, dagerîn
turn [turn] *n* çivane, fitil, nobe
turn around [turn erewnd] *v* piçikandin
twenty [twêntî] *num* bîst
twin [twin] *n* cêwî, hemzik
twins [twins] *n* hemzik

type [tayp] *n* qism
typical [tipikul] *adj* xarû

U

ugly [uglî] *adj* beter, bêteher, bixok, qebe
ultimatum [ultimêytum] *n* oltîmatom
umbrella [umbrêla] *n* çetir, seyvan
uncivilized [unsivilayzd] *adj* bêmedenîyet
uncle [unkl] *n* kak
unclean [unklîn] *adj* ḧeram, necis
unconquerable [unkanqwurabul] *n* altnebûyl
unconscious [unkanşus] *n* bêḧiş
under [undur] *prep* bin
understand [understend] *v* fahm, kirin, tê gihîn,
    têgihaştin
understanding [understending] *adj* bîrbir,
    aquilmend, serederî, te'eqol, ziqet
underwear [undurwêr] *n* binîş
undisturbed [undisturbd] *adj* e'qilremîde
undoubted [undewtid] *adj* bêşik
undress [undrês] *v* weranîn
unemployed [unimployd] *adj* bêxebat
unemployment [unimploymênt] *n* bêxebatî
unfair [unfêr] *n* bêdad, bêheq

unfaithful [unfêysful] *adj* bêşerie't

unfortunate [unforçunat] *adj* bêçar, dêran,
   felekreş, kulmal, mudbir
unfulfilled [unfulfild] *adj* bêmiraz
ungrateful [ungrêytful] *adj* bêminet
unhappiness [unhepînis] *n* elem, bextxirabî
unhappy [unhepî] *adj* bextreş, bedbext, bêxur,
   bêmiraz, mixab, stûxwar, perîşan, talektor
union [yûnyun] *n* girêdanî
unique [yûnîk] *adj* tekane, tenê
unit [yûnit] *n* ta, tek
unite [yûnayt] *v* hevxistin
unity [yûnitî] *n* tevhevbûn, tewhîd, wehîdî,
   yekbûn, yekîtî
universe [yûnivurs] *n* alet, cehan, gerdûn, gêhan,
   serwêt
university [yûnivursitî] *n* ûnîvêrsîtê, zanîngeh
unjust [uncustêd] *adj* bêe'dalet
unknown [unnown] *adj* bênav
unlawful [unloful] *adj* bêdad, bêqanûn
unlocked [unlakd] *adj* vekirî
unlucky [unlukî] *adj* teşqele
unmannered [unmenurd] *adj* bêterbyet
unmarried [unmerîd] *adj* bêjin

unpleasant [unplêzunt] *adj* bêlezet, delû
unproductive [unproduktiv] *adj* bêhasil
unprofitable [unprafitabl] *adj* bêxêr
unqualified [unqwalifayd] *adj* bêhunur
unreliable [unrilayubl] *adj* bêîtbar
unrest [unrêst] *n* nedîncî
unripe [unrayp] *adj* xavî, kal
unruly [unrûlî] *adj* bêîtae't, lewand
unscrupulous [unskrûpyûlus] *adj* bêîman
until [until] *prep* hingî, ta
unusual [unyûjûal] *adj* bêresa
upset [upsêt] *adj* dilgiran, dilbirîn, xemgîn, portmijî, qelibî, serabin, şewişî
upside-down [upsayd-dewn] *adv* berepaş
use [yûz] *n* fayîde
useful [yûzful] *adj* xalis, kêr, kardar, mifade
useless [yûzlês] *adj* bêfitîya, bêxêr, e'bes, hawa, qels
usual [yûjûul] *adj* e'detî

V

vacant [vêykunt] *adj* vala
vagrant [vêygrunt] *adj* rewindayî

vague [vêyg] *adj* bêĥal
vain [vêyn] *adj* bêfitîya, e'bes
vainly [vêynlî] *adv* bêfitîya
valley [velîy] *n* dehl, tûş
valuable [velyûubl] *adj* fayîdekar, qîmetdar, nerx
value [velyû] *n* fayîde
various [veryus] *n* cûr-cûr
vegetable [vêctubl] *n* êmîş
vein [vêyn] *n* derem
vengeance [vçncins] *n* enteqam, qesas
verity [vêritî] *n* têtî
veranda [vurenda] *n* heywan, ẍorfe
vertical [vurtikul] *adj* kîp, tîk
very [vêrî] *adv* xeylî, pir, tewrî, zehf, zehftir
vice [vays] *n* cîhgirtî
victim [viktum] *n* dîtiye, feda, gorî, ĥeyran, qurban
victor [viktur] *n* altker
victory [vikturî] *n* mizeferîyet, zefer
village [viluc] *n* gund
vine [vayn] *n* saq
vinegar [vinigur] *n* sihik
violator [vayulêytur] *n* wêranker
violence [vayulins] *n* tade
virgin [vurcin] *n* e'zra
visage [vizic] *n* dêmûrû, rû

visible [visubl] *adj* belû, berbiçav, dîhar, e'yan, xuya

visit [visit] *n* serdan

vitamin [vaytumin] *n* vitamîn

voice [voys] *n* aheng, deng, deyn, seda

volcano [volkêynow] *m* agirdiz

volume [valyûm] *n* celd

vomit [vamit] *v* vereşandin

voter [vowtur] *n* bijarkar

vulgar [vulgur] *adj* qubet

vulgarity [vulgeritî] *n* qubetî

W

wage [wêyc] *n* dexl, heqxebat

wail [wêyl] *n* çarîn, hele-hel

waiter [wêytur] *n* dergevan

wake [wêyk] *v* rakirin

walk [wok] *v* çûyîn, gerîn, meşîn *n* seyran, rewal

wall [wol] *n* dîwar

wander [wandur] *adj* gerîn

wanderer [wendurur] *n* berdîwar, rêwî

wandering [wenduring] *n* terkeser

war [wor] *n* ceng, genc, pirxaş

wardrobe [wordrowb] *n* îşkav

ware [wêr] *n* kala

warm [worm] *adj* germ
warmth [worms] *n* germî
warrior [woryur] *n* cengçî
wash [waş] *v* werdan
watch [waç] *v* eseh
water [wotur] *n* cirav
waterfall [woturfol] *n* çirik, gurgure
watermelon [woturmêlun] *n* qarpûz, kal, şebeş, zeveş
wave [wêyv] *n* çelq, delxe, mewcan, perav, pêşî, tîpî *v* raweşandin
way [wey] *n* beravan, esibil, rê, ûslûb, wesîle
weak [wîk] *adj* aciz, alçax, çilazok, ixtîyar, zeîf, kêmhêz, bêhêz, lawaz, tutar
weakness [wîknis] *n* alçaxî, bêganî
wealth [wêls] *n* dewlet, dengiz, dewlemendî, maldarî
wealthy [wêlsî] *adj* maldar, pî
weapon [wêpun] *n* alem, çek, tifing, top
weapons [wêpins] *n* cebirxane
wear [wêr] *v* anîn
weather [wêzur] *n* hewa
weave [wîv] *v* hûnandin
wedding [wêding] *n* de'wat, nikeh, ors
wedding ring [wêding ring] *n* gustîl
Wednesday [wênsdêy] *n* çarşem

week [wîk] *n* ḧeftê
weep [wîp] *v* vine-vin, zarîn
weigh [wêy] *v* pîvan
weight [wêyt] *n* mêzîn
weights [wêyts] *n* kêşan
well [wêl] *n* bêrim *interj* ca
well known [wêl nown] *adj* belû, bilîmet,
    berbiçav, eşref
West [wêst] *n* ẍerb, meẍrîb
Western [wêsturn] *adj* ẍerbî
wet [wêt] *adj* ter, şil
wetness [wêtnis] *n* terayî
whale [wêyl] *n* neheng
what [wat] *conj* ku
what? [wat] *interj* ha?
wheel [wîl] *n* çerx
when [wên] *pron* çiçax *conj* kengê *adv* liku
where [wêr] *pron* kîderê *adv* liku
where (at) [wêr et] *adv* kuder
where (to) [wêr tû] *adv* kuva, kuda
which [wiç] *pron* ça, ya
whirlwind [wurlwind] *n* bobelat
whisper [wispur] *n* pite-pit
whistle [wisl] *v* fîkandin *n* fîte-fît, fişe-fiş, fîşîn,
    tîqîn

white [wayt] *adj* belek, beyaz, gewr, kevej, kej, qerqaş

whole [howl] *adj* temam

wholeness [howlnis] *n* temamî

why [way] *inter* bo *prep* çiman

wicked [wikid] *adj* mifsid, neçê

wickedness [wikidnês] *n* neçêyî

wide [wayd] *adj* berek, pehn

widow [widuw] *n* pîrebî, jinebî

widower [widuwur] *n* jinmirî

wide [wayd] *adj* fireh, fereh, biber

width [wids] *n* berînî, berahî, firehî, fireyî, pehnayî

wife [wayf] *n* hurmet, kulfet, zêc, jin

wild [wayld] *adj* wehş, yaban

wild goat [wayld gowt] *n* ahû

wildness [wayldnês] *n* wehşî, yabanî

will [wil] *n* heq, hemd

window [winduw] *n* pencere

wine [wayn] *n* meya, şerab

wineglass [wayngles] *n* fîncan

wink [wink] *v* qirçimandin

winner [winur] *n* altker

winter [wintur] *n* zivistan *adj* zivistanî

wisdom [wisdum] *n* e'rifî

wise [wayz] *adj* bilîmet, ahil, e'rif, ferzan,
    xweyhiş
wish [wiş] *n* arzû, berîya, e'rbab, xwestek, xwezî,
    minêkarî, miraz, vên, viyan
wit [wit] *n* tûjî
with [wis] *prep* bi
wither [wisur] *v* çirmisîn
witness [witnês] *n* şade
wolf [wolf] *n* gur
woman [wûman] *n* afret, hurmet, nîsa, jin, jinik,
    pîrek
wonder [wundur] *n* e'cêb, e'cêbî, ḧeyret, mûcize
    v e'cibîn
wonderful [wundurful] *adj* delal, fayiq, e'zîm
    wood [wud] *n* êzing
word [wurd] *n* axawik, bêje, gotin, gilî, qewl,
    qezî, kelam, peyv, peyvik, ştexilî
work [wurk] *n* berhem, xebat, îş, kar, xizmet,
    şixul
worker [wurkur] *n* e'melker, hodax, xebatkar,
    îşker, karker, şixulkar
world [wurld] *n* alet, cehan, dinya, gêhan, e'lem
worm [wurm] *n* kurm
worn [worn] *adj* kevn
worry [wurî] *n* cefa, fikare, xem, helecan,
    serêşanî

wound [wûnd] *n* kew, qereh
wrap [rep] *v* pêçandin *n* zerf
wrestling [rêstling] *n* tirat
wrinkle [rinkl] *n* çîn
write [rayt] *v* meşq, nivîsandin
writer [raytur] *n* nivîsevan
writing [rayting] *n* nivîsar
wrong [rong] *adj* xar

Y

yard [yard] *n* dermal
yell [yêl] *v* qîjandin, qarîn, xurîn, qûjîn
yellow [yêluw] *adj* qîçik, zer
yes [yês] *part* belê, ê
yield [dakhwäryn] *v* daxwerin
yolk [yowk] *n* zerik
you [yû] *pron* tu
young [yung] *adj* biçûk, cahil, can, ciwan, nestêl, nûber
young man [yung men] *n* bişkorî, lawko, rewal
young person [yung pursun] *n* wuşoq
young woman [yung wumen] *n* qîz
younger [yungur] *adj* çûk
youngest [yungist] *adj* çûk
your [yor] *adj* a, ê, eu, u

youth [yûs] *n* cahilî, ciwanî, xort, xortanî, lawanî, zelam

Z

Zazan (name of Kurdish tribe) [zazan] *n* Zazan
zeal [zîl] *n* bizav, te'esob
Zend (name of Kurdish tribe, living in the North-West of Iran) [zênd] *n* Zênd
Zili (name of Kurdish tribe) [zîlî] *n* Zîlî
zoltan (money) [zoltan] *n* zoltan
Zoro (name) [zoro] *n* Zoro
Zoroastrism [zarowastrizm]*f* agirperesî, zerdeştî
Zozan (name) [zozan] *n* Zozan
Zurba (name) [zurba] *n* Zurbe

HIPPOCRENE FOREIGN LANGUAGE DICTIONARIES
Modern • Up-to-Date • Easy-to-Use • Practical

Afrikaans-English/English-Africaans Dictionary
0134   ISBN 0-7818-0052-8 $11.95 pb

Albanian-English Dictionary
0744   ISBN 0-7818-0021-8 $14.95 pb

English-Albanian Dictionary
0518   ISBN 0-7818-0021-8 $14.95 pb

Arabic-English Dictionary
0487   ISBN 0-7818-0153-2 $14.95 pb

Arabic-English Learner's Dictionary
0033   ISBN 0-7818-0155-9 $24.95 hc

English-Arabic Learner's Dictionary
0690   ISBN 0-87052-914-5 $14.95 pb

Armenian-English/English-Armenian Concise Dictionary
0490   ISBN 0-7818-0150-8 $11.95 pb

Armenian Dictionary in Translation (Western)
0059   ISBN 0-7818-0207-5 $9.95 pb

English-Azerbaijani/Azerbaijani-English
0096   ISBN 0-7818-0244-X $11.95 pb

Bulgarian-English/English-Bulgarian Practical Dictionary
0331   ISBN 0-87052-145-4 $11.95 pb

Byelorussian-English/English-Byelorussian Concise Dictionary
1050 ISBN 0-87052-114-4 $9.95 pb

Cambodian-English/English-Cambodian Standard Dictionary
0143 ISBN 0-87052-818-1 $14.95 pb

Catalan-English/English-Catalan Dictionary
0451 ISBN 0-7818-0099-4 $8.95 pb

Classified and Illustrated Chinese-English Dictionary (Mandarin)
0027 ISBN 0-87052-714-2 $19.95 hc

An Everyday Chinese-English Dictionary (Mandarin)
0721 ISBN 0-87052-862-9 $12.95 hc

Colloquial Navajo: A Dictionary
282 ISBN 0-7818-0278-4 $16.95

Czech-English/English-Czech Concise Dictionary
0276 ISBN 0-87052-981-1 $11.95 pb

Danish-English/English-Danish Practical Dictionary
0198 ISBN 0-87052-823-8 $14.95 pb

Dutch-English/English-Dutch Concise Dictionary
0606 ISBN 0-87052-910-2 $11.95 pb

Estonian-English/English-Estonian Concise Dictionary
1010 ISBN 0-87052-081-4 $11.95 pb

Finnish-English/English-Finnish Concise Dictionary
0142 ISBN 0-87052-813-0 $9.95 pb

French-English/English-French Practical Dictionary
0199 ISBN 0-7818-0178-8 $8.95 pb

Georgian-English/English-Georgian Concise Dictionary
1059 ISBN 0-87052-121-7 $8.95 pb

German-English/English-German Practical Dictionary
0200 ISBN 0-88254-813-1 $6.95 pb

English-Hebrew/Hebrew English Conversational Dictionary
(Revised Edition)
0257 ISBN 0-87052-625-1 $8.95 pb

Hindi-English/English-Hindi Practical Dictionary
0442 ISBN 0-7818-0084-6 $16.95 pb

English-Hindi Practical Dictionary
0923 ISBN 0-87052-978-1 $11.95 pb

Hindi-English Practical Dictionary
0186 ISBN 0-87052-824-6 $11.95 pb

English-Hungarian/Hungarian-English Dictionary
2039 ISBN 0-88254-986-3 $9.95 hc

Hungarian-English/English-Hungarian Concise Dictionary
0254 ISBN 0-87052-891-2 $8.95 pb

Icelandic-English/English-Icelandic Concise Dictionary
0147 ISBN 0-87052-801-7 $8.95 pb

Indonesian-English/English-Indonesian Practical Dictionary
0127 ISBN 0-87052-810-6 $11.95 pb

Irish-English/English-Irish Dictionary and Phrasebook
1037 ISBN 0-87052-110-1 $7.95 pb

Italian-English/English-Italian Practical Dictionary
0201 ISBN 0-88254-816-6 $6.95 pb

Japanese-English/English-Japanese Concise Dictionary
0474   ISBN 0-7818-0162-1 $11.95 pb

Korean-English/English-Korean Dictionary
1016   ISBN 0-87052-092-X $9.95 pb

Kurdish-English/English-Kurdish Dictionary
0218   ISBN 0-7818-0246-6 $11.95

Latvian-English/English-Latvian Dictionary
0194   ISBN 0-7818-0059-5 $14.95 pb

Lithuanian-English/English-Lithuanian Concise Dictionary
0489   ISBN 0-7818-0151-6 $11.95 pb

Malay-English/English-Malay Dictionary
0428   ISBN 0-7818-0103-6 $16.95 pb

Nepali-English/English Nepali Concise Dictionary
1104   ISBN 0-87052-106-3 $8.95 pb

**Norwegian-English/English-Norwegian Dictionary
(Revised Edition)**
0202   ISBN 0-7818-0199-0 $11.95 pb

Persian-English Dictionary
0350   ISBN 0-7818-0055-2 $16.95 pb

English-Persian Dictionary
0365   ISBN 0-7818-0056-0 $16.95 pb

Polish-English/English-Polish Standard Dictionary
0665   ISBN 0-87052-882-3 $22.50 hc

Polish-English/English-Polish Standard Dictionary
0207   ISBN 0-7818-0183-4 $16.95 pb

Portugese-English/English-Portugese Dictionary
0477 ISBN 0-87052-980-3 $16.95 pb

English-Punjabi Dictionary
0144 ISBN 0-7818-0060-9 $14.95 hc

Romanian-English/English-Romanian Dictionary
0488 ISBN 0-87052-986-2 $19.95 pb

Russian-English/English-Russian Standard Dictionary with Business Terms
0440 ISBN 0-7818-0280-6 $16.95 pb

English-Russian Standard Dictionary
1025 ISBN 0-87052-100-4 $11.95 pb

Russian-English Standard Dictionary
0578 ISBN 0-87052-964-1 $11.95 pb

Russian-English/English-Russian Concise Dictionary
0262 ISBN 0-7818-0132-X $11.95 pb

Concise Sanskrit-English Dictiontary
0164 ISBN 0-7818-0203-2 $14.95 pb

Scottish Gaelic-English/English-Scottish Gaelic
285 ISBN 0-7818-0316-0 $8.95 pb

English-Sinhalese/Sinhalese-English Dictionary
0319 ISBN 0-7818-0219-9 $24.95 hc

Slovak-English/English-Slovak Concise Dictionary
1052 ISBN 0-87052-115-2 $9.95 pb

English-Somali/Somali-English Dictionary
0246 ISBN 0-7818-0269-5 $29.50

Spanish-English/English-Spanish Practical Dictionary
0211 ISBN 0-7818-0179-6 $8.95 pb

Swahili Phrasebook
0073 ISBN 0-87052-970-6 $8.95

Swedish-English/English-Swedish Dictionary
0761 ISBN 0-87052-871-8 $19.95 hc

English-Tigrigna Dictionary
0330 ISBN 0-7818-0220-2 $34.95 hc

English-Turkish/Turkish-English Concise Dictionary
0338 ISBN 0-7818-0161-3 $8.95 pb

English-Turkish/Turkish-English Pocket Dictionary
0148 ISBN 0-87052-812-2 $14.95 pb

Twi-English/English-Twi Dictionary
0290 ISBN 0-7818-0264-4 $11.95 pb

Ukrainian-English/English Ukrainian Practical Dictionary
1055 ISBN 0-87052-116-0 $8.95 pb

Ukrainian-English Standard Dictionary
0006 ISBN 0-7818-0189-3 $14.95 pb

Urdu-English Gem Pocket Dictionary
0289 ISBN 0-87052-911-0 $6.95 pb

English-Urdu Gem Pocket Dictionary
0880 ISBN 0-87052-912-9 $6.95 hc

English-Urdu Dictionary
68 ISBN 0-7818-0222-9 $24.95 hc

Urdu-English Dictionary
0368   ISBN 0-7818-0222-9 $24.95 hc

Uzbek-English/English-Uzbek
0004   ISBN 0-7818-0165-6 $11.95 pb

Vietnamese-English/English-Vietnamese Standard Dictionary
0529   ISBN 0-87052-924-2 $19.95 pb

Welsh-English/English-Welsh Dictionary
0116   ISBN 0-7818-0136-2 $19.95 pb

A New Concise Xhosa-English Dictionary
0167   ISBN 0-7818-0251-2 $14.95 pb

**English-Yiddish/Yiddish-English Conversational Dictionary
(Romanized)**
1019   ISBN 0-87052-969-2 $7.95 pb

Yoruba-English/English-Yoruba Concise Dictionary
0275   ISBN 0-7818-0263-6 $11.95 pb

Zulu-English/English-Zulu Dictionary
0203   ISBN 0-7818-0255-5 $29.50 pb

(Prices subject to change)
TO PURCHASE HIPPOCRENE BOOKS contact your local
bookstore, or write to: HIPPOCRENE BOOKS, 171 Madison
Avenue, New York, NY 10016. Please enclose check
money order, adding $4.00 shipping (UPS) for the first bo
and .50 for each additional book.